W9-BJL-208

DISCARDED

Center Stage

A Curriculum for the Performing Arts

Grade Four
Grade Five
Grade Six

LAMAR UNIVERSITY LIBRARY

Center Stage Contributing Writer:

Fleda Evans
Drama Educator
California State University, San Jose

Center Stage Consultants:

Paul Blumenthal
Special Education Consultant
School District of Philadelphia

Leora Chwalow
Early Childhood Consultant
Solomon Schechter Day School
Bala-Cynwyd, Pennsylvania

Center Stage Reviewers:

Jackie Erceg
Art Specialist
Tracy School District
Tracy, California

Jan Ingram
Fifth Grade Teacher
Denton, Texas

Center Stage

A Curriculum for the Performing Arts

Wayne D. Cook

Contributing Writer
Fleda Evans

Grade Four
Grade Five
Grade Six

Dale Seymour Publications

Managing Editor: Diane Silver
Product Manager: Bev Dana
Project Editor: Lois Fowkes
Production/Manufacturing Manager: Janet Yearian
Production/Manufacturing Coordinator: Barbara Atmore
Design Manager: Jeff Kelly
Cover design: Rachel Gage
Illustrations: Rachel Gage
Text design: Jeff Kelly

Acknowledgments: page 30: "Jabberwocky" is from Lewis Carroll's *Alice's Adventures in Wonderland and Through the Looking Glass;* page 176: "When the Hare Brought the Sun," from *Dramatized Folk Tales of the World,* edited by Sylvia E. Kamerman, is reprinted by permission of Plays, Inc. Publishers, 120 Boylston Street, Boston, MA 02116-4615.

Story scripts for "The Bunyip," "The Two Sisters," "The Horse of Seven Colors," and "Johnnycake" are from *Story Chest: Treasured Tales from Many Lands,* by Steve Osborn; Addison-Wesley Publishing Company, 1992. The text for "The Rainbow Goblins" is from *The Rainbow Goblins* by Ul De Rico; copyright © 1978 Thames and Hudson; reprinted by permission of Thames and Hudson.

Limited reproduction permission: The publisher grants permission to individual teachers to reproduce the story scripts and student pages as needed for use with their own students. Reproduction for an entire school district or for commercial use is prohibited.

Copyright © 1993 by Dale Seymour Publications. Printed in the United States of America.

Grades 4–6
Order number DS31156
ISBN 0-86651-575-5

2 3 4 5 6 7 8 9 10–ML–97 96 95 94 93

This Book is Printed
on Recycled Paper

Contents

About the Author

Wayne Darby Cook had his first professional theatre experience while serving in the military, at which time he decided to pursue a career in the theatre. Mr. Cook received his B.A. in Theatre from Point Park College in Pittsburgh, Pennsylvania, and subsequently studied drama with Brian Way at the Theatre Centre in London. It was at the Centre that he was awakened to the potential power of creative dramatics, and directed his efforts to working with students and teachers.

Mr. Cook has been a drama instructor at the Theatre Centre in London; California State University, Long Beach and Penn State University; and drama consultant for the Pennsylvania Department of Education. He has worked with students of all ages, from preschoolers to teachers in training. Mr. Cook has worked with inner-city students, students at risk, and prison inmates. He has written drama curriculum for the Glendale and Chula Vista school districts in California, the California Visual and Performing Arts State Framework, and the Academy of Visual and Performing Arts at UCLA.

Mr. Cook was creator and host of a weekly television program for young adults and has had numerous television, film, and stage roles. He continues to act professionally, and performs in a one-man show, dramatizing the poetry of Langston Hughes.

Mr. Cook is currently the Program Administrator for the Artists in Schools program of the California Arts Council in Sacramento.

Dear Teachers . . .

It is my passionate belief that the arts, and in particular drama/theatre, change people's lives! I've seen it happen! I've seen it with preschoolers discovering the world around them and the wonderful world inside them. I've seen it with elementary school children who become involved in class for the first time, or who speak for the first time with confidence and respond positively rather than negatively to school.

I've seen it with the so-called delinquent teenager who through drama discovers a talent and interest, and therefore a sense of self-worth never before experienced. I've seen it with prison inmates while working as an artist in our correctional facilities. Some of these inmates will never leave the system, yet they develop a new awareness of themselves and begin to take responsibility for their lives. Some of them have told me that if they had had the opportunity to experience the arts in their younger lives, they might have made different choices and might have avoided the correctional system altogether.

I find the trends in education—the ways of attempting to find out how and what to teach children—fascinating. My experience as an actor and drama specialist working within the educational community has been varied, to say the least. I can remember earlier in my career working for the Pennsylvania Department of Education as a drama consultant. My task was to travel around the state presenting workshops on the power of drama techniques and how drama could be used in the classroom. The approach at that time was not so much teaching drama as a discrete discipline, but rather using drama to teach other subjects.

I can remember standing in front of a group of administrators and teachers at workshops and challenging everyone there with the statement that drama could do just about anything in the classroom. No subject was off limits; I could use drama in science, social studies, math, and language arts.

To test my assertion, teachers presented problems in specific subject areas. On the spot, I described a drama experience that could achieve the stated learning goal, or at least enhance the skills necessary for knowing and understanding the particular subject area.

What I didn't understand at that time was that the way I was using drama to teach other subject areas is the very essence of what drama is all about, and in fact is one of the reasons I am in this art form. Drama incorporates problem solving, creativity, and the ability to use old information in new ways. New perspectives are discovered, and in the discovery process, holistic thinking is increased. These are indeed the skills employed by artists in this art form.

Drama and education are inseparable. All of the skills that drama/theatre techniques utilize are inherent in human knowledge and experience. When I work with classroom teachers, I now begin with what teachers already know naturally about drama. They are already skilled in instructing 30 or more children at once. They can stimulate 30 minds; they can present an interesting environment in which to grow; they can give children the skills to make connections to their identities as individuals; and they present information in a way that helps children understand the correlation between mere information and the ways in which this information will affect their lives.

Drama experiences do not exist apart from other experiences, nor are they experiences that only a few gifted children have. Drama is what we, as adults and children, involve ourselves in every single day of our lives. Drama is the journey, not the destination. Drama/theatre offers you the world in your classroom, an opportunity for both you and your students to solve real problems and challenges. This curriculum can be the beginning of your exploration into that world.

Start to evaluate the drama that you already do in your classroom. I'm sure you will realize that the technique you use to heighten perception about a concept is indeed a skill that is part of drama/theatre. Only you can begin to make such connections in the classroom, and you can use this curriculum as your guide.

An important resource to this curriculum is the artist living in your community. Local artists provide a link between community and school—a way to motivate and inspire children and adults alike in the processes of drama/theatre. With a true collaboration between the educational and artistic communities, you will succeed in preparing literate, sensitive, and creative problem solvers to effectively lead all of us into and beyond the year 2000.

I applaud the work that you have already done in the education of our youth, and I hope that *Center Stage* will inspire you to include drama in that education. As you involve your students in these activities and have questions, look to that playful part of your own heart and soul for answers. The search can be as interesting and delightful as knowing the direct path we must go.

Within each of us there is a song, a rhythm, a speech, or a movement that has roots from which to grow and expand. Children love to move; they love to imagine; they love to pretend to be different people, animals, or objects. What they need is someone to provide a safe environment for that growth to occur. Drama/theatre is a wonderful way for children to experience their worlds, both real and imagined. The challenge is yours.

Sincerely,

Wayne D. Cook

Preface

Drama curriculum is not about creating professional actors, although the experience may spark those who have the calling. A drama curriculum is about life, about preparing students to think responsibly and creatively, which in turn will affect their quality of life. Drama gives students the opportunity to experiment with life from many perspectives, to challenge old assumptions and beliefs, and to look at a problem through many eyes. Drama gives students the confidence to reach out, and it prepares them to make better decisions.

Each student brings his or her own life's experiences to the creative dramatics process. Drama connects students to their environment, to each other as human beings, and to themselves. Drama excites. It motivates! It teaches the joy of learning and the joy in discovery. It teaches ways to solve problems which can be enlightening and liberating as each individual contributes to the solution.

The art discipline of drama/theatre includes a wide range of activities and experiences geared toward developing the individual skills of the child. It also provides opportunities for the acquisition of knowledge that represents the heritage of drama/theatre, both past and present.

Drama/theatre is an art form. The unique value of the theatre experience is that it involves students as active rather than passive learners. Through experiences in drama/theatre, the students will be able to:

- Experience success and the joy of discovery.
- Develop the "self." Students will learn to discover, express, and accept themselves.
- Learn to communicate effectively.
- Solve problems inventively in both real and imagined situations.
- Learn from society, past and present, drawing from the rich contributions of multicultural groups that make up the American heritage.
- Use critical and creative skills.
- Understand drama/theatre as an art form.
- Approach other art forms with insight.

The most important single factor in the use of drama in the classroom is the teacher. For drama/theatre to flourish in basic education, the teacher must believe that creative dramatics works, and must consciously create the time and provide the resources for drama/theatre activities to happen in the classroom.

Introduction

PROGRAM DESCRIPTION

Center Stage is a complete, discipline-based drama/theatre curriculum in two books, one for grades K–3, the other for grades 4–6. The materials contained here cover the primary grades, and consist of lessons for three grade levels (K–1, 2, 3) with story scripts, resources, and other information for the teacher. Each grade level contains 30 lessons, which build sequentially within and across the grade levels to provide a continuum of activities and experiences that foster individual growth and development. *Center Stage* also provides strategies to include the arts in other content areas and practical suggestions about time, resources, commitment, and class management styles.

PROBLEM SOLVING

In every lesson of *Center Stage* students work on problem solving, either individually or cooperatively. Many lessons within *Center Stage* involve observing, communicating, comparing, and categorizing not only to better understand dramatic concepts, but also to understand oneself and one's relation to the world.

Part of the problem-solving process is the dramatization itself. A good director of a play expects his or her actors to experiment with their roles. Even though the form or structure of the play remains basically the same, the actors bring something new and different to each rehearsal. By experimenting with characterizations, moods, vocal delivery, and ways of moving, the actor brings life to the playwright's words and intentions.

It is the same for students involved in creative dramatics; although the content and structure of a session need to be established, students find solutions through the freedom of using their creative energies within specific boundaries.

CREATIVE DRAMATICS

The particular form of drama/theatre activity used throughout *Center Stage* is creative dramatics. Creative dramatics is drama for the players, not the audience. A student begins with what he or she knows, and using imagination, experiments with that knowledge to create something new and to gain more knowledge. Through creative dramatics, *Center Stage* gives students this opportunity to experiment. Creative dramatics can be extended to formal play performance, but the emphasis in this curriculum is on the development of the individual—the process rather than the product. The culmination of a development of the individual—the process rather than the product. The culmination of most creative dramatics activities in *Center Stage* is a sharing of a story, poem, or movement, allowing students to realize the results of the problem-solving process in which they were involved.

INTEGRATING DRAMA WITH OTHER CONTENT AREAS

Education has moved towards a more holistic approach to the child. Many educators no longer concentrate on each content area separately, but focus on the total curriculum, realizing that all parts must fit together as a balanced whole. They also teach to the differences in children, using the cognitive and affective curriculum to meet the needs of kinesthetic, visual, and auditory learners.

In both science and the arts, students use critical thinking skills to observe, compare, order, and categorize the sights, sounds, and movements in the world around them. Certain scientific topics, such as light, sound, and perception are particularly appropriate areas to integrate with the arts.

Both the social studies and the drama curriculums place much emphasis upon the ideas, values, and beliefs of many people from many lands who have contributed to a vast body of knowledge. Students should recognize that literature and art reflect the inner life of a culture. To support this learning, *Center Stage* introduces stories, fables, and fairy tales that incorporate conflict and raise value issues that are both interesting and age-appropriate.

Drama and language arts are obviously interrelated. Oral language skills are integral to the process of drama. Children learn to move, to understand relations of movement to nonverbal communication, and then to speak. A continuous sequence of skill development in language arts is the body and soul of drama/theatre. Students' experiences in role-playing, leadership, and decision making—for example, when they plan classroom publications cooperatively, dramatize reactions to a novel, or engage in formal speaking situations—provide models for comparable roles in their lives.

In both mathematics and the arts, students learn how to analyze problems and select strategies. Some strategies that carry over from drama to math include:

- Making a model
- Drawing a picture
- Organizing information in a table or chart
- Finding a simpler related problem
- Acting out the situation

- Restating the problem
- Looking for patterns
- Guessing and checking the result
- Working backwards

In both mathematics and drama, it is important that students feel free to take risks, and that they see that there are many ways to arrive at the "right" answer.

In *Center Stage,* Connections activities demonstrate how drama activities can enhance another subject. These activities can act as a springboard for the integration of drama into the content areas.

A MULTICULTURAL CURRICULUM

Arts education is a superb vehicle for creating a bridge across cultures to foster mutual understanding and tolerance. Many lessons in *Center Stage* draw upon the wide variety of literature available to students that is representational of the diverse world community in which we live. As the world becomes smaller through technology, the importance of using literature that includes all people in all lands becomes greater. Through drama/theatre, students compare stories from different cultures, put themselves in others' shoes, and begin to understand how all of us in the world community can learn from each other.

In teaching a multicultural curriculum, it is important to go beyond the first step of learning about cultural holidays and historical figures to infusing every area of the curriculum with exploration and comparison of the similarities and differences of the peoples of the world. Lessons in *Center Stage* stress the value of diversity, and introduce historical, critical, and aesthetic issues.

It is also important to recognize and draw upon the strengths of the diversity of cultures within the classroom. Lessons in *Center Stage* are open-ended with the multicultural classroom in mind, precisely so that each teacher can adapt the activities to the wide range of backgrounds in his or her particular class.

ORGANIZATION   Each grade level, identified by an on-page tab, begins with an overview of the subjects covered, along with the table of contents. Each lesson, throughout the six grade levels of *Center Stage,* is organized in the following manner: the planning section, which consists of the Component, the Subject, the Objective, Materials, and special notes; the body of the lesson, which is divided into Warm Up, Explore, Develop, and Evaluate sections; and additional information, which contains Connections (to other content areas), specific suggestions for Special Needs students, and Resources.

COMPONENT

Lessons in *Center Stage* are organized by the four components in a discipline-based arts curriculum: Aesthetic Perception, Creative Expression, Historical and Cultural, and Aesthetic Valuing. The purpose of the lessons within each of these four components is as follows:

Aesthetic Perception   These lessons guide students in developing a fuller awareness of the nuances of light, color, sound, movement, and composition. Heightened perception sensitizes the individual to the world and provides a stimulus for imagination and creativity. Aesthetic awareness also enables students to comprehend and respond to the elements of an object or event and to express and appreciate it in greater depth.

Creative Expression   These lessons give students the opportunity to originate, create, perform, and interpret drama/theatre activities. Direct personal involvement is necessary for understanding the structure and language of drama/theatre. Creative expression enables students to know themselves and to appreciate one another's uniqueness.

Historical and Cultural   In these lessons, students develop a broad base for understanding artists, their works, their evolution, and their effects on society in the past and present. Learning the importance of drama/theatre activities to various cultures, past and present, helps students gain appreciation and understanding of these cultures and of their own heritage.

Aesthetic Valuing   These lessons enrich the student's awareness and response to beauty in art. To develop aesthetic values, students study the sensory, intellectual, emotional, and philosophical bases for understanding drama/theatre and increase their ability to make judgments about artworks. Students develop criteria for arriving at personal judgments.

SUBJECT

The subject heading for each lesson falls into one of these broader general categories upon which the lesson is built.

Subject areas in *Center Stage* include:

Sensory and Emotional Awareness   Creative dramatics increases students' visual, aural, tactile, and kinesthetic perception of their environment. This ability to perceive is basic to creative expression and aesthetic appreciation. Lessons concentrate on the use of the five senses, emotions, and sensations—real or imagined.

Rhythm and Movement   Movement is the external expression of an internal idea, intention, or feeling. Activities in rhythm and movement develop cooperation and cohesiveness as a group. Movement is an essential element of drama and a basis for all physical communication.

Pantomime   Nonverbal communication of an action, an activity, a mood, a feeling, or an idea offers students practice in self-expression, thus developing their ability to communicate through an intricate language of symbolic and individualized gestures.

Oral Communication   The voice is an instrument for the expression of meaning and feeling, whether in speech or nonverbal sound. In practicing vocal skills, students also learn receptive, or listening skills.

Discipline   Through drama students learn the skills to concentrate on the task at hand and develop social responsibility to other members of their group.

Storytelling   Storytelling is a special form of oral communication, the oral tradition of passing stories on from one generation to another.

Improvisation   Improvisation is the creative, cooperative, and spontaneous dramatic response to rapidly changing and unanticipated dramatic stimuli. A creative problem is presented with no preconception of how it will be solved, thereby permitting everything in the environment (animate or inanimate) to serve the experience.

Characterization   Exercises in characterization are geared towards the development of real people onstage under imaginary circumstances. The focus is on ways of moving, talking, and feeling that are unique to a particular individual.

Playmaking   Most lessons in playmaking center around an original story improvisation. The story may be a real-life situation or an imagined one. In the intermediate grades, students are expected to analyze the components of a story or play and use those components as they create their own work. The improvised story is carefully structured and planned, played, evaluated, and replayed with no formal audience. As students become more adept at creative dramatics, they occasionally may perform for an audience. In Grade 6 the lessons culminate in a formal dramatic production.

Technical Elements   Scenery, lighting, props, costumes, make-up, and sound are all part of drama/theatre. These technical subjects are important in developing an overall understanding of drama/theatre and become increasingly useful as students begin to perform before an audience.

OBJECTIVE

For each lesson a statement of a specific goal relates directly to the subject area and to the four major components of Aesthetic Perception, Creative Expression, Historical and Cultural, and Aesthetic Valuing. The objectives are sequential in nature and focus on the creation of original dramatic and visual art, the discussion of aesthetics of art, and the investigation and appreciation of the historical and cultural contributions of our multi-ethnic community.

MATERIALS

Each lesson lists supplies and materials that may be needed. These include visual arts materials, informational resources, and community resources. Because many lessons are built around a specific piece of literature, that source is also identified. However, this selection is only a suggestion; other sources may also be effective. At the intermediate level, students are expected to keep individual notebooks of reference material. The Materials section often lists scripts or notes students have created or information they have been given in previous lessons.

WARM UP

The Warm Up is a three-to-five-minute activity. It can be used as a self-contained lesson—if the purpose is simply to introduce a few dramatic concepts—or it can function as an introduction to a comprehensive creative drama lesson. This format allows effective ways to communicate complicated and abstract ideas to students as well as introducing them to the various skills used in drama/theatre, such as listening and vocalization, concentration, improvisation, and movement. The Warm Up activity is designed to lead the students directly into Explore.

EXPLORE

Explore gives students a chance to try out some of the ideas they have developed during Warm Up. The activity here often involves some creative drama experimentation as well as discussion. Warm Up and Explore together will take about 15 minutes. (At this intermediate level, the Explore section sometimes takes longer to allow for research or in-depth discussion. These extended lessons are identified in the Note at the beginning of the lesson.)

DEVELOP

Develop gives students a chance to convey through body movement and language the ideas and concepts presented. Students may work in groups or individually. Most lessons, from Warm Up through Develop, will run approximately 45 minutes. Develop fully explores the objective listed by giving students the opportunity to try out their own ideas in discussion and dramatization. It is a sustained activity that often involves risk-taking and cooperation and invites active participation by all the students.

When the Explore section of a lesson is extended, the Develop section usually requires a longer time period also. By the time students are ready for structured rehearsals in Grade 6, the lessons sometimes go beyond the Warm Up, Explore, Develop format to focus on one particular process in formal theatre.

EVALUATE

Student evaluation   *Center Stage* offers questions for student discussion and/or suggestions for an evaluation activity, such as writing or drawing. The evaluation reflects the objective of the lesson and allows students to participate in their own growth.

Teacher observation   In general, questions are presented for teachers to consider while students are involved in an activity. These questions also reflect the objective of the lesson and are guidelines to key behaviors that should be observed.

CONNECTIONS

Specific activities are offered that relate the concepts, skills, and techniques used in drama/theatre to the mathematics, science, social studies, language arts, and other arts curriculums.

SPECIAL NEEDS

When appropriate, specific ways to involve students with special needs are suggested. (General guidelines for working with special needs students are discussed further on pages xxi-xxii.)

RESOURCES

Resources provide both classroom materials and references that help involve students in story development. Resources also include particular recordings and videotapes that help create a mood or motivate movement activities. To provide background in drama/theatre and historical perspectives, materials are listed for the teacher's reference, as well.

TEACHING CENTER STAGE

LESSONS

Each teacher must approach drama/theatre activities from the place where he or she is most comfortable and confident. With *Center Stage* as a resource, that confidence should grow. The material in this guide serves as a solid basis from which to begin a program of drama in the classroom. As you gain experience, make notes on what is particularly successful for you. Feel free to add to or delete from the lessons according to your own style and your students' abilities.

Some of the later lessons at each grade level involve review and extension of skills taught earlier, so ideally the lessons should not be taught out of order. It is certainly acceptable to present a lesson out of order to meet specific needs, but realize that you may have to introduce or review a dramatic concept for a more complete understanding by your students.

The materials or books listed in a particular lesson are not the only ones that will work. Others with which you are more familiar may be substituted. Use the source listed and the accompanying techniques as a model for involving the students creatively and dramatically through literature.

Before teaching a lesson, go over it in your mind's eye. Try to visualize the amount of time each segment of the lesson will take. Such analysis will help in having a well-paced lesson with interesting and smooth transitions from one activity to another. Avoid delays by having all the materials needed for an activity organized before the lesson. One of the easiest ways to lose the interest of the students is to allow them to stand or sit idly while you gather materials. Be prepared.

Each lesson in *Center Stage* is cumulative—the Warm Up section leads directly into Explore, and Warm Up and Explore provide the impetus for Develop, the activity session. For teachers who are just beginning to experiment with drama in the classroom, or students with limited attention spans, the lesson may be ended after Warm Up or Explore. Keep focused on the lesson objective, even if you are using this shorter form of the lesson. If you stop the lesson after the Warm Up or Explore section, be sure to provide closure by asking students one or two questions to review what they have been discussing.

The culmination of each Develop activity in *Center Stage* is the sharing of a story, poem, or movement. Sharing does not mean that students passively watch others (although they could), but rather that they actively participate in the results of the process with which they were involved. Following the creative session, a few minutes should always be devoted to evaluating what has been accomplished. Bring students back together if they have been working in groups, and ask open-ended questions in a positive, nonthreatening, and constructive manner. By reflecting upon and internalizing the experience, students' sensibilities and perceptions about their experience will be heightened.

Keep your instruction simple, focused, and open-ended, so that students can discover the joy of learning by doing. Their creative thinking skills will be strengthened, and you will have the reward of enthusiasm and intellectual curiosity from your students.

ASSESSMENT

STUDENT EVALUATION

Assessment is an important part of arts education. Part of the evaluative process in drama involves sharing the ideas students have worked out. In the beginning stages of drama/theatre, students should be given the choice of whether or not they want to share their story, scene, or improvisation with the entire class. No pressure should be placed upon them to share, since the process rather than the end product should be emphasized. As students become more confident in what they do, sharing becomes a natural extension of group activity.

In the primary grades, evaluation was usually a simple discussion about the activity, focused on the students' involvement, their ability to work together, and elements of the activity that were successful, or that should be changed next time. A discussion could include such questions as, "What did you like about the ending of the story?" "Was there a particular movement that helped you know what that character was feeling?" or "What new ideas for your own story did you get from seeing this scene acted out?" At the intermediate level, however, students should be able to analyze dramatic structure and content in much more detail, and questions can focus on plot conflict and resolution and characterization. Possible questions are included in each lesson.

When discussing a student's opinion about a scene or story, always ask, "Why did you like the story or scene? What happened in the story or scene that gave you the feeling that you liked it?"

Have students interact during evaluation. One group may discuss its improvisation, story, or exercise with another group. The discussion should be positive. There is no room for negative evaluation at this stage in the drama process.

TEACHER OBSERVATION

Educators must be accountable for what students learn. Recently, educators have praised teacher observation as an effective way to assess the learning process in school arts programs.

Through observation, the teacher has the advantage of seeing the growth of each student. The teacher can evaluate whether students are actively involved and whether they use problem-solving skills to create dramatic art. The teacher can evaluate the students' confidence level as they approach the arts, and how students' growth in the arts translates into growth in other subject areas.

Through observation, the teacher can determine the direction an activity should take or how long an activity should continue. For example, if students have a high unfocused energy level when entering the room, beginning with a low-key, focused activity would be in order.

For each lesson of *Center Stage*, questions are provided for the teacher to consider during and after the lesson. If many of the answers to these questions are negative, the presentation of the activity should be reviewed. Perhaps directions were not clear enough. Perhaps an abstract concept was not sufficiently discussed for students to proceed with an activity. Perhaps ground rules were not carefully laid out, or perhaps the activity itself was too long or too advanced for the students. Lessons should be carefully analyzed and revised according to students' needs, and if necessary, repeated in the modified form.

SPECIAL NEEDS   *Center Stage* is a curriculum for the mainstream classroom. Recognizing, however, that special needs students are often mainstreamed, many lessons in *Center Stage* include specific suggestions for adapting a particular activity for this audience. Students are given appropriate yet challenging opportunities for creative expression—e.g., learning impaired students experience sequencing, the visually impaired experiment with body movement, and hearing impaired students participate in a rhythm activity through feeling vibrations.

The general suggestions that follow will help you work with the particular special needs students in your classroom.

Mentally Impaired   The less able a mentally impaired student is, the more difficult it is for her or him to understand the abstract. Therefore, adapt activities so that they are as concrete as possible. Repeat directions often, and have the students physically move through the directions to understand them better.

Learning Impaired   Many of the *Center Stage* lessons provide opportunities for success for learning impaired students as they become physically involved in the full range of activities—music, expressive movement, pantomime, and the re-creation of stories. Be prepared to offer help with organization, as well as to rephrase a concept or instruction, show a physical example, or present the concept from a different angle.

Physically Impaired   Encourage the physically impaired to participate as fully as they can in lessons involving movement. Partial movement should be accepted according to each student's abilities. Challenge these pupils to find effective and safe ways to express themselves in movement lessons.

Socially and Emotionally Impaired   With socially and emotionally impaired students, use the emotions of story and play characters to explore and work with the emotions and feelings of students themselves. Sensitivity to others, to animals, and to the environment, as well as good working relationships in a group can also be developed through drama activities.

Hearing Impaired   The hearing impaired use many modes of communication, including sign language, electronic voice amplification, writing, and lip reading. Learn and use the method that is most successful with your students. Many of the activities involving music can be used with these pupils, as they compensate for their hearing loss to some degree by feeling the music's vibrations through their chairs and the floor. However, when necessary and feasible, use visual stimuli in place of auditory stimuli to achieve the stated objective.

Visually Impaired An important fact to recognize in working with visually impaired individuals is that only a minority are "totally blind." The range of severity of visual impairment is wide: some students can perceive objects, while others may be limited to color perception or light and shadow only. Adapt the lessons according to the needs of your individual students. Obtain audiotapes, Braille, and large print materials from local agencies and libraries for the visually impaired; have a visually impaired student work with a helpful classmate; substitute tactile (mosaic, sculpture, relief paintings, or maps) and auditory stimuli for visual stimuli.

Many visually impaired individuals lack experience with radical changes of their bodies in space. Most of the movement activities can benefit them in this area.

Having special needs students in a mainstream classroom provides unique opportunities for the mainstreamed students as well as the special needs students for learning from each other and developing respect and social responsibility. Be patient, sensible, and flexible as you adapt the *Center Stage* program to the abilities of your special needs students, and work toward the goal of the fullest participation possible for *all* students.

TEACHING TIPS   CHOOSING DRAMA/THEATRE MATERIALS

As you become more comfortable with the models in this curriculum, you may want to select your own materials for creative dramatics, either to provide variety, or to suit the specific needs of your students. Keep the following suggestions and criteria in mind as you make your selections.

Ideas The simplest way to begin creative dramatics is with a single idea. How an elephant moves, what a wave looks like, what it feels like when one sees a birthday cake are all examples of ideas for creative dramatics. Moving from the dramatization of an idea to the dramatization of a series of ideas to form a story is an easy step.

Stories A story chosen for creative dramatics must be suited to the age and taste of the students. It must challenge them, but not be too difficult to dramatize. It must meet special literary and dramatic standards: The plot must be simple, logical, and full of action with not too many incidents. The characters and their dialogue must seem natural and believable. The story must have emotional appeal, a strong climax, or turning point, and a quick and satisfying ending.

Most stories contain a conflict between good and evil, and students should be led to distinguish between right and wrong. However, refrain from overt moralizing or stating ethical truths. Children want to see cause and effect and judge for themselves, and the influence of the story is far greater if they are allowed to do so.

Historical Events   Historical events can be used for creative dramatics. An imaginary story may be developed around the event if necessary to add strong dramatic appeal, a strong climax, or a quick and satisfying ending.

Poetry   Poetry, when used for creative dramatization, should be simple and clear to the students. Students should be able to understand what the poem is about and to share in the feeling behind the words. The poem should contain words that are rich in sensory and associative meaning, and the subject matter should give new and everyday experiences importance and richer meaning. When a poem is chosen for rhythmic interpretation, it should have a good rhythm and a compatibility of sound and subject. If chosen to develop a mood, a poem should contain ideas that lead students to a deeper understanding of the emotion expressed. If a poem is chosen for its story content, it must meet the same requirements as those of a good story for dramatization.

Music   If music is used with creative dramatics, it should entertain students and hold their interest; it should be musically suitable to their age group; it should stimulate creative activity; and it should provide a satisfactory emotional and educational experience at the students' own level of development.

Although a leader provides the dramatic material, the students, with their own ideas, determine how the material should be developed and dramatized. Every individual has innate creative abilities. If these are encouraged they will grow; if they are suppressed and discouraged, they disappear. A warm and trusting relationship between teacher and students allows students to freely express their ideas and lose their self-consciousness.

RULES AND LIMITS FOR CREATIVE DRAMATICS

Limits and structure can give students a sense of security as they explore creatively within the structure. For activities, develop the limits with genuine concern for students' safety and comfort. When students are new to creative dramatics, set simple, understandable rules. Say, for example:

"The first rule about drama is that we never, ever laugh at one another. We can laugh *with* one another if something is funny, but we never laugh *at* one another.

"The second rule about drama is that whenever I say, 'Freeze,' you must freeze. That means your mouth as well as your body.

"The third rule is that any kind of violence—tripping, pushing, pulling—will stop the drama activity immediately."

Give students room to imagine and create, but if rules are broken, stop the drama experience. Usually students enjoy the drama experience so much that peer pressure on any offenders will cause them to abide by the rules.

Acquaint students with the rules of good audience etiquette for both creative dramatics and a staged performance. If the group attends a live theatre performance, insist that they arrive promptly and remain quiet while the performance is going on, not getting up or otherwise causing a disturbance. They should refrain from eating or drinking in the theatre, applaud to show appreciation, and leave the auditorium in an orderly manner after the performance. Creative dramatics is not so formal, of course, but still requires consideration for the players.

GROUPING

Once the concepts are introduced and students have been given guidelines, they can work on their own or in groups to complete a task. The objective of having students work in groups to solve problems should be developing the spirit of cooperation and collaborative skills. These skills must be practiced, however, and such practice often results in loud, sometimes messy, and seemingly disorganized classroom behavior. Nonetheless, resolving disagreement is a worthwhile goal, and the process will become smoother as students find ways to work out differences of opinion.

Drama/theatre activities naturally lend themselves to group work, but each teacher must determine whether his or her class is ready for this responsibility. Activities should be teacher led at first, and directions should always be clear and complete.

To determine whether your class is ready for group work, assign a group lesson, and observe group dynamics. Ask yourself these questions:
- Are individuals or groups actively working on the creative problem to be solved or are they looking or wandering around the room?

- Are they constantly asking for help?
- Can the group choose characters or focus their attention without arguing or bickering?

Usually a group that is ready for this responsibility will quickly assemble and begin the process of discussion, casting, and rehearsing. However, if the class does not seem to be ready, go through the process with one group of students to provide modeling for the others.

BREAKING INTO GROUPS

There are creative and effective ways of grouping and pairing students so that they gain the fullest benefit of the lesson. Decide whether your students should work in pairs, small groups, or as a whole group. When breaking the class into large and small groups, consider the following procedures:

- Count off by fours or fives to create equal groups.
- Count off by pairs: A and B, or one and two.
- Send a boy and girl pair to each of several designated spots in the room.
- Give the class a math problem on dividing the entire class into equal groups of, say, four each.
- Use the alphabetical order of first or last names to create groups.
- Use other categories; for example, children who have younger brothers; children who have specific pets; children who are wearing blue socks or red shirts.
- Allow the class to divide themselves into four or five equal groups.

CLASSROOM ENVIRONMENT

Creating a special mood when the students are entering the classroom will heighten their anticipation and interest about what is going to happen. In the classroom setting, the mood can contribute to the success of a lesson. For example, if the lesson focuses on stories that take place in different environments, the teacher might play *Close Encounters of the Third Kind,* or another mysterious musical recording; he or she might also close the blinds. Then the teacher could begin the lesson in a whisper, to stimulate students' imaginations about different environments.

Many drama activities can be done in the classroom even while students are in their seats. However, an open space is an ideal location. Either clear a space within your classroom or secure the auditorium or multipurpose room for the creative drama activity. Make sure that whatever space is used is relatively free from obstruction and safe for all students, including those with special needs.

Introduction to Grade Four

The lessons in Grade 4, as at every level, are sequential and cumulative. At this level students may exhibit a wide divergency of background and abilities in drama/theatre. Individual students may profit by a review of some of the techniques from earlier grades, particularly in the areas of sensory and emotional awareness and rhythm and movement.

Because the developmental level of the lessons in Grade 4 is more sophisticated than at earlier levels, some background and review is necessary for all students. Therefore, the sequence of lessons begins with an overview of sensory and emotional awareness, rhythm and movement, and oral communication, before moving on to improvisational techniques and a broader understanding of the theatre.

Students who have participated in the *Center Stage* curriculum at Grades 1–3 will need less review than those who have not, but it is not necessary to have studied drama in previous grades to participate in *Center Stage* at Grade 4.

Expectancies for Grade 4 are that students will:

1. Grow in awareness of the senses and their relationship to the creative process.
2. Perceive rhythm and movement as the external expression of an inner idea or feeling.
3. Develop the voice as an instrument of communication.
4. React spontaneously and creatively to situations requiring problem solving.
5. Adapt simple materials for improvisation and recognize some of the basic elements of drama.
6. Gain some knowledge of the physical theatre.
7. Grow in critical evaluative skills.
8. Continue to develop an appreciation of drama in the arts.
9. Grow in knowledge of their own cultural heritage and the heritage of others.

Contents of Grade Four

Sensory Walk

COMPONENT   Aesthetic Perception

SUBJECT   Sensory Awareness

OBJECTIVE   Working in pairs, students experience a variety of visual, tactile, auditory, and olfactory sensations to increase their perception and sensory awareness.

MATERIALS   A number of small tables; cassette tape player with earphones and tape of sound effects (or rhythm instruments, egg beater, bird whistle, ball to bounce); different small objects to observe: a rough stone, a small rubber ball; objects to smell: a piece of fruit, garlic, popcorn, perfume, flowers; objects to taste: lemons, cookies, apples, oranges; toothpicks; tablecloth; timer; blindfold

Note: Warm Up describes one station, and Explore and Develop each describe two, but the order of stations does not matter. For a shorter lesson, you may wish to have pairs of students visit one or two stations only. Or you may want to schedule extra time to complete this activity to let each pair of students fully explore the sensory stations. Be aware of any dietary restrictions students have.

WARM UP   Tell students that they are going to take a "sensory walk." Describe the walk as a visit to five sensory stations. At each station, or table, students will find various stimuli for one sense—sight, taste, smell, touch, or sound. In pairs, one student will lead a partner through the various sensory experiences provided at each station.

Select five single students, one to stay at each station and rearrange the items on the table, clean up, or do whatever is needed so that others can complete the experience at that station. Divide the remaining members of the class into pairs. Have one student at a time take his or her partner to each table. As one pair finishes with the first station, another pair can begin, so that there is a steady flow of students moving from one station to another.

GRADE 4

At the "sight" station, display a collection of small objects. The leading partner should instruct the other student to take 20 seconds to look at the objects and remember as many items as possible. Then the first student covers the table with a cloth and the partner writes down all the objects that she or he can remember. If time permits, have the two switch roles, changing the objects, so that the second student can also have the visual experience.

EXPLORE

For the remaining four sensory stations, have one partner in each student pair blindfold the other. After two stations, students may switch roles. The "touch" station will have on the table a number of objects of different textures, such as a small shaggy teddy bear, a piece of fruit, a rough stone, and a small rubber ball. The blindfolded student is to be led to that area where he or she will handle and then attempt to identify the objects. Have the person assigned to that area record the student's guesses for later reference.

For the "smell" station, the blindfolded student is led to another table on which are a number of items that have distinctive odors, such as garlic, popcorn, perfume, flowers, and an orange. Again, have the student try to identify each item by its scent. The person assigned to the station records the student's responses for later use.

DEVELOP

The "hearing" station is a table on which there is a tape recorder with earphones. Have the blindfolded student sit down and put on the earphones. The student listens to a tape of various mechanical and natural sounds such as whistles, voices, horns, wind, cars, rain, boats, and airplanes.

If a tape recorder and sound effects tape are not available, provide a box of various rhythm instruments (triangle, wood blocks, small drum) and assorted items that make sounds: an egg beater, bird whistle, a ball to bounce, and so on. The first student makes sounds for the blindfolded partner to identify.

The "taste" station is a table with cookies, raisins, and small portions of different fruits such as lemons and apples on toothpicks. The first student carefully feeds the blindfolded partner small bites of different foods and writes down what that person thinks the food is. (Ask students about food allergies before starting this portion of the activity.)

As each student pair progresses from station to station, they should talk about their sensations with each other.

EVALUATE

Student evaluation: Ask the students, "How did it feel to have to trust another student to lead you to each station with your eyes covered? How did it feel to be the person who was responsible for safely leading another person from station to station? At which station were the sensory objects most difficult to identify? Why? Which station did you enjoy most? Why? Which sense do you think you rely on most in everyday life?"

Teacher observation: How well were students able to identify the various foods, objects, sounds, and smells? Were the leading partners sensitive to the students with their eyes covered? Did the students seem to increase their sensory awareness with this exercise?

CONNECTIONS

Social Studies: Have students take a tour of the school, keeping in mind the insights they gained from the activity. Have students evaluate the accessibility of school resources for disabled students. Discuss what changes might be necessary to accommodate the needs of blind, deaf, or physically challenged students.

SPECIAL NEEDS

For visually impaired students, the "sight" station could involve the students handling the objects and then describing them. Let the hearing impaired students use the rhythm instruments and/or sound-making objects themselves. Encourage them to describe the sensations they feel.

RESOURCES

Brandt, Keith. *Five Senses.* Troll Associates, 1985.

Living Sound Effects, Vols 1, 3, 7. Bainbridge Entertainment Company (tape recording of environmental sounds)

Suzuki, David. *Looking at Senses.* John Wiley & Sons, Inc., 1991.

Van Der Meer, Ron, and Atie Van Der Meer. *Your Amazing Senses.* Alladin Books (Macmillan), 1987.

Sensory Associations

COMPONENT	Aesthetic Perception
SUBJECT	Sensory Recall/Pantomime
OBJECTIVE	Students use sensory recall to convey weather conditions in improvising a scene.
MATERIALS	None required

WARM UP

Ask the students if anyone can define *sensory recall* (the ability to remember various sensory experiences associated with persons, places, or things). Ask the students for examples of sensory recall, and to explain what made the experience so important that the student recalled it. Then discuss how such an experience might be used in drama/theatre. For instance, a visit to the ocean might be remembered by the smells associated with it, and meeting someone at a train station by the noise the train made as it clattered into the station. The more vivid an actor's remembered sensations are, the more realistic a dramatization will be.

EXPLORE

Choose one of the examples suggested by the students that took place outdoors, and ask what the weather conditions were at the time of the experience. Have the student try to convey the climate conditions through pantomime. (Pantomime is nonverbal communication, demonstrating an idea or activity, a feeling, or a character, without words.)

If, for example, the student visited the ocean on a hot summer day, the student might pantomime taking off a sweatshirt or other wrap, rubbing sunscreen lotion on her or his arms and legs, and lying out on the beach to enjoy the sun. Ask the other students for ideas on how to convey the sense of heat, and have one or two pantomime their idea of a hot day. Some might add the idea of distress, acting thirsty and weak because of the heat.

DEVELOP

Tell each student to think of a particular weather condition, then consider how best to convey that condition nonverbally. Have students think of what physical movements, gestures, or facial expressions they could use to convey specific meaning. Give the students a few moments to rehearse, and then have them share their improvisations. Following each student's pantomime, have the rest of the class try to identify the particular weather conditions each student was trying to convey. Comment on how physical movement, gestures, and facial expressions help to interpret the climatic condition and with it, the setting. Others in the class may have additional suggestions for interpreting a particular condition.

EVALUATE

Student evaluation: Discuss what worked and what didn't work in the improvisations, and why. Ask the students for other situations in which sensory recall would be used. How can they use sensory recall in drama/ theatre?

Teacher observation: In your opinion, do the students now have a clearer idea of sensory recall? Did all the students participate in showing a climatic condition? How effective were the individual scenes?

CONNECTIONS

Science, Mathematics: Have each student choose a major city listed in the daily weather section of the newspaper. Tell students to keep track of the high and low temperature and precipitation amounts every day for a week. Have students then use the information to make a temperature graph and a precipitation graph to show rain or snow amounts. Display the labeled graphs on a bulletin board.

RESOURCES

Benedetti, Robert. *Actor at Work.* Prentice Hall, 1990.

Powers of Observation

COMPONENT   Creative Expression

SUBJECT   Observing Objects and Events

OBJECTIVE   Students strengthen the observation skills needed in drama/theatre by focusing on sensory details of experiences.

MATERIALS   None required

WARM UP   Review Lesson 2, in which students were asked to recall certain sensory experiences and to use their imaginations to reproduce them. In order to pantomime a sensory experience, students had to have noticed the detail in that experience. Ask students to close their eyes and picture in their minds the room at home where they eat. Then ask several students to describe the room, both visually and by remembered smells, textures, tastes, and sounds. Define *observation* as noticing the detail in what we see, hear, taste, smell, and feel. Ask the students how they can use their powers of observation in drama. Lead them to the idea that what is carefully observed and conveyed to others contributes to the creative effort and the richness of performance.

EXPLORE   Have students close their eyes, then try to recall as many details as they can remember about the classroom. What is hanging on the walls, if anything? Where? How many chairs and/or tables are there? What are the colors of the objects in the room? What is written on the board? and so on. Then have students open their eyes and check their recall. Do they see some objects that they hadn't noticed before?

Discuss with students how we tend to look at things every day without really "seeing" them. We look at objects and at actions without consciously noting what they are or what is happening. Ask the students, "Why would observation be important for an actor in a play?" (An actor must be aware of details to be able to convey them to an audience.)

DEVELOP   While students are seated at their desks, ask them to imagine, or see in their "mind's eye" the sequence of actions necessary to complete various tasks. Present such examples as:

1. peeling and eating an orange
2. brushing teeth
3. manicuring nails
4. putting on shoes
5. putting on and taking off a coat
6. tasting a strong cheese
7. walking barefoot on wet grass, hot sand, cold tile

Divide the class into pairs. Have one student pantomime a task, either one of those listed or another everyday task. The second student observes the first one, and then describes what he or she saw the other doing.

For example, if a student is pantomiming walking on wet grass, the observer might say, "When you first carefully put your foot down, your face looked shocked, as though you were feeling something cold. By the way you shook your foot, it looked as though it might have been wet. You wiggled your toes, feeling something with your feet, and then your face looked as though you were enjoying the feeling on your feet."

Switch roles; have the listener perform a task and the partner describe what he or she observes.

After each pantomime is completed, have students point out what movements, expressions, or gestures helped identify the activity, and suggest additional details that might improve the pantomime.

EVALUATE

Student evaluation: As a class, discuss details of individual pantomimes that effectively conveyed an experience. Was it difficult to show another person exactly what a particular task was? Why? Ask students how being aware of details of objects and events is important in drama/theatre.

Teacher observation: Were pairs of students able to give each other helpful suggestions for details to convey an experience? Which task seemed easiest for students to portray, and why? Did students seem to gain an awareness of the importance of observation in relation to drama/theatre activities?

CONNECTIONS *Mathematics:* Present students with a variety of number sequencing activities. Write a random series of numbers on the chalkboard for students to study. Then erase the numbers and see whether students can remember them in order. Write them in a different order and see whether students can unscramble them. Write the sequence again, substituting one number for another, and ask whether students can spot the new number.

Creating Mood with Color

COMPONENT	Aesthetic Perception
SUBJECT	Color Perception
OBJECTIVE	Students use color as motivation for movement and characterization activities.
MATERIALS	Enough 8-by-4-inch pieces of colored cellophane so that each student has several different colored rectangles

Note: This lesson could be done in two sessions. A natural division would be between Explore and Develop.

WARM UP

Give each student several different colored pieces of cellophane and tell students to hold the red one up to their eyes and look through it. Ask the students whether the color creates a particular mood in the room. If so, ask them to describe the mood. An answer might be, "The red glow makes me think about the sun on a hot summer day. It makes me feel hot!" Repeat the experience with as many colors as students have, and ask how the moods created by the colors are different.

EXPLORE

Divide the class into small groups. Have one group move while the others watch. Challenge the students in one group to make still shapes with their bodies that are suggested by a specific color. Ask, "How can you shape your body to represent how the color red makes you feel?" The students watching can hold the specific color of cellophane over their eyes to help maintain the mood.

Then ask students in the group to imagine a character that represents that color. Have students bring their shapes to life and begin moving individually as their characters.

Ask, "How would you move throughout the open space using the color red as motivation? Think about the kinds of movements you want to do, and how these movements relate to a character. I may stop you at any time and ask you why you are moving the way you are."

Let students move freely for a few minutes. Then say, "Freeze," and ask several students to explain their movements. Challenge the students in another group to make shapes and move as particular characters with the motivation of another color. Have the students watching give their opinions on whether the movements captured the mood of the color.

DEVELOP

Read the story *The Rainbow Goblins* (page 291 of CENTER STAGE) as dramatically as possible, and have the students concentrate on the different scenes, locations, and characters of the story. (The story is about the adventures of seven goblins, each named for a color.)

Tell students that they can use some of the movements they created in Explore to improvise a scene with the characters from *The Rainbow Goblins*. Ask, "What kinds of movement would each character have? What would distinguish one character from another?" Have individual students experiment with the kind of movement that would be associated with a particular goblin. Ask each student to tell why that character would move in that certain way.

Recall specific locations in the story where the action takes place, such as the rocks the goblins crawl over when they are looking for rainbows, the cave in which they sleep, and the valley of the hidden rainbows. Identify specific actions that could be improvised for each location.

In groups of seven, one student for each character in the story, have students improvise various scenes from the story using both movement and dialogue. Allow the students enough time to plan, rehearse, and then share their improvisation with the class.

Following the sharing, discuss the effectiveness of each character's movements. What made each of the characters distinctive? Ask individual members of each group to show their movements again and to evaluate their own styles in conveying the character and mood of the scene.

EVALUATE

Student evaluation: Discuss with the class whether looking through different colors of cellophane was an effective stimulus for movement. Ask, "How did the colors affect your emotions? How were the colors portrayed in the characterizations?"

Teacher observation: Could students transfer the ideas and mood generated by color into movement activities? How effectively were the students able to convey the moods of the different characters? In the groups of seven, did all the students participate fully?

CONNECTIONS   *Language Arts:* Have students write a poem or story about their favorite color. To get started, they should list objects that are their favorite color. Have students explain why they like the color and how it makes them feel.

SPECIAL NEEDS   Keep in mind that most visually impaired individuals can perceive color. Only those who are severely impaired with minimal to no light perception will not be able to participate in the Warm Up and Explore sections of this lesson. For Develop, use determining characteristics such as size, shape, odor, sound, texture, feelings, and age to help the students distinguish each character's style of moving.

RESOURCES   De Rico, Ul. *The Rainbow Goblins.* Thames Hudson, Inc., 1978. (This book recently went out of print, but the text is in the Appendix of CENTER STAGE.)

LESSON FIVE

Emotions as Themes of Poems

COMPONENT   Aesthetic Perception

SUBJECT   Emotions

OBJECTIVE   Students listen to poetry to identify emotions used as themes in poetry, and create a scene that conveys an emotion.

MATERIALS   *Talking to the Sun: An Illustrated Anthology of Poems for Young People,* by Kenneth Koch and Kate Farrell

WARM UP   Discuss *theme* with students. The theme of a story or play is its central thought, idea, or significance of action. The plot in a story or play tells what happens, but the theme expresses an idea about life that the author or playwright wishes to convey. Poems, while they may have a message about life, often have a mood or an emotion as a theme.

Tell the students to think about the emotion or mood used as a theme in each of the following poems as they are read aloud. Read, "To an Isle in the Water," by William Butler Yeats (love), "Little Fish," by D.H. Lawrence (happiness), "Miss Blue's Child," by Langston Hughes (sorrow and loneliness), and "Autobiographia Literaria," by Frank O'Hara (loneliness and joy). Ask the students what they think is the theme of each poem, or the expressed emotion. Write students' answers on the board.

EXPLORE   Remind students of Lesson 4, in which they created improvisations using moods and characters suggested by colors. In this activity they are to use the emotions conveyed in a poem to motivate an improvisation. For example, say, "You thought that the emotion, or theme, in 'Miss Blue's Child' was loneliness. What do you think made the person speaking the poem lonely? Can you imagine another situation in which someone was lonely?" Write one or two situations on the board. Ask similar questions for each of the poems read.

DEVELOP   Select one of the situations suggested by students to develop into a scene. Ask first, "Who are the people involved, the characters?" Write the list on the board. Then ask, "What will they be doing?" For example, there might be two people saying goodbye. Ask where they are. Establish the location, then explore what the characters might be saying to each other (dialogue).

Finally, remembering Lesson 4, ask students what movements are needed to convey the emotion, and decide on the way the characters will move.

After the *who, what, where,* dialogue, and movements of the scene have been established, ask for volunteers to play the scene. After the scene has been played, ask the rest of the class such questions as, "How did the dialogue convey the emotion of the poem? Did the movement help show what the character was feeling? What other dialogue could be added to make the emotion clearer? Are there other movements that could make the emotion easier to identify?"

Select other volunteers to replay the scene, utilizing the suggestions made by the class. Ask the questions again. Repeat the process with another poem. Again, emphasize the movements necessary to convey the emotion.

EVALUATE

Student evaluation: The two scenes showed two different emotions. How did the actors show the differences between them? How were the emotions in the scenes shown by movement? Do you think one scene was more interesting to create than the other? Why?

Teacher observation: Were students able to convey the emotional themes? Did the students use their bodies creatively to convey emotion? Did the students utilize both movement and dialogue to create a scene? Did students understand *theme* as it is used in poetry?

CONNECTIONS

Language Arts: Have students name different emotions, and write their responses on the board. Then divide the class into groups and have students work together to think of synonyms for each word. Encourage students to list as many synonyms as they can. If they wish, they could write a short poem with their emotion as the theme, using as many of the synonyms as possible.

RESOURCES

Koch, Kenneth, and Kate Farrell. *Talking to the Sun: An Illustrated Anthology of Poems for Young People.* Henry Holt and Company, 1985.

Movement Study

COMPONENT   Aesthetic Perception

SUBJECT   Movement/Characterization

OBJECTIVE   Students use animal comparisons to visualize behavioral traits for characterization.

MATERIALS   None required

WARM UP   A variety of similes and metaphors are commonly used to compare people and animals. Some examples are: "cute as a kitten," "clumsy as a bear," "quiet as a mouse," "making a pig of himself," and "snake in the grass." Ask the students what these mean. Can they think of others? Write students' suggestions on the board.

EXPLORE   Discuss with students the usefulness of animal comparisons for drama/theatre activities. Because animals are familiar, and they bring an immediate picture, or visualization, to mind, they become a model of movement or behavior that an actor can imitate. Select one or two of the similes or metaphors that students have suggested, and ask students how seeing the picture of that animal in the mind's eye would give them clues for movement in a scene. Ask a volunteer to demonstrate, for example, moving "with catlike grace."

DEVELOP   Move students to an open space and let them all experiment with moving like a particular animal. You may wish to start with the example from Explore. As students move, point out specific catlike movements of various students, and how their observation of cats has helped them in imitating the movement.

Then have students experiment with moving like other animals, such as a lion, a deer, a bear, a fox—whatever examples students have suggested. Before students begin to move, ask for descriptions of the movement and behavioral characteristics of each animal to stimulate students' imaginations.

Define *characterization* in drama/theatre as imitating the individual and distinctive traits of a character in a play to portray that person or being to an audience. Ask students what characters from stories read in class have characteristics or traits of certain animals. What character would act or move like a mouse, a bear, or a deer? If students had read *Heidi,* for example, they might imagine the grandfather to be gruff and bearlike. Ask, "If you had to portray that character in a drama, how would it help to imagine how an animal moves?" Have students try moving as a particular character, using an animal as a comparison. Then select one or two students to demonstrate their movements for the class.

EVALUATE *Student evaluation:* Ask students, "How many similes or metaphors could you think of that compare the behavior of people to animals? Did animal similes and metaphors help you to understand people and characterization? Which animals were the easiest to imitate? Which were the most difficult? Why?"

Teacher observation: In your opinion, did using the similes and metaphors help the students understand the concept of characterization? Were the students able to use the different animals to generate ideas for movements? Did students use their bodies freely in interpreting the movements of animals?

CONNECTIONS *Science:* Have students explore animal characteristics in terms of their adaptations to the environment. Suggest that students focus on a habitat, such as ocean, desert, island, or polar region. Then have them choose an animal that is able to survive there, and find out how it lives there and what makes it able to survive. Students' research may be presented in oral reports or in an informal discussion.

SPECIAL NEEDS Some visually impaired students will not have observed animal behavior and movement. For these students, have a classmate model the animal movement while maintaining physical contact with the visually impaired student. Then have the visually impaired student try to imitate what she or he has felt.

Controlled Movement

COMPONENT	Creative Expression
SUBJECT	Action in Slow Motion
OBJECTIVE	Working in pairs, students concentrate on disciplined movements to give them aesthetic form.
MATERIALS	None required

WARM UP
Say, "Without bumping those around you, raise your hands into the air as fast as you can! Without hurting yourselves, put your hands down as fast as you can! Now, when I say 'go,' raise your hands very slowly, as slowly as this [demonstrate very slowly for the students]. Now put your arms down as slowly as you can!"

Ask the students, "What is the difference between the two motions?" (control) Tell the students that control of the body is important in almost all of our activities. For the athlete, the dancer, and the actor it is especially important to have absolute and complete control of their bodies. One of the ways to understand how we move and to learn to control our bodies is by practicing actions in slow motion.

EXPLORE
Challenge students to pantomime other actions in slow motion. Ask them to pick up and put down a pencil. Have them stand up and walk in slow motion to an open space, and then find places for themselves where they will not bump into one another. Suggest other simple movements to pantomime, such as bending down to tie a shoe, tossing and catching a ball, opening and closing a door, petting a dog, and eating an ice cream cone. Challenge students to do each action as slowly as possible.

Ask the students, "What did you have to do physically and mentally to slow down your actions? What muscles did you use? How is using those muscles in slow motion different from moving them at normal speed?

DEVELOP
Divide the class into pairs. Tell students that each pair is going to cooperate in pantomiming an activity. Assign each pair an activity such as playing catch, picking up a chair and moving it, washing and drying dishes, putting fallen leaves into a large bag, or making change. Allow time for the pairs to experiment with moving in slow motion together.

Now tell students that they are to act singly again and add characterization (see Lesson 6) to their slow motion pantomimes. Each student is to choose one of the following characters and actions to perform in slow motion:

A 70-year-old fisherman in a boat struggling to land a big fish.

A 4-year-old boy picking up and carrying a heavy bag full of groceries.

A strong mountain climber having a difficult time climbing a steep mountain.

A teacher in a classroom writing an assignment on the board.

An astronaut raising a flag on the moon.

Challenge the students to make the characters interesting by visualizing the character and actions chosen in the mind's eye first, then bringing the picture of the character to life with slow motion actions.

EVALUATE

Student evaluation: Ask students, "Could you maintain the slow motion throughout the activity? What helped you? What made it difficult? Do you think slow motion is more or less difficult than normal movement? Was portraying someone else in slow motion more or less difficult than being one's self? Why?"

Teacher observation: Were the students able to slow down their body motions for these activities? Did students cooperate when working in pairs? Were they able to portray specific characters in slow motion?

CONNECTIONS

Art: Have students use crayons, pencils, pens, chalk, or paint to draw a picture that conveys the idea of either fast or slow motion. Students are to use only lines in their pictures; lines may be curved and may intersect, but no solid shapes are to be used. Compare drawings and have students try to determine the "speed" of each picture.

RESOURCES

Way, Brian. *Development through Drama.* Humanities Press, 1967.

Communicating Emotion Through Movement

COMPONENT   Aesthetic Perception

SUBJECT   Movement and Emotions

OBJECTIVE   Students become aware of and respond to the communicative potential of drama/theatre by exploring nonverbal methods of communication.

MATERIALS   None required

WARM UP

Explain to students that movement is nonverbal communication and is used in drama/theatre just as much as the spoken word. Physical movements can tell in many ways how a person feels and what is happening to him or her.

Ask the students, "How do we show how we feel? What are some of the movements we make to express an emotion? What happens to your faces and bodies when you are happy? Sad? Angry? Upset? Puzzled?" Ask students, "How do you show some of these expressions with the rest of your body?" Answers might include: stamping your foot, standing with your arms folded and looking away, jumping up and raising your arms, shrugging your shoulders, and so on.

Ask the students if they can think of any other movements that show how a person feels. Make a list of the movements with their related feelings on the board.

EXPLORE

In an open space have the students show postures and movements that portray the various emotions or moods the class has talked about. Then have students continue to act out a particular emotion by adding other movements to it. Tell students, "If you have been showing happiness by smiling and jumping up in the air, you might add a little skip."

Have one student demonstrate his or her original movement, then follow it with other movements that also show this emotion. For example, if a student originally stamped her foot, she might fold her arms and frown, or throw her hands in the air. Have students use the list on the board to select emotions and their related movements, and then experiment with adding other movements to the first one.

GRADE 4

DEVELOP

Tell students that you are going to ask them to walk in ways that express certain feelings arising from specific situations. As they move, they must think about how they are feeling inside, and how that feeling will be shown in their external movement and gestures.

As you describe the situations below, have students imagine being in them, and express their emotions through movement by walking across the room as though the situation had just happened to them.

You are late for school.

You are angry because you can't watch your favorite TV program.

You are sad because your team just lost a ball game.

You are happy because your father cooked your favorite food for dinner.

You are going to the dentist for a checkup.

You are going to the toy store to buy a present for your best friend.

Let all students experiment with movement motivated by each particular emotion and situation. Then ask for volunteers to demonstrate their movements, and have the class suggest additional movements to portray each particular feeling and situation. Ask also for descriptions of characters that might be in that situation. Let the student repeat the movement using the suggestions to see whether the emotion is portrayed more clearly, and whether becoming a particular character improves the improvisation.

EVALUATE

Student evaluation: Ask students, "Were you able to move across the room in ways that showed how a character was feeling inside? How does movement, or nonverbal communication, help to develop a character?"

Teacher observation: Do the students understand the relationship of movement to the portrayal of feeling and mood created by an actor? Were the students able to "put on" the assigned feelings so that the movements in a particular situation became more believable to them and the viewer?

CONNECTIONS

Science: Explain that animal species communicate nonverbally in many situations, including when they are mating, fighting, sensing danger, warning each other of danger, and marking their territory. Have each student choose an animal and study the manner in which it communicates. Then have each student demonstrate for the class his or her animal's method of communication.

RESOURCES

Center Stage: Creative Dramatics Supplement. (contains "How Are You Feeling Today?" poster) Available from Dale Seymour Publications.

Character Study

COMPONENT	Creative Expression
SUBJECT	Observation
OBJECTIVE	Students use perceptual skills to experience, create, understand, and evaluate drama/theatre as they transform what they have observed into aesthetic form.
MATERIALS	None required

Note: A day or two before the lesson, ask the students to observe carefully someone at home or in the community who is unknown to the rest of the class. Students are to note the way the person walks, talks, and moves.

WARM UP

Tell the students that every human being is unique in the way he or she moves, talks, and thinks, and that this very diversity makes the world an interesting place to be. (You may need to spend some time at this point in the lesson discussing diversity in language, race, or physical ability. Insist on respect for all differences, and emphasize the fact that while the actor observes to identify unique characteristics, the actor also constantly works to identify with and understand the feelings of the character he or she portrays.)

Ask the students to think for a moment of the differences in their own classmates. They all move and speak in distinctive ways. Ask, "Could you identify one of your friends if you could only see or hear that person walk or talk, without seeing his or her face or other identifiable features?" Give students a chance to respond.

EXPLORE

Give the students a few minutes to recall their observations of the person they selected (see *Note* above). Have students describe the person they observed, telling the way that person walked, talked, and gestured.

Move the students to an open space, and have one of the students who described someone repeat the description. Ask students to walk about, not touching each other, as they imagine the person described would walk. Point out that each student sees the described person a little differently in his imagination, and portrays him or her that way. Ask the student who gave the description to comment on the accuracy of the portrayals. Although none of the students may match the exact movements of the person described, each student should be able to translate some of the description into movement and gesture. An actor follows this process in developing a characterization.

DEVELOP   In the open space, ask each student to re-create the walk and gestures of the particular person she or he observed. Then bring the class together again, and ask individual students to describe the person they re-created. Have them demonstrate the movements of that person again. Ask them to say, "Good morning. How are you?" in the manner of the person they re-created. Ask the class, "Do you know somebody like this person?" Point out that being able to portray persons other than themselves is one of the most important skills of actors.

EVALUATE   *Student evaluation:* Ask the students what challenges they had to overcome to portray or convey the essence of persons other than themselves. Could they pick out unique characteristics of movement, speech, and posture of the people they observed?

Teacher observation: Were students able to describe or move with the physical characteristics of another person from observation? Did students seem to understand the relationship of this experience to what actors do in the theatre?

CONNECTIONS   *Social Studies:* Write on the board some famous quotations from historical figures in your current state history unit. Have students interpret how the words were said, adding gestures and movement. Then let groups of students each choose one quotation to perform.

SPECIAL NEEDS   To varying degrees, both visually and physically impaired students may have to restrict their re-creations to the manner of speaking and whatever movements and gestures they have been able to observe or can reproduce. Also, the essence of another person is quite abstract, and its observation and portrayal could be very difficult for the mentally impaired.

RESOURCES   Stanislavski, Constantin. *Building a Character.* Theatre Arts Books, 1977.

Nonsense Words

COMPONENT   Creative Expression

SUBJECT   Communicating Through Actions

OBJECTIVE   Students communicate meaning through voice inflection as they give nonsensical directions for a set of actions.

MATERIALS   About 20 small strips of paper on which are written simple tasks such as moving a chair, picking up a pencil, or setting a table, and several nonsense words

Note: This lesson could be divided into two sessions. A natural break would be between the Explore and Develop sections.

WARM UP   Ask the students, "How many of you have made up words that don't make any sense and sound like gibberish? Do the words you make up have special meanings for you? Do you sometimes share these words with special friends and make up a language of your own?" Allow students the opportunity to share various nonsensical words. Ask them for definitions of the words they make up.

Tell the students you have made up a nonsense word, *mellopap.* Say, "Now I just made up that word. I will tell you what it means; it is a new kind of cereal to eat. Would you like some of my *mellopap?*" Give students a chance to make up some new words of their own and tell what they mean.

Explain to the students that even though a word has no real meaning, we sometimes can convey meaning by the way we use the voice to say the word. A change in the tone or pitch of the voice is called an *inflection,* and is very important in conveying meaning. (Demonstrate *inflection* by changing the pitch and tone of your voice as you say the word *extraordinary.*) The rate of speed and the volume also help to convey meaning.

Ask various students to say the word *well* using two different inflections, and then ask them to explain what the word meant each time. Point out that as some of the meaning of the word *well* was conveyed by its inflection, so can nonsense words be given meaning by inflection.

EXPLORE   Give one student a strip of paper with several nonsense words on it, and a simple task to complete, such as moving a chair or picking up a pencil.

Let that person give directions for the task in nonsense words, adding gestures if necessary, and choose another student to follow the directions. Be sure that the person talking uses only nonsense words! Let several pairs of students try this process until they are comfortable with the idea.

Then repeat the exercise with a more complex task, such as setting a table for dinner, or making a bed. Give various students opportunities to perform, and ask others to suggest different inflections for communicating the direction.

DEVELOP   Divide the class into pairs. Give one student in each pair a strip of paper with a task and nonsense words on it. That person will direct the other to complete that task, using gibberish, and gestures if necessary. The gibberish can be what is written on the strip, or the student may make up new nonsense words. The student taking directions may ask questions, but only in gibberish. Tasks on the strips might include putting a toy together, planting a garden, making a pizza, and feeding a cat. Give students ample time to plan and rehearse the scenes.

Following the planning and rehearsing, allow the pairs to share their scenes with the rest of the class.

EVALUATE   *Student evaluation:* Ask students to recall the definition of *inflection*. Do they understand how inflection conveys meaning? Ask, "What gave you the clues about what was happening between the two people? Was it gibberish and voice inflection only, or did gestures convey part of the meaning? Was the person following the directions able to understand what he or she was to do? Was the person using the gibberish consistent? What would help to make the scenes clearer?"

Teacher observation: Could students communicate with gibberish? Did all of the pairs participate? Did students investigate various ways of utilizing the voice, body, and gestures to convey different ideas in the improvisations?

CONNECTIONS   *Mathematics:* Let groups of students invent nonsense words for the numbers from 0 to 9 and give each other multiplication problems using the nonsense words.

SPECIAL NEEDS   You may have to limit the scope and length of the scenes for mentally impaired students.

Improvisation from Literature

COMPONENT   Creative Expression

SUBJECT   Improvisation

OBJECTIVE   Students use their imaginations to interpret and dramatize a famous nonsense poem.

MATERIALS   One copy for each student of "Jabberwocky," from *Alice's Adventures in Wonderland and Through the Looking Glass,* by Lewis Carroll (page 30)

Note: You may wish to do this lesson in two sessions, dividing it between Explore and Develop.

WARM UP   Review Lesson 10, in which the students used nonsensical words and created improvisations using gibberish. Ask the students, "How many of you have read *'Alice's Adventures in Wonderland and Through the Looking Glass?'*" (Some students may be familiar with the animated film.) Explain to the students that these stories were written in Great Britain more than one hundred years ago, in 1868, for the entertainment of a little girl. The books are full of nonsensical situations and people, as well as nonsense words.

Say, "I am going to read the poem 'Jabberwocky' from *Alice's Adventures in Wonderland.* The poem is made up of real and nonsense words." Tell the class that the real words in the poem give clues to what the nonsense words might mean. Determining whether the nonsense words are names of things (nouns), are actions (verbs), or describe something (adjectives and adverbs) can also help detect meaning. Ask the students to listen carefully to discover what the poem is about and to see if they can decide which nonsense words are nouns, verbs, adjectives, or adverbs.

Read the poem to the students. Reread it several times if necessary.

EXPLORE   Review previous lessons in which the students used movement to interpret various characters, often creating a mood or portraying a particular emotion.

Give students a copy of "Jabberwocky" and ask them to circle as many nouns as they can, then decide which are characters that could be dramatized. Characters could include the slithy toves, borogroves, manxome foe, Jabberwock, Jubjub bird, and Bandersnatch. Have students put X's on the action words (verbs) and parentheses around the words that describe (adjectives and adverbs).

Say, "Use the verbs and adjectives and adverbs to help you think about how these creatures would look and how they would move. They aren't human, but rather strange-looking and strange-sounding creatures. Since these characters are unique, and the words have no real meaning, there is no right or wrong way to portray them. Use your imaginations to make a character that satisfies you."

Move the students to an open space to explore various ways of physically portraying the different characters. Have each student choose a character. Ask such questions as, "How does your creature move? How is it shaped? Does your creature do something that we have never seen before?" As the students move, continue asking questions that will help them develop a definite characterization for each creature.

DEVELOP　　　Continue this activity by improvising a scene based on the characters, setting, and mood created by the poem.

First, cast the various characters based on the students' interests and abilities. Allow a number of students to play the same character. For example, the slithy toves may be four or five students moving together within an established area. Some of the students could be inanimate objects such as a Tumtum tree.

Next, decide on the setting, mood, and playing area. Discuss the settings in which the action will take place. Students might imagine that the action happens in a magical forest or marsh. It is night, with a full moon to light the scene. Ask students to describe sounds that could be heard in such a magical place.

Decide whether one person will read the poem as the students act out the characters, whether individual students will each read certain parts of the story, or whether groups will recite parts as a chorus. Experiment with a number of ways to read the poem; then determine which would work best.

Establish guidelines for the different characters entering the playing area when their names are mentioned in the poem.

Finally, establish the action that takes place. Assign some students to create the sounds that may be heard in this magical place, and then play the improvisation of the poem from the beginning to the end.

Replay the story to give all the students an opportunity to experience a number of characters.

EVALUATE

Student evaluation: Ask students, "Did the nonsense words in the poem give you any clues about the characters or their actions? What were the clues? What did you like about your character? Did observing others' characters help you to create your own? How? Which parts of the poem did you enjoy dramatizing, and why? What would you change if you were to perform the story again?"

Teacher observation: Did the students use what they had learned from Lesson 10 about nonsense words to create different characters? How creative were the students in reading parts of the poem and in developing nonhuman creatures? Could students use the nonsense words as stimuli in creating a movement piece to the poem?

CONNECTIONS

Physical Education: Divide the class into teams of four for a "Jabberwocky Relay Race." Assign one person on each team to be one of four creatures developed for the poem improvisation. That person must use the movements of the creature from the improvisation as he or she runs.

RESOURCES

Carroll, Lewis. *Alice's Adventures in Wonderland and Through the Looking Glass.* Putnam Publishing Group, 1963.

Jabberwocky

'Twas brillig, and the slithy toves
Did gyre and gimble in the wabe:
All mimsy were the borogroves,
And the mome raths outgrabe.

"Beware the Jabberwock, my son!
The jaws that bite, the claws that catch!
Beware the Jubjub bird, and shun
The frumious Bandersnatch!"

He took his vorpal sword in hand:
Long time the manxome foe he sought—
So rested he by the Tumtum tree,
And stood awhile in thought.

And, as in uffish thought he stood,
The Jabberwock, with eyes of flame,
Came whiffling through the tulgey wood,
And burbled as it came!

One, two! One, two! And through and through
The vorpal blade went snicker-snack!
He left it dead, and with its head
He went galumphing back.

"And hast thou slain the Jabberwock?
Come to my arms, my beamish boy!
O frabjous day! Callooh! Callay!"
He chortled in his joy.

'Twas brillig, and the slithy toves
Did gyre and gimble in the wabe:
All mimsy were the borogroves,
And the mome raths outgrabe.

—Lewis Carroll

Practicing Concentration

COMPONENT	Aesthetic Perception
SUBJECT	Concentration Skills
OBJECTIVE	Students practice their concentration skills with exercises stressing the ability to focus in the midst of distractions.
MATERIALS	None required

WARM UP

Ask the class whether anyone can define *concentration*. The definition should be close to "keeping one's mind and attention on one particular object, scene, or idea." Add, "Concentration in drama/theatre is being able to focus your attention in spite of the presence of the class, audience, or other distractions. Concentration requires conscious effort and practice."

Provide an open space with enough room for the students to move around. Challenge them with a series of movement and concentration activities, such as, "When I say 'go,' I want you to walk around the room without touching another person, and when I say 'freeze,' I want you to freeze, no matter what position you are in."

Emphasize the importance of not touching, and listening for the "go" and "freeze" commands. Discuss how concentration played a part in students' abilities to follow the commands.

EXPLORE

Divide the class into pairs. Say, "You and your partner are to walk around the room in different directions without touching anyone else. You are to keep eye contact—that is, look at each other's faces, at all times. You and your partner should move freely throughout the space, away from each other, but always keeping the eye contact. To keep from bumping anyone else, you also have to be aware of other people, but don't lose the eye contact with your partner. Start when I say 'go,' and stop when I say 'freeze.'"

Give the students a number of "go" and "freeze" commands in order to observe their abilities to concentrate on the directions. Challenge all the students to keep focused on the activity. Discuss with students how well they were able to concentrate. Were they distracted by anything or anyone?

DEVELOP

Give four or five students copies of the same book, preferably one of their current texts, and have students enter a circle and sit on the floor or in chairs. Have the students turn to a particular page in the book. Select one student to read that page aloud. Tell the readers that when you say "go," the one student will begin reading aloud as the others follow along in the books silently. They should try to focus all of their attention and concentration on the reading.

Select another five or six students to distract the readers. They can sing, dance, talk loudly, tell jokes, run around the readers, and so on. They must not touch the readers in any way, nor come inside the circle. Warn the remaining students that they are to follow good audience etiquette by keeping absolutely silent.

Begin the activity by saying, "Go." After a few minutes, say, "Stop." Ask the readers how it felt to try to concentrate with all the distractions around them. Was the student who was reading aloud able to keep going? Could the silent readers hear the student who was reading aloud? Did they comprehend what was read? Have the readers relate to the class some of the content of the passage read. Ask others in the class whether the readers seemed to be distracted or whether they seemed to be concentrating fully on the reading.

Change the readers and the distractors and continue with the activity. (Be aware that this could be a loud activity.) Discuss concentration again, and how it relates to the actor in drama/theatre. Ask students, "How do actors learn to concentrate on what is happening on the stage, and be aware of the audience without letting the audience distract them?"

EVALUATE   *Student evaluation:* Ask students, "Were you able to keep eye contact when you were working with a partner? How easy or difficult was it to concentrate on reading with the distractions? Can you think of situations in your own life in which good concentration skills would be helpful? How can concentration exercises help an actor perform her or his role on the stage during a performance? Why is it important that the audience remain quiet?"

Teacher observation: Were students genuinely trying to concentrate? Were they able to do so while being distracted? Why, in your opinion, were some students able to concentrate better than others? Did the students seem to understand the concept of concentration better following this exercise? Could they understand how an actor must use concentration skills in the theatre?

CONNECTIONS   *Language Arts:* Create 15–20 pairs of cards with literary titles and authors for students to use to play Concentration. Have students match identical literary titles or titles and authors. Pairs (or teams) of students arrange the cards face down. A player then turns up two cards. If the cards match, the player gets another turn; if not, the cards are replaced and the other player turns up two cards to attempt a match. The player matching the most pairs wins.

SPECIAL NEEDS   Many visually impaired students will not be able to maintain eye contact during the Explore section of the lesson. Have them touch fingertips and try to maintain this contact. Learning impaired pupils may have a great deal of difficulty concentrating on reading while others attempt to distract them.

Developing a Logical Sequence

COMPONENT Aesthetic Perception

SUBJECT Sequence

OBJECTIVE Students arrange several events in sequential order, and create a story from a given set of events or descriptions.

MATERIALS Sets (one set per student) of five 3-by-5-inch cards that list related pieces of information, with one piece of information on each card, so that the list can be put into some kind of order. You may use one list for all the sets or you may choose to have a different list for each set.

WARM UP Define *sequence* as the order in which events happen or steps in a task are performed. Relate sequence to everyday activities such as washing one's face. In what order are the actions performed? Does one usually dry one's face before washing it? What is the sequence of action in preparing a hamburger to eat? Is the meat put on a bun before it is cooked? What other activities must be done in sequence? List students' suggestions on the board, and discuss the sequence of action for each activity.

EXPLORE Write on the board a sequence of actions for an activity, but write them in random order, and have the students number the actions sequentially. For example, write "Opening a Present" on the board, and under it, write:

playing with a toy
receiving a present
untying ribbon
finding a toy inside
lifting off box top

Ask the students to number the actions so that the activity is logical and correct.

Point out that there is a beginning, a middle, and an end to the sequence of action. Say, "If this were a story, what part would be considered the beginning? The middle? The end?" Ask the students to pantomime the actions of the story at their desks. They can add story elements by imagining, for example, that they are a child who has never had a toy before and who is given a wonderful bicycle; the setting could be a special restaurant that the child chose; and the present could be opened in the evening.

DEVELOP

Give each student five cards with related information on them, so that the information could be used to create a story. A set of five cards might have written on them:

changing colors in the moonlight
the magical stone
into a deep, deep pool
freed from the powerful spell
trying to get away

Challenge each student to write a story using the information on the cards. Students will need to add sequence, characters, settings, and actions. They may add information to make a logical beginning, middle, and end. Let students know that, unlike the sequence in Explore, this sequence has no correct order except the one they create. Tell the students to think about their stories as possibilities for dramatizations. Emphasize creativity and logical sequence, rather than grammar or spelling.

Allow enough time for students to write their stories, and then ask several students to share their stories with the entire class. Let the class comment on the sequence of actions. Was it logical? Was each part related to the part preceding it, and to the one following after? Was the story interesting?

EVALUATE

Student evaluation: Ask students, "What are examples of everyday activities that need to be done in sequence? Was it easy or difficult to decide on a logical order for five actions? Why? What process did you use to create a story from the information on the cards?"

Teacher observation: Were the students able to understand sequence and how it pertains to stories in drama/theatre activities and their own stories? Did most students individually create a story from the sequence cards? Were the students aware of the beginning, middle, and end in their stories? Did the students use the information on the cards imaginatively?

CONNECTIONS

Science: Have students make a poster showing a sequence of events found in nature. Possibilities include the water cycle, the life cycle of a butterfly, the eruption of a volcano, a year in the life of a Canada goose, a year in the life of a bear, and so on. Discuss the posters and display them in the classroom.

SPECIAL NEEDS   Read aloud to visually impaired students the information written on the sequence cards, or provide Braille cards. With emotionally and mentally impaired students, create the story as a class, giving the students the opportunity to suggest creative information for the story. Allow those students who are able the opportunity to write their stories on their own.

RESOURCES   McCaslin, Nellie. *Creative Drama in the Classroom*. Longman, 1990.

Scher, Anna, and Charles Verrall. *Another One Hundred Plus Ideas for Drama*. Heinemann, 1987.

Sequential Development in Stories

COMPONENT   Creative Expression

SUBJECT   Sequence

OBJECTIVE   Students create a story using the five W's
and a logical sequence of events.

MATERIALS   Cassette tape recorder and blank tape

WARM UP   Remind students of Lesson 13, in which they put events in order and
created a story with a beginning, middle, and end. Tell students that they
are going to play the Add On game, in which they will be adding on
events in a logical sequence to create a story. Review the five W's, and tell
students to include them as they create the story. Tape record the story so
that you can review it later.

Have the students sit in a circle. Begin telling a story, and stop at a certain
place. For example, start by saying, "Once upon a time there was a little
boy who had always wanted to fly. One day he went to the top of a high
mountain, looked over the edge, and . . .[stop]"

Point to a student, who will then continue the story from the place you
left off. After a few moments, say, "Stop." Let the storyteller point to
another student to continue from where she or he left off. Continue the
story-telling process until the story reaches a natural closure.

EXPLORE   Tell the students that you will play the tape of the recorded Add On story,
and ask them to listen to check that the sequence of events is logical, and
that each of the five W's can be identified.

Play the tape. Ask the students to identify the five W's in the story. Who is
the story about? Who are the other characters? What is happening?
Where does the story take place? When does it happen? Why do all the
events happen? Then ask, "Is there a beginning, middle, and end to the
story? Should any of these events be put in a different order?"

DEVELOP   Remind students that in Lesson 5 they discussed *theme*. Review, if necessary, the definition of theme as the central thought or idea of a play or
story. Ask what they thought was the theme of the taped story. Tell students that they will be working in small groups to develop sequentially an
original story, and that they will begin with a basic idea or theme.

Divide the class into groups of four to six, and challenge each small group to think of a theme for a story. Using the taped story as a model, one student provides the beginning of the story, then the others add characters and events as they think of ones that could logically follow. Remind the students to use the five W's in creating their story. Give groups enough time so that they are not rushed in developing a story line, and so that someone in the group can write down the main sequence of events. Allow each group to share its story with the class. If time permits, have the groups dramatize parts or all of their stories.

EVALUATE

Student evaluation: As a class, discuss the process that each group went through to develop its story. What was the hardest part of the collaboration? What was the easiest? Could you create a logical sequence of events in each story? Did you use the five W's? Did everyone in the group participate?

Teacher observation: How imaginative were the students in improvising on a given story line? Were the individual groups able to work cooperatively with one another? Did using the taped model seem to provide structure for the small groups to create a story?

CONNECTIONS

Mathematics: Write a sequence of numbers on the chalkboard. Include enough numbers to establish a definite pattern. Then have students take turns supplying a number to continue the sequence. Suggest that students create their own number sequences and share them with the group. For example: 1, 6, 3, 8, 5, 10, 7. . . $(x + 5 - 3)$; 3, 9, 7, 21, 19, 57, 55, 165, 163. . .$(x \times 3 - 2)$; 1, 3, 6, 10, 15, 21, 28, 36, 45, 55, 46, 38, 31. . . $(1 + 2 + 3. . .+ 10 - 9 - 8. . .)$

Story Components in Drama

COMPONENT	Creative Expression
SUBJECT	Theatre Vocabulary
OBJECTIVE	Students learn appropriate drama/ theatre terms and their meanings, and use the concepts to create and dramatize the beginning of a story.
MATERIALS	Cassette tape player; tape recording of mystery movie themes

GRADE 4

WARM UP

Remind students that there are three very simple parts, or components, of a story—the beginning, the middle, and the end. The beginning introduces the characters, the setting, and the situation, problem, or conflict the characters are facing. The middle tells how the characters work to solve the problem. The ending tells how the problem or conflict is solved.

Choose a book, a story, television program, movie, or play that the students are familiar with, and decide what could be considered the beginning, the middle, and the end.

EXPLORE

Discuss with the students other terms that also describe elements of a dramatized story. Some of these terms were introduced in Grade 3 of CENTER STAGE, but you may need to introduce them to students new to the program. Some terms may be new to all the students.

Plot: What happens in the story, or the events as revealed through the action and dialogue of the characters.

Conflict: The tension or struggle between two or more characters, or between a character and some kind of force. Conflict can also be two opposing ideas.

Climax: The turning point of the action, usually an exciting part, in which some kind of change takes place that will bring about the resolution, or outcome of the story.

Resolution: The final unfolding of the solution to the complications or conflicts in the plot.

Analyze a well-known story such as "Jack and the Beanstalk" in terms of plot, conflict, climax, and resolution. What is the plot of this story? (What happens in the story? Ask students to give the actions in sequence.) What is the main conflict in the story? (What does the main character want, and what does that person have to overcome to get it?) What is the climax of the story? (What event is the turning point of the story and decides the outcome?) What is the resolution of the story? (Does the main character achieve what he or she wants? If so, how? If not, why not?)

Ask students to name the other elements of a story, such as setting (time and place) and mood. Have students identify each of these elements in "Jack and the Beanstalk."

DEVELOP

Have the class create and outline the elements of a story, then set up the beginning so that events can follow in a logical sequence. Start by choosing a mood or kind of story, for example, a mystery. Have students suggest characters and a sequence of events. List the suggestions on the board. Have students construct the plot, the conflict between characters, the climax, and the resolution.

Then in groups of five or six, improvise a beginning for the story. Perhaps a jewel theft has occurred, but the thief is unknown. The main character might hear a scream and run into the library to find a person who has been poisoned. Encourage the students to be detailed and specific in their interpretation of characters and events as they invent the beginning of the story.

Let each group plan, rehearse, and share its beginning of the story with the entire class. If possible, provide mysterious mood music at the beginnings of the scenes.

EVALUATE

Student evaluation: Ask students to explain the purpose of the beginning, the middle, and the end of a story. What are *plot, conflict, climax,* and *resolution?* What part does *theme* play in a story?

Teacher observation: Were the students able to work together to develop logical beginnings to the story they created? Are the students clear on the concepts of plot, conflict, climax, and resolution?

CONNECTIONS

Social Studies: Analyze an exciting event in state history from students' current social studies unit in terms of plot, conflict, climax, and resolution. Create a class poster that shows the characters and the historical sequence of events.

Analyzing Stories for Dramatization

COMPONENT	Aesthetic Valuing
SUBJECT	Criteria for Playmaking
OBJECTIVE	Students become aware of the techniques used to change a narrative story into a play, and make suggestions for dramatizing a particular story.
MATERIALS	A chart of the techniques for changing a story into a play (see Develop)

Note: Keep story notes for later dramatization.

WARM UP   Ask the students what steps they take when they improvise a scene for presentation to the class. List students' responses on the board. Answers should include: choosing a theme or story, deciding on the characters, planning the action, planning the dialogue, rehearsing, presenting the scene.

EXPLORE   Explain to the students that not all stories can be dramatized. Stories must meet certain criteria, or standards, to be suitable for dramatization. Write "Criteria for Dramatization" on the board. Ask the students what kind of story would make a good play. List their answers on the board. Lead students to include the following criteria:

The plot should be dramatic in nature, and full of action.

The story should have strong characters.

The story should provide opportunity for dialogue.

The story should have enough characters so that several people can be in it.

Other considerations for choosing a story:

The story should be suitable to the age and understanding of the players and the audience.

The story must have a theme that is important to the audience.

The story must be enjoyable or appealing in some way.

Ask students to list examples of books they know that have been dramatized successfully as plays or movies.

DEVELOP   Tell students that you would like them to listen to a folk tale to evaluate its suitability for a drama. "The Bunyip" is a folk tale from Australia, where native people called Aborigines have lived for thousands of years. Tell students that Australia is famous for its kangaroos, koalas, black swans, and other unusual animals found only in Australia. Maybe students can name some of the animals. The people in Australia speak English, but it sounds different from American English. The native people have a language of their own.

Read the story of "The Bunyip," which is in the Appendix of CENTER STAGE. Ask the students, "Does this story have action and offer opportunities for movement? What are the action scenes? Are there several strong characters? Who are they and what are they like? Are there opportunities for dialogue? Can some of the descriptions in the story be changed to dialogue to help identify the setting? Can you give an example? Would you enjoy acting out this story?"

Show students a chart with the following information, and allow time for them to read it and ask questions. Explain any unfamiliar vocabulary.

To change a story into a play:

1. Get rid of unnecessary scenes, characters, and plots that aren't important to the main story.

2. Arrange the scenes or actions in the order of the time they happened. (no flashbacks)

3. List the number of scenes necessary to tell the story, and briefly describe each one. Are there ways to combine the scenes? (Too many scenes make the story difficult to follow.)

4. Identify sections of narrative (descriptive storytelling) that can be changed to dialogue.

Then read the story again, and ask students afterwards what needs to be done to make this particular narrative story a drama.

If time permits, the students may wish to try out some of the actions or dialogue in the story. Allow individual students to demonstrate actions they think would be appropriate, or ask groups of students to develop portions of the dialogue. Keep notes, or have students keep notes, in case the class wishes to extend this lesson to a complete dramatization of the story at some future time.

EVALUATE

Student evaluation: Ask students, "What do you think is the most important criterion or standard for selecting a story for dramatization? Why? Which of the steps in changing a story into a play do you find the easiest? Which do you think is the most difficult? Why?"

Teacher observation: Were the students able to draw from the story the necessary elements for dramatization? Did all the students participate in volunteering information and ideas? Did this lesson make students more aware of dramatic elements in stories, and what needs to be done to create a play from a story?

CONNECTIONS

Social Studies: Have students look through magazines and newspapers to find a current events story to share with the class. Have students present their stories in a TV newscast format. Suggest that students confine their stories to less than two minutes. Have them concentrate on the essential facts, main people involved, background information, and sequence of events (beginning, middle, and end) in preparing their stories.

RESOURCES

Center Stage: Creative Dramatics Supplement. (contains an audiotape of "The Bunyip") Available from Dale Seymour Publications.

Themes and Stories

COMPONENT	Historical and Cultural
SUBJECT	Themes in Children's Literature
OBJECTIVE	Students analyze and compare themes in children's literature, both folk tales and contemporary fiction.
MATERIALS	None required

Note: In Lesson 20 students are to perform the improvisations developed here. Keep a record of the groups and their chosen themes to help students recall their improvisations. You may wish to divide this lesson into two sessions.

WARM UP

Review Lesson 5, in which *theme* is discussed. The theme of a story is the underlying thought or message of the story, not to be confused with the *plot*, or action. Sometimes the theme can be expressed as an underlying idea about life ("goodness will win," for example), and sometimes it is expressed in a word, such as "peace," or "intolerance."

Tell the students that the theme, "kindness will be rewarded," is well known in folk and fairy tales. Ask students how many stories they can think of in which this theme occurs. Examples may include: "Beauty and the Beast," *Mufaro's Beautiful Daughters,* by John Steptoe, and the Aesop fable, "The Lion and the Mouse."

EXPLORE

Name some stories the class has read together, and see whether students can identify the themes. Ask the students to suggest other themes in well-known stories. Have them name a theme and think of a story that illustrates that theme. Some suggestions might be discrimination (*The Hundred Dresses,* by Eleanor Estes, and *Maria Teresa,* by Mary Atkinson), friendship (*Who Needs Espie Sanchez?* by Terry Dunnahoo, and *Jennifer, Hecate, Macbeth, William McKinley, and Me, Elizabeth,* by E.L. Konigsburg), growing up (*And Now Miguel,* by Joseph Krumgold and *Slake's Limbo,* by Felice Holman), or greed (the Grimms' *The Fisherman and His Wife,* and *The Stonecutter,* a Japanese folk tale). Make a list on the board of the themes students suggest.

DEVELOP Divide the class into small groups of five or six. Each group is to select a theme from those listed on the board and create a story scene based on that theme. Have each group plan, cast, and rehearse the scene and share it with the entire class. After each group's presentation, allow time for the other students to comment on how the theme was conveyed in each scene, and to give suggestions for additional dramatic details.

EVALUATE *Student evaluation:* Ask the students, "How successfully did you establish the theme for your story in one scene? Were the viewing students able to identify the theme in your dramatization? What could you have done to make it clearer? Does knowing the themes of stories help you to understand and enjoy them? Why or why not?"

Teacher observation: Were the students able to identify themes in children's literature? How effective were the students in developing the themes in their scenes? Did all of the students participate in identifying themes?

CONNECTIONS *Art:* Divide the class into groups. Assign a color to each group. Explain that each student is to draw or paint a picture with the color assigned as the theme. When the pictures are done, have each group compare the depictions of their color and discuss similarities and differences in interpretation.

RESOURCES Atkinson, Mary. *Maria Teresa.* Lollipop Power, 1979.

Center Stage: Creative Dramatics Supplement. (contains an audiotape and script of "The Stonecutter") Available from Dale Seymour Publications.

Dunnahoo, Terry. *Who Needs Espie Sanchez?* Dutton, 1977.

Estes, Eleanor. *The Hundred Dresses.* Harcourt Brace Jovanovich, 1974.

Grimm, Jacob, and Wilhelm Grimm. *The Fisherman and His Wife.* Greenwillow Books, 1978.

Holman, Felice. *Slake's Limbo.* Dial Books, 1975.

Konigsburg, E.L. *Jennifer, Hecate, Macbeth, William McKinley, and Me, Elizabeth.* Atheneum, 1967.

Krumgold, Joseph. *And Now Miguel.* Crowell, 1953.

Lonsdale, Bernard J., and Helen Mackintosh. *Children Experience Literature.* Random House, 1973.

Common Themes in Literature

COMPONENT   Historical and Cultural

SUBJECT   Themes of Good and Evil

OBJECTIVE   Students discover that throughout time people of diverse cultures have dealt with common themes, and then dramatize a story with the theme of good against evil.

MATERIALS   *Saint George and the Dragon,* by Margaret Hodges; "Repaying Good with Evil," a folk tale from Mexico.

Note: "Repaying Good with Evil" contains a reference to alcoholic drink; this reference can be left out of the story without changing the theme or the plot. You may wish to divide this lesson into two sessions, one to read the two stories, the other to dramatize one of them.

WARM UP   Tell the students that one of the most common themes throughout all time in stories, poems, and plays is "The good guys against the bad guys." This is another way of saying "Good versus evil." Read the story, *Saint George and the Dragon,* by Margaret Hodges. Help students locate the setting (Egypt) on a map. Tell the students that this story is ancient, with origins dating back almost 800 years to 1200 A.D. Point out that stories of today, in many cultures, deal with the same issue of good versus evil. Ask, "How does the author demonstrate the theme in the story? Who or what represents good? Who or what represents evil? What are the qualities in the hero that help him triumph over evil?

EXPLORE   Read, "Repaying Good with Evil," a folk tale from Mexico. Help students locate Mexico on a map. This story originated at least 500 or more years later than *St. George and the Dragon.* It is a very different story, yet it too deals with the theme of good and evil.

Ask students what the similarities and differences are in each author's presentation. Ask such questions about both stories as, "Are the bad characters in the stories always bad from the beginning of the stories? Do the characters use special powers in the stories? Does the good always win, or right always triumph in the end?"

DEVELOP   Choose one of the stories to dramatize. Identify the scenes that demonstrate the good and the evil. Discuss how the theme is shown in that scene. Who or what represents good? Who or what represents evil? How is goodness shown? How is evil shown? Does the good triumph by physical power or by some other means?

After analyzing the content, make a list on the board of the scenes that could be dramatized to show the theme most clearly. Have students put the scenes in order. Ask, "What is the beginning of the story? The middle? The end? Who are the characters involved? Where do the scenes happen?"

Select a group of students to play each scene. Give each group a few minutes to plan and rehearse its scene. Encourage the students to consider the different ways in which the story could be communicated—pantomime, dialogue, or a combination of both.

While the players are planning their scenes, tell the remaining students to ask themselves the following questions as they watch the dramatizations: Is the beginning well established? Does the order of the scenes make the story clear? Do the actors stay in character (concentrate and focus on their parts)? Are the characters clearly defined? Is the theme clearly demonstrated in each scene?

After the dramatizations are given, let the class analyze the performances in terms of the above questions, and suggest ways of enhancing the performances. Students are to note especially the positive aspects of the performances, and which particular movements and dialogue demonstrated the theme of the story.

EVALUATE   *Student evaluation:* Ask students, "Why do you think the theme of good versus evil is found in so many stories? Is evil always defeated in the stories you read? Compare some of the different story outcomes. In your dramatizations, which quality—good or evil—was more challenging to show? Why?"

Teacher observation: Could the students grasp the concept of the "good versus evil" theme? Were they able to translate their understanding of the theme into an effective dramatization?

CONNECTIONS   *Art History:* Bring several illustrated art reference books into the classroom. Select a few groups of students to research paintings that have as their theme goodness or evil or the conflict between the two. Tell students to use the books you have provided. Have each group keep notes on the names of the paintings, the artists, and when they were painted, and present its findings to the rest of the class.

SPECIAL NEEDS   This lesson provides a good opportunity to explore the issue of good versus evil in the lives of socially and emotionally impaired students. Try to lead them into drawing parallels in their own lives.

RESOURCES   Hodges, Margaret, retold by. *Saint George and the Dragon*. Little, Brown and Company, 1990.

Janson, H.W., and Anthony F. Janson. *History of Art for Young People*. Abrams, 1987.

Rugoff, Milton, ed. *A Harvest of World Folk Tales* (contains "Repaying Good with Evil.") The Viking Press, 1949.

Ruskin, Ariane. *Nineteenth Century Art*. McGraw Hill, 1968.

Ruskin, Ariane. *Seventeenth and Eighteenth Century Art*. McGraw Hill, 1969.

Sound Voyages

COMPONENT   Creative Expression

SUBJECT   Drama with Sound Effects

OBJECTIVE   Students imagine and create auditory stimuli to tell and dramatize stories.

MATERIALS   Cassette tape player and blank tape (optional)

Note: This lesson could easily be divided into two sessions, with a break between Explore and Develop.

WARM UP   Ask the students to imagine taking a "sound voyage." Tell them that a sound voyage is an imaginary trip taken with special attention paid to the sounds that identify the settings. Let students suggest the destination of such a sound voyage, and then ask what sounds might be heard along the way. For instance, a student might describe a journey to Mars as follows: "I can imagine riding in a space ship and hearing the hum of its big engines as we move through space. A space ship horn beeps as we pass another space ship. The stars whir as they twirl around at great speed, and a comet whooshes by."

Ask the students to suggest other destinations for sound voyages. List the ideas on the board, and ask questions to add details and sounds to each voyage suggested.

EXPLORE   Divide the class into small groups of four to six students, and have each group choose one of the ideas suggested for a sound voyage for improvisation. Challenge group members to use their imaginations to create sound effects that bring to mind their chosen setting. Have students share with the others in their group the pictures in their mind's eyes as they think about their method of travel, their destination, and the sounds that would be heard along the way.

Have each group make a list of the sounds they want to try to reproduce, and then suggest that the students explore different ways of making the sounds. Help them to use materials in the classroom creatively. For instance, pencils clicking together might be a useful sound effect. Also explore the use of the voice and the body in making the sounds.

Each group should plan the scene, rehearse, and then evaluate their scene among themselves. Suggest that some of the students describe the scene and the others provide the sound effects, or that the group record the sound effects and play them during the scene.

Ask each group to discuss the effectiveness of the sounds they used to convey the images of their voyage and their destination. What were some of the interesting and creative ways of making sounds? Could some of the sound effects be combined to make interesting new sounds?

DEVELOP   Now ask each group to develop a story using their chosen environment and sound effects. Have them discuss the possibilities for characters, objects, events, and emotions to be included in their story. They should also talk through a possible beginning, middle, and end to the improvisation. Have groups cast, rehearse, and share their dramatizations and sound effects with the rest of the class.

EVALUATE   *Student evaluation:* Ask students, "What images came to mind as you listened to the sounds in the dramatizations? Which sound effects do you think most effectively conveyed a particular setting? Which did you enjoy the most? Why?" Compare the similarities and differences in the various settings in the dramatizations.

Teacher observation: Could the students offer imaginative ideas for different sound voyages? Were the students able to translate their images into improvisations? Was there a creative use of sound effects? Were there definite beginnings, middles, and ends to the scenes?

CONNECTIONS   *Language Arts:* Have students brainstorm words that describe. Examples might include *chatter, squeak, groan, splat, thump.* Allow invented words, too, that are onomatopoetic. List students' words on the board, and then ask students to use their words in sentences.

SPECIAL NEEDS   Ask hearing impaired students to create a sight voyage, or even a motion voyage, in which they concentrate on such factors as speed, vibrations, direction, and shifting positions on their way.

Theatrical Stages

COMPONENT   Aesthetic Perception

SUBJECT   Theatre Vocabulary/Playing Areas

OBJECTIVE   Students identify and learn the terms for different types of performing areas, and experiment with performance in each one.

MATERIALS   One copy for each student of the diagrams and descriptions of the three kinds of stages (page 53); pictures of the insides of theaters, showing the stages and the audiences

Note: If possible, schedule a field trip to a community theater when the theater is empty, to provide firsthand observation of a stage.

WARM UP   Ask the students to recall the last time they were in a theater in the community, or the last time they saw a play or live performance of some kind. What did the stage or playing area look like? Where was the stage in relation to the audience?

Ask a few of the students who responded to go up to the board and draw the stage area and show where the audience was sitting. Compare students' examples.

EXPLORE   Tell students that dramatic activity can occur in almost any kind of open space. Explain that *playing area* can be defined as a cleared space for dramatic activities without a designated place for the audience.

Discuss the times you have moved furniture around the classroom to make a space for a dramatic activity. If appropriate, point out that there was no concern for where the audience would sit, since performing for an audience was not the focus of the activity.

Give students the copy of the diagrams and descriptions of stages to look at as you describe them. Refer to the examples of stages given by students in Warm Up, and identify each by the terms listed on page 53. These are the formal terms used to describe traditional playing areas or stages.

In your classroom or in an open space, arrange chairs or desks to represent the three kinds of stages discussed. Or arrange the students sitting on the floor to represent the three kinds of playing areas. Have a few students at a time stand within the different stage and playing areas to get a sense of how each of the three areas would feel if the students were performers.

DEVELOP   Using the improvisation developed in Lesson 17, allow the students in one group to perform their scene in each of the different stage areas. Following the performances, discuss the different feelings students had in performing and viewing from the three kinds of stage areas. What were the differences? What were some of the problems presented by the different playing areas? Allow other selected groups to perform in the different playing areas. What are their reactions to the areas?

EVALUATE   *Student evaluation:* Ask students, "Did some of the improvisations seem better suited to one stage than another? Why? Did the different playing areas make you change anything about your improvisations? What elements did you change? Why? What playing areas are the most difficult for the audiences to see? Why? How would this affect your presentations?

Teacher observation: Can students identify and describe the features of the different kinds of performing spaces that actors use? Did students' performances change in any way from one playing area to another? Why or why not?

CONNECTIONS   *Language Arts:* Have students write a newspaper article by the theatre critic announcing the opening of the new theater. Have them use the terminology from the activity to describe the type of stage the new theater has and tell how it will affect different kinds of performances.

SPECIAL NEEDS   To give a severely visually impaired student a sense of a stage's configuration and the location of the audience, be sure that student has a chance to stand on the makeshift "stages" and "feel" the audience in front, on three sides, and on all four sides.

RESOURCES   Craig, Edward. *Towards a New Theatre, Forty Designs for Stage Scenes.* Ayer Company Publishers, 1913.

Theatrical Stages

Proscenium Stage: a stage with the audience seated on one side, usually directly in front of the playing area.

GRADE 4

Thrust Stage: a stage with the audience seated on three sides. The stage extends, or thrusts out into the audience space. This kind of stage is sometimes called a runway, and is often used for fashion shows and award shows on TV.

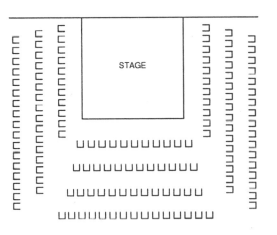

Arena Stage: a stage with the audience seated on all four sides or all around the playing area. The actors are surrounded by the audience. A performance on this type of stage is sometimes called "Theatre-in-the-Round."

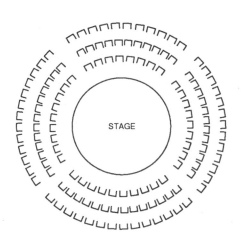

COPYRIGHT © DALE SEYMOUR PUBLICATIONS

Stage Areas and Directions

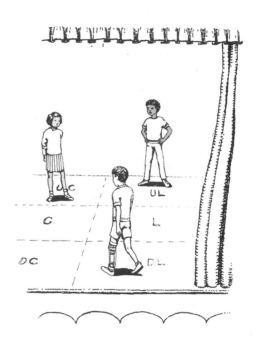

COMPONENT   Aesthetic Valuing

SUBJECT   Theatre Vocabulary/Careers

OBJECTIVE   Students identify and use appropriate vocabulary to describe different areas of the stage and an actor's movement from one part of the stage to another.

MATERIALS   One copy for each student of the diagram and description of stage areas on page 56.

WARM UP   Tell the students that every job or profession has its own unique words, phrases, and abbreviations that are recognized and understood by other people in that same profession. Sometimes people outside the profession understand the words, too, but often they seem like a different language. For example, a computer expert might talk about "floppy disks," "cursors," "icons," "GOTO," and so on. (Students will probably know many computer terms.) Ask students to name a few professions, perhaps those of their parents, for which they know some of the special words, and list the professions and some of their vocabulary on the board.

Explain to the students that the theatre community also has its own language which is understood by most people in the profession. Students already know some drama/theatre vocabulary. Have them name drama/theatre words that they know. (*character, plot, conflict, climax, resolution; proscenium, thrust,* and *arena stages*; and so on)

EXPLORE   Draw a diagram of a stage on the board (see the diagram on page 56), and give students a copy of the diagram for their notebooks. Indicate the name of each area and its abbreviation as you point out the different locations on the stage. Explain that stage areas are defined by the position of the actor as she or he faces the audience. Note that for some stage areas you will have to indicate the position of the actor.

Very specific areas on the stage are indicated by the abbreviations alone, or in combination, such as DR, for Downstage Right. (See the diagram.)

After you have introduced and discussed the stage areas and their abbreviations, erase the letters and ask selected students to come to the board and write the correct abbreviations in each area of the diagram. Point out to students that once the actors know these terms it is easier for the director to give them movement directions from one area to another.

DEVELOP

Mark off a stage area in a large open space. Define the borders of the stage and the audience area. Ask selected students to stand in specified areas.

Tell students that another term used in theatre to define the movement of an actor from one stage area to another is *cross*. Ask specific students standing in one stage area to cross to another stage area. For example, say, "_____, cross from up left to down center." Give as many students as possible the opportunity to stand and move in the various stage areas. Then let students give crossing directions to each other.

Review the names of the stage areas and their abbreviations. Remind students that the areas are defined as the actor faces the audience!

EVALUATE

Student evaluation: Ask students to name some of the terms they learned to indicate stage directions, as well as the abbreviations. Ask students to give some stage directions using these terms. Ask students why such a particular vocabulary is necessary. Do they think it is useful?

Teacher observation: Were the students able to recognize the locations on the stage and the appropriate abbreviations? Were they able to follow the stage directions?

CONNECTIONS

Mathematics: Draw a diagram of the stage on the chalkboard. Assign a number at random to each section of the stage. Present students with addition and subtraction problems described only by stage directions. For example: *up left + center = x; down right − up center = x.*

SPECIAL NEEDS

Due to perceptual problems, learning impaired students may have difficulty in grasping the directionality involved in this activity until they physically move their bodies to the defined stage areas.

To give severely visually impaired students a sense of a stage's dimensions and the location of each area on the stage, have a responsible classmate accompany the student to the school auditorium. There they can walk the length and breadth of the stage and explore it. Another aid could be a large piece of cardboard or other flat material to which you have glued yarn defining the various stage areas. Label the areas with Braille letters.

Stage Areas

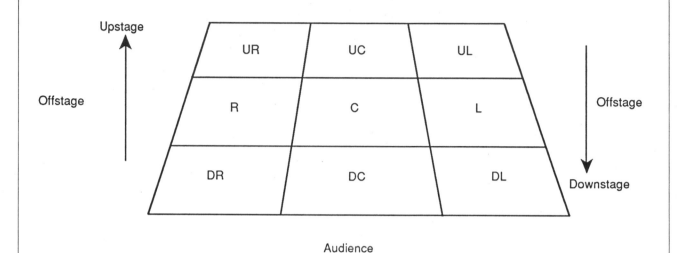

Upstage

Offstage

Offstage

Downstage

Audience

Upstage (U): the general area toward the back part of the stage

Downstage (D): the general area toward the audience

Center stage (C): the area right in the middle of the stage

Stage right (R): the area to the right of center stage, as the actor faces the audience

Stage left (L): the area to the left of center stage, as the actor faces the audience

Offstage: off the acting area of the stage, or any part of the stage not enclosed by the setting

Wings: either side of the stage out of sight of the audience

COPYRIGHT © DALE SEYMOUR PUBLICATIONS

Designing a Set

COMPONENT	Aesthetic Valuing
SUBJECT	Technical Theatre/Careers
OBJECTIVE	Students learn the role of the set designer in drama/theatre, and practice designing a set by making a rendering for a drama.
MATERIALS	*Scene Design and Stage Lighting,* by Oren Parker et al; five or six cardboard boxes; tagboard strips, glue, paper, pencils, crayons or colored pencils; paint

Note: Keep a record of the students in each group, and have them save their set renderings and/or models for Lesson 23.

WARM UP

Ask the class whether anyone can tell the others what a *set* is, and what *set pieces* are (the stage environment for a dramatic performance, and free-standing pieces within it). Show the students various renderings of sets (artists' sketches) from a resource book such as the one listed in Materials; then show pictures of the completed sets. Discuss students' reactions to the finished sets. Did they look the way students imagined them to look?

Describe the role of the set designer in the theatre as one who creates the physical environment for the action of a play. The director (the person who trains the actors for the play, and directs their movements on the stage) works with the set designer to decide the general layout of the scenery, while the designer selects or decides on the coloring and decoration.

Point out to the students that when they planned improvisations, they often needed some kind of furniture arrangement and plan for the playing area suitable for the particular action. Review some improvisations students have done and the settings needed for them.

EXPLORE

Tell the class that in formal theatre, the set designer (also called the scene designer) makes a rendering, like the pictures they saw in the book, after having discussed with the director the needs for the environment or setting. A *rendering* is a detailed drawing of the playing area. The set designer makes one for each different setting in the play. The renderings help the director visualize the action, because the actors' movements and groupings must be planned around the size, shape, and arrangement of the furniture or whatever is needed to create the environment for the play.

Divide the class into groups of five or six. Say, "Suppose that you are set designers, and you must draw a rendering of a set. Think of a specific story or scene you have improvised, or create one from your own imagination. You are going to design the environment for one scene in the story. What will be in the environment? Will you have walls, chairs, tables, a doorway, and so on? Will you have rocks and trees? Will the environment be fantastical or real? Will it suit the mood of the story?" Let each group discuss and decide upon a scene, and then the set that would be needed for that scene. Encourage the students to think of as many details as possible. It may be helpful for them to make a list.

DEVELOP

Ask each group to picture in their mind's eye the action that takes place in their scene, and to make a rendering of the area for the action to happen. Give the groups at least twenty minutes to work together planning and drawing their settings.

Choose a group to discuss the specifics of their rendering. You may want to hang the renderings on the wall so that the students can view each other's creations. Ask questions, and encourage others in the class to ask questions. Does the rendering show a setting for a story already written, or did the students create their own story? What set pieces are involved? Is there enough space for the actors to move about? Does the design of the setting fit the mood of the story?

Often a model is made of a set to help further visualize the action. If students are interested, and if time permits, give each group a cardboard box. Have them cut out one side of the box so that three walls and a floor are left, and create a model from their rendering. Also give students some tagboard strips to cut and fold to represent set pieces. They will also need to cut doors and windows, perhaps paint the walls, and glue down the set pieces.

EVALUATE

Student evaluation: Ask the students, "What did you consider when you created your rendering? What challenges did you face in designing the set and drawing it or creating a model?"

Teacher observation: Were the students able to visualize an environment and translate their visualization into a theatrical set? Did the students seem to understand the need for a rendering of the stage set? Did students increase their awareness of the set designer's job in drama/theatre?

CONNECTIONS   *Language Arts:* Give each group copies of another group's set rendering. Have each group use the rendering to determine the play subject. Encourage students to study the details that have been provided to get a feel for the scene, mood, and characters that the set designers had in mind. Then tell each group to make up a scene that could be dramatized with that particular set. Compare their scene with the scene the original group had in mind.

SPECIAL NEEDS   Have a responsible classmate work with a severely visually impaired student to design a set for a story and create it with a cardboard box. The two students can then orally describe the set to the class.

RESOURCES   Parker, Oren W., et al. *Scene Design and Stage Lighting.* Holt, Rinehart and Winston, Inc., 1990.

The Technical Element of Drama/Theatre

COMPONENT   Aesthetic Valuing

SUBJECT   Technical Theatre/Careers

OBJECTIVE   Students develop an understanding of and appreciation for the jobs necessary to aesthetic and technical theatre.

MATERIALS   Set renderings and/or models from Lesson 22

WARM UP   Tell the students that there are three elements in the theatre:

1. the organization (often a producer), which deals with the business side of a dramatic production;

2. the artistic element, which consists of the directing, acting, speech, and set and costume design; and

3. the technical element, which consists of the lighting, set construction, properties, sound, costumes, and make-up.

Write the list of technical areas on the board. Review the meaning of each term, and then ask the students to tell what they think the various purposes of each of the technical areas might be. The answers should include the following:

Lighting: to provide enough light on the acting area so that the audience can see the action, to set a mood, and to establish time of day.

Sets, or scenery: to create an environment that defines the acting area. Set pieces on the stage also help the director indicate location to the actors.

Properties (props): to help an actor play a role; to add to the reality of the production. Props include everything an actor handles.

Sound: to add to the reality of the production; to create a mood. This technical area includes all the sound effects that are essential to the production, but not the music before the production.

Costumes: to help an actor play a role; to add to the reality of the production. Costumes are anything the actors wear.

Make-up: to add to the reality of the production and to make an actor more visible to the audience. Each actor usually puts on his or her own make-up, but when special effects are required, a makeup technician is used.

EXPLORE

Divide the class into the same groups in which they worked in Lesson 22, and ask them to recall the story and the set used for the rendering in that lesson. Ask students to think about how all the areas of technical theatre would affect that story. Say, "If you were to present your story on the stage, what lighting would you use to suggest the environment? What sound effects would you use? What would be used for scenery and set pieces? What props do the actors need? What costumes do they need? Is special make-up needed? For which characters?

Have one student in each group write down the needs for one technical area of the group's story. Students should refer to the group's rendering or model from Lesson 22.

DEVELOP

Have the students in one group set up the stage area to suit their story and set, using items of furniture found in the classroom to substitute for set pieces (a chair for a rock, for example). Ask the student who wrote down the scenery and set pieces to explain what they are, using the rendering or model as a visual aid, and also to define the acting area (the major space in which the actors move). The student responsible for lighting should tell what that would be, naming any special effects such as, "A spotlight should shine here," or, "There is a red glow in the mouth of the cave."

Have the student responsible for properties explain what props are needed and where they are on the stage ("a big pot, and a spoon for stirring, in front of the cave"). The student responsible for costumes should describe those ("Gruff wears a tiger skin around his body"), and the student who kept notes on make-up should describe any special effects needed ("Gruff has a long beard").

Give each group a chance to describe the technical areas of their scene, and let the class evaluate the presentations and suggest possible additions.

EVALUATE

Student evaluation: Ask students, "Were you able to think of ways in which lighting, sound, costumes, props, and makeup might enhance your production? Can some simple technical elements for improvisations be provided in the classroom? Which ones? What people other than the actors are needed to put on a play?

Teacher observation: Were the students able to use their renderings from the previous lesson to add the technical aspects to their improvisations? Did students have creative ideas for the technical areas?

CONNECTIONS   *Science:* Have students work together in groups to determine the sets, lighting, costumes, and props needed to dramatize a natural phenomenon, such as a volcanic eruption, a hurricane, an earthquake, and so on. Have students present their production plans to the rest of the class.

RESOURCES   Adix, Vern. *Theatre Scenecraft.* Anchorage Press, 1981.

Pillbrow, Richard. *Stage Lighting* (Illustr). Applause Theatre Book Publishers, 1990.

Creating Characters with Costumes

COMPONENT	Creative Expression
SUBJECT	Costumes
OBJECTIVE	Students use hats as costume pieces to create characters and improvise a story.
MATERIALS	Various hats as costume pieces

Note: Borrow a variety of hats from your local community theatre, or use your own collection of hats; use hat linings inside the hats for health purposes.

This lesson could be divided into two sessions. A logical break would be between Explore and Develop.

WARM UP

Bring out from a costume box a hat that represents a particular profession, such as a firefighter's hat, and ask, "Who might wear this particular hat, and when would it be worn?" As students identify each hat, return it to the costume box and bring out another. Other hats might include a baker's cap, a police officer's cap, a baseball cap, a cowboy hat, a lady's flowered hat, a bike helmet, a construction worker's (hard) hat, and so on.

Discuss with the class that a costume identifies a character; it tells the audience whom the actor is portraying. Ask students to picture in their minds' eyes the character represented by a doctor's white coat, a tennis dress, and a king's crown.

Tell the students that the actor must spend a great deal of time studying a character and what he or she does to be able to portray that character believably. Besides studying the character, wearing a costume often helps an actor "become" a certain character. Often the costume influences the way the actor moves. For example, if the character is an animal, the costume sometimes limits the physical movements the actor can make. If a woman wears a hoop skirt, she moves quite differently from the way she moves when she is wearing blue jeans. Ask students to think of other examples.

EXPLORE

Place the box with the assortment of hats in front of the students in an open space. Challenge them to pantomime an action the character represented by the hat might do. Have several volunteers in turn each choose a particular hat, put it on, and pantomime an action that might be done by a person wearing the hat.

Following each pantomime, ask the viewing students about the improvisation. Did wearing a costume piece seem to help the miming student to "become" a certain character? How did the costume piece help to identify the action?

DEVELOP   Divide the class into groups of five or six. Ask one student from each group to choose five or six hats from the box. Using the hats as motivation, the group is to create a story that will incorporate the characters who would wear the selected hats.

Have the groups plan, rehearse, and share their stories with the class.

EVALUATE   *Student evaluation:* Ask the students, "Did wearing a hat help you get a feel for your character? In what way? Were you able to think of some unique or unusual things for your character to do? How does wearing a costume help an actor?"

Teacher observation: Were the students able to use the hats as motivation to create a character? Were they able to combine their characterizations to create an improvisation as a group?

CONNECTIONS   *Music:* Have students use a hat to create a character and then sing a familiar song in that persona. Song possibilities include "Yankee Doodle," "Mary Had a Little Lamb," and "Twinkle, Twinkle, Little Star."

RESOURCES   Cummings, Richard. *One Hundred One Costumes for All Ages, All Occasions.* Plays, Inc., 1987.

Analyzing a Dramatic Work

COMPONENT	Aesthetic Valuing
SUBJECT	Performance Analysis/Theatre Vocabulary
OBJECTIVE	Students use drama/theatre vocabulary and ethical standards when analyzing a dramatic performance.
MATERIALS	None required

Note: If the students have seen a school play or other performance together, use it as a basis for this lesson. If not, assign ahead of time a specific TV performance to be viewed by all the students.

WARM UP Write on the board, "Theme," "Plot," "Conflict," "Climax," and "Resolution."

Remind the students of Lesson 5, in which *theme* was defined, and Lesson 17, in which various common themes were explored. Recall with students that *theme* is the central thought or idea of a story or play. Ask the students to identify and explain the theme of the observed performance. Write it on the board.

EXPLORE Review the story components of plot, conflict, climax, and resolution discussed in Lesson 15. Ask the students, "Was the plot, or action, of the story clear? Did it move smoothly from one event to another?" Ask a volunteer to briefly outline the plot, and write a short description of each component on the board.

Remind the students that conflict is two opposing ideas or forces. Usually in a play, one person wants something, and another person or force tries to prevent him or her from getting it. Ask, "What was the conflict in the performance we saw? Was it good versus evil? Did someone want something and try to get it, or did someone do something wrong and try to escape the results?" Ask for two or three volunteers to dramatize briefly the scene that showed what the conflict was.

Ask the students, "What was the turning point, or climax, of the story? How was the conflict or problem resolved, or brought to an end? Was everyone in the story happy with the way things worked out? Who was not, and why?" Write students' answers on the board.

DEVELOP   Add "Value" to the list on the board, and ask the students, "What of value did you find in the performance that you could apply to your own lives?" Define *value* as a quality or idea that is worth something in terms of social principles or moral standards. For instance, students might have admired the hero for his or her courage in the face of danger, or a family for helping someone in distress, or another character for turning in to the police some money that she or he had found.

If the story involved violence or unkindness, ask, "How could the violence or unkindness in this story have been avoided? What other ways can problems be solved?" Encourage students to think of practical and moral solutions to problems that do not involve danger to themselves.

Select two or three students to role play an alternate solution to the conflict that was shown in the viewed performance. If students have ideas for several solutions, allow different groups to improvise these solutions.

Have students say which solution they think is most realistic, and which resolution would be the one that most people would view as "right." Are the two the same?

EVALUATE   *Student evaluation:* Ask students, "Was the performance you saw like many others you have seen, or did it have a special meaning for you? What values did you see in the performance that you could apply to your own life?"

Teacher observation: Do students understand the concepts of theme, plot, conflict, climax, and resolution? Did the students demonstrate understanding of the meaning of value in a performance? Was there a consensus of opinion on the value of the dramatic event? Did all the students participate in the discussion?

CONNECTIONS   *Social Studies:* Have small groups of students each choose a current event described in a newspaper or magazine article or television newscast, and evaluate the story. Ask students to identify the theme, plot, conflict, climax, and resolution, and describe the principal characters. Have the groups each present a brief synopsis of the story for the class. Discuss the values of the people involved in the current event.

The Living Newspaper

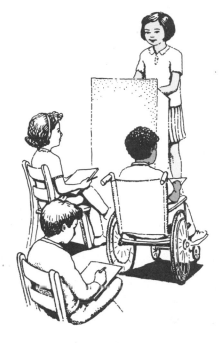

COMPONENT   Historical and Cultural

SUBJECT   Current Events

OBJECTIVE   Students create a dramatization from a current news event.

MATERIALS   Current newspaper stories
Note: You may wish to have students listen to or watch a news broadcast or read the newspaper ahead of time, so that they will be familiar with current news stories.

WARM UP

Ask the students, "How many of you read the daily or weekend newspaper? How many of you watch the news on TV? How are a newspaper article and a TV newscast different? Which do you like better, and why?"

Read aloud a short, simple article from a current newspaper, and ask for volunteers to act out the story.

Tell students about "The Living Newspaper," which did what the student actors have just done. "The Living Newspaper" was the only federally funded theatre company in America. It lasted little more than three and a half years, from October, 1935 to July, 1939, but it made a very important contribution to American theatre. "The Living Newspaper" presented dramatizations to inform the audience about important issues of the day. Topics for the dramatizations were selected from newspapers or magazines.

EXPLORE

Ask the students, "If 'The Living Newspaper' existed today, what news stories do you think would make good dramatizations?" Write students' responses on the board, and have students explain why each story would make a good dramatization. Responses may be from a variety of areas, from serious international events, to professional sports, to events involving popular music stars. Respect all suggestions made by the students.

DEVELOP

Select one of the suggestions from those on the board, preferably ones that involve other ethnic groups or cultures and persons different from those with whom the students come in daily contact. Ask students to give the *Who, What, Where, When,* and *Why* of each situation. Tell the students that they are to present this news event creatively and dramatically in a short, concise scene. Unlike a newscaster, who would sit and tell the information, they are to dramatize the information so that an audience would find it interesting.

Ask students to tell what happens first, what events make up the middle of the story, and what events end the story. Decide together on characters, action, and dialogue, and put the scene together sequentially.

Select the needed number of students to dramatize the scene for the class. Following the presentation, evaluate students' work and decide on any changes. Then ask another group of students to replay the story. Allow as many students to participate as time permits.

EVALUATE   *Student evaluation:* Ask students, "Was the information presented in the dramatization accurate? Can you think of other ways the information could have been dramatized? How easy or difficult was it to dramatize a news event? Why? Can you think of any news programs today that might have been influenced by 'The Living Newspaper'?" (Sometimes these programs are called "docudramas.")

Teacher observation: Were the students able to provide a variety of stories that were current and interesting news events? Were the students able to improvise an effective dramatization from the news story? Did all the students participate in this activity?

CONNECTIONS   *Social Studies:* Have students work in groups to create a "Living Newspaper" story about an important event in their state's history. Be sure students provide information about *Who, What, Where, When,* and *Why,* and explain the significance of the event.

Writing and Dramatizing a Scene

COMPONENT	Aesthetic Perception
SUBJECT	Playscripts
OBJECTIVE:	Students become aware of the structural differences between stories and plays, and begin writing a playscript.
MATERIALS	"Catching a Thief," from *American Folk Tales and Songs,* by Richard Chase

WARM UP

Remind the students of Lesson 16, in which they heard the story of "The Bunyip" and identified the criteria for a story to be dramatized. Review briefly the criteria listed in Explore, Lesson 16.

Ask the students to think carefully about the criteria while you read "Catching a Thief." Tell the students that instead of improvising the action, this time they will create a formal play from the story. A formal play requires a written playscript, so that the actors know exactly what to do and what to say, and so that the play will be the same each time it is presented. After reading "Catching a Thief," have students check the story against the criteria for dramatization, to be sure that the criteria are met.

EXPLORE

Ask students, "How many of you have read a play?" What does it look like on the page?" Show the class the written script on pages 176–178. (Lesson 13 in the Grade 3 level of CENTER STAGE describes the differences in detail between a story and a play.) Ask students to point out the words that describe the action and the words that are the dialogue. Discuss that the dialogue is written by naming the speaker, adding a colon, and then writing the words the speaker is to say. The description of setting or action is enclosed in parentheses, and is often in italics.

On the board, write this example of description from "Catching a Thief":

(The scene is a cabin. On one wall is a fireplace with cooking pots in it. A table and a few chairs are in the room. There is a door to the outside, and another door to another room. An old man and woman are seated by the fireplace.)

Ask the students what could happen first. An answer might be, "There is a knock on the door." Add "There is a knock on the door." to the description written on the board. Ask the students what could happen next. If it is description of an action, add it to what is already on the board; if it is speech, write it on the board in dialogue format. What follows is an example of possible dialogue for the scene. Note that description of action is incorporated.

Old Man: Wife, someone is knocking on the door.

Wife: I wonder who could be out this time of night. It is dark and very late.

Old Man: I'll go see who it is.

(He goes to the outside door and opens it. The Preacher is standing there.)

Preacher: Good evening, I am Preacher Jones. It is very dark and late, and I need a place to stay.

DEVELOP

Continue asking the students the sequence of events until the first scene of "Catching a Thief" (perhaps until the Preacher retires for the evening) is complete. There will probably be several erasures and changes before the students are satisfied with the action and speech. When the scene has been completed to the students' satisfaction, ask selected students to read the lines that the characters speak.

Ask several students to arrange the furniture or set pieces in an open area, as they did in Lesson 22. Ask other students to take their places as characters, following the written description. Have students move and speak according to the written directions and dialogue.

Point out to the students that they have been following formal theatre procedure. The lines actors speak are memorized and are always the same, as is the action. Playwrights create the plays in their imaginations, and "hear" the lines in their heads and "see" the actions before they write them down as formal scripts.

If desired, a student could copy the script that is on the board so far, so that the activity can be extended to another lesson, and the play can be completed.

EVALUATE

Student evaluation: Ask students, "What is the difference between the improvisations done in the classroom and a formal play? Would you rather improvise a scene, or read the lines from a playscript? Why?"

Teacher observation: Can all students identify a few features of a playscript? Did students use knowledge gained in previous lessons to determine dialogue and action for the play? Did all of the students participate in the creation of the play?

CONNECTIONS   *Language Arts:* Write a sample of dialogue, either original or excerpted from a published play, on the chalkboard. Omit all of the punctuation. Have students take turns coming to the board and adding punctuation to the sample. Point out that the use of exclamation and perhaps even question marks—as in the case of "Really." or "Really!" or "Really?"—may depend on one's interpretation of the scene and the character's feelings.

RESOURCES   Chase, Richard. *American Folk Tales and Songs.* Dover, 1971.

Creating a Shadow Puppet

COMPONENT   Historical and Cultural

SUBJECT   Shadow Puppetry

OBJECTIVE   Students learn some of the techniques of shadow puppetry, make a shadow puppet, and experiment manipulating the puppet.

MATERIALS   *The World of Puppets,* by Rene Simmens, or other resource book; visual arts materials such as scissors, construction paper, pencils, cardboard; an adjustable lamp; light fabric such as sheeting

WARM UP   Ask the students whether they know what a shadow play is. Ask: "Are shadow puppets or plays given today? Where?" In the United States, the plays are mostly given at children's parties, and are not performed in the theatre as they are in Asian countries. Tell the students that the simplest form of shadow puppetry is the projection of the hands' shadow against a wall.

Set up a strong light source (an adjustable lamp) and shine the light against the wall. Give students the opportunity to place their hands between the light and the wall to create shadows. Have students move and shape their hands to form shadows representing various objects. Small objects in the hands can aid, enlarge upon, or improve the shadows when used imaginatively.

EXPLORE   Give students a brief overview of shadow puppetry, and show pictures from a book, or prints of puppets as used in different cultures around the world. Shadow plays have one of the longest histories in theatre. Some research indicates that shadow plays started in China in the 11th century, but other research seems to show that they began as far back as the second century B.C., in India. The date may be uncertain, but shadow puppetry is unquestionably Asian in origin. In Asia today, shadow play is used to teach history through storytelling and for religious purposes, as well as for entertainment and art.

Shadow plays are performed behind a screen, or fabric stretched over a frame, which separates the audience from the figures and from those who make the figures move. A light source behind the screen shines on the screen. The operator of the figure or puppet manipulates the puppet from behind or below the screen, between the light source and the screen, thus throwing the shadow of the puppet onto the screen for the viewers to see.

The puppets are cutout figures, or any device of the desired shape that will make the appropriate shadow on the screen. Because they show only the shadow, the figures need not be three-dimensional. The voice of the puppet might or might not be that of the operator, but the audience does not see the performers who are singing or speaking the puppets' lines.

DEVELOP

A simple shadow show can be made as follows: To make a screen, stretch a piece of light fabric such as muslin across a doorway, or between two objects that will hold it taut. Place a light source (the adjustable lamp) a few inches behind and above the screen. Cut out simple figures in silhouette; attach them to a rod or stiff piece of cardboard. The operator holds the rod or stiff cardboard, and places the cutout figure lightly against the screen, in front of the light. The operator may move the figure back and forth and up and down, creating an illusion of movement for the viewers on the other side.

Help students discover that only a very few shapes can be on the screen at one time, that the distance from the screen defines the sharpness or softness of the shadow, and that scenery can be made and fastened to the screen.

Read aloud, or have students read the story "The Two Sisters," from the Appendix of CENTER STAGE. Have each student make one of the characters from the story, and experiment with that character as a shadow puppet. For another lesson, let students develop a dramatization with the shadow puppets they have made.

EVALUATE

Student evaluation: What stories or plays or scenes from previous lessons could be adapted for use with shadow puppets? What are some advantages of shadow puppets over live actors? What materials other than cutout silhouettes can you think of that would make interesting shadow puppets?

Teacher observation: Did students already have some information about shadow puppets? Where did they get their information? Did the students become aware of some of the technical aspects and requirements of shadow plays? Were students imaginative in their construction and use of the puppets?

CONNECTIONS   *Science:* Explain to students that an eclipse occurs when a shadow is cast by one celestial body on another. Have students make a diagram of a solar eclipse and a lunar eclipse. They should show the relationship of the sun, the earth, and the moon and identify the *umbra* and *penumbra* for each.

SPECIAL NEEDS   With visually impaired students, keep in mind that all but the most severely impaired can perceive light and shadow, although to varying degrees, and may or may not be able to see the finer details of the puppet shadows, that is, sharp versus soft edges, shape differences, and so on. Allow students who are having difficulty to feel the hands or figures creating the shadows.

RESOURCES   Brandon, James R., ed. *On Thrones of Gold: Three Javanese Shadow Plays.* Harvard University Press, 1970.

Center Stage: Creative Dramatics Supplement. (contains an audiotape of "The Two Sisters") Available from Dale Seymour Publications.

Simmens, Rene. *The World of Puppets.* Elsevier Phaidon, 1975. (This book is out of print, but may be available in your library.)

Van Ness, Edward C., and Shita Prawirohardjo. *Javanese Wayang Kulit, An Introduction.* Oxford University Press, 1986.

Stories for further dramatization:

Brown, Marcia. *Shadow.* Charles Scribner's Sons, 1982.

_____. *Once a Mouse.* Charles Scribner's Sons, 1961.

Goble, Paul. *The Girl Who Loved Wild Horses.* Bradbury Press, 1980.

Lawrence, Jacob. *Harriet and the Promised Land.* Windmill, 1968.

Longfellow, Henry Wadsworth. *Paul Revere's Ride.* Greenwillow, 1985.

Osborn, Steve. *Story Chest: Treasured Tales from Many Lands.* Addison-Wesley Publishing Company, 1992.

Poetry in Chorus

COMPONENT   Historical and Cultural

SUBJECT   Choral Speaking

OBJECTIVE   Students learn some of the history of
             Greek chorus and perform poetry as a
             chorus.

MATERIALS   *Talking to the Sun: An Illustrated Anthology
             of Poems for Young People,* by Kenneth
             Koch and Kate Farrell; poetry collections
             or other resources from the language arts
             or social studies curriculum

WARM UP   Ask students whether they have ever performed in a chorus, either singing
or reading. To demonstrate an example of a chorus, have students recite
together a verse that everyone knows, such as "Mary Had a Little Lamb."
Ask, "How can all the members of the chorus stay together as they speak?"

Ask the students for whatever information they have about different kinds
of choruses. What does being part of the chorus mean in a music class?
Have students ever heard a chorus in the theatre? Tell the students that a
chorus is a group of people who sing, speak, or dance together.

Explain that the idea of a chorus has its roots in ancient Greece, where it was
part of religious celebrations. As Greek theatre developed from the ancient
Greek religious experience, the chorus became a vital part of the theatre.

In ancient Greece, the performers who sang and danced and recited narrative as a group were called the Chorus. The Chorus commented on the
events in the story, and was treated in the drama almost as a single character.

EXPLORE   Using a familiar rhyme like "Mary Had a Little Lamb," have the class try
different ways to deliver the lines of the poem. Have students experiment
with pitch, inflection, volume, and tempo. Ask them to concentrate on
each sentence and the different ways it could be delivered. Students
should plan the recitation and present it. Ask, "What could be done to
make the choral speaking more effective?" Have students incorporate the
suggestions and present the poem again.

DEVELOP Ask, "What is necessary to be able to work effectively together as an ensemble or chorus? Can one person be the star? What would happen to the choral effect if one person was more noticeable than the others? Can you see opportunities to move as a group while you speak? Remember that the Greek chorus danced or moved as well as spoke and sang."

Have students say one line together, perhaps "Row, row, row your boat, gently down the stream," and suggest movements that they must all do together. They could sway back and forth or make a rippling motion with their hands for the stream, but they have to decide when to move, and watch each other to be sure that they all move together.

Divide the class into groups of five to eight students and allow each group to choose a short selection from a poetry anthology (or assign selections in the interest of time) that could be interpreted chorally. Remind students to add movement to their presentation, if possible. Have each group plan, practice, and share its choral speaking activity with the class.

EVALUATE *Student evaluation:* Describe the experience of using a poem as a choral speaking presentation. Did having to read the poem instead of saying it from memory make it harder? What other kinds of materials besides poems might make good choral speaking presentations?

Teacher observation: Did students seem to understand the idea of a Chorus as it was used in Greek theatre? Were the students able to recite something together? How effective were the students in using pitch, inflection, volume, and tempo while speaking together? Were students able to develop some sort of group movement for their choral speaking?

CONNECTIONS *Music:* Have students practice and then perform the song, "She'll Be Comin' 'Round the Mountain." Let each group that performed together during the lesson sing one of the verses, and have the whole class join in on the chorus. Encourage each group to think of appropriate sound effects to add to their verse: "Toot, Toot!" "Hi, Babe!" "Whoa Back!" and so on.

RESOURCES Brockett, Oscar G. *History of the Theatre.* Allyn & Bacon, 1990.

Gullan, Marjorie. *Speech Choir.* Ayer Company Publishers, Inc., 1937.

Koch, Kenneth, and Kate Farrell. *Talking to the Sun: An Illustrated Anthology of Poems for Young People.* Henry Holt & Company, 1985.

A Special Celebration

COMPONENT	Creative Expression
SUBJECT	Performance
OBJECTIVE	Students use a story as motivation to plan a celebration, implementing ideas and techniques about drama/theatre that they have learned over the year.
MATERIALS	*I'm in Charge of Celebrations*, by Byrd Baylor; *Festivals: Ideas from Around the World,* by Elizabeth Honey et al; materials for costumes, props, scenery, or lighting (see Develop)

Note: Allow two or three extra class sessions to plan and rehearse the celebration.

WARM UP Ask the students, "What is a celebration?" Elicit from students the idea that *celebration* means a public and formal ceremony to mark a special occasion. Ask, "What are some of the special occasions people celebrate? How do people celebrate in different homes and in different countries?" List the responses of the students on the board.

EXPLORE Read *I'm in Charge of Celebrations* to the class. Have the students name the different locations or settings in the story. Discuss the reasons for the various celebrations that the character speaks about, such as Dust Devil Day, Rainbow Day, Green Cloud Days, and The Time of Falling Stars. Ask, "Are these the usual traditional holidays we celebrate? What if we thought up all new holidays? What would you like to celebrate? Ask students to choose something in their lives that they care very much about. Make a list of students' suggestions on the board, next to the list of traditional celebrations.

DEVELOP Have the class choose one of the invented holidays for their own class celebration. Perhaps they would like to have a Class Pet Day, or an All-Sports Day, or a Favorite Foods Day. After they have chosen their theme, let the class plan an appropriate celebration, using the drama/theatre knowledge they have gained this year. If, for instance, the class decides on a Class Pet Day, some students could work out a short skit that demonstrates the value of pets in their lives. Some students might be able to have a parent bring their pet to class (either in a cage or otherwise controlled). Those who do not have a pet, but would like to have one, could give a short talk on the pet they would like to own. The class should decide whom to invite—perhaps parents or another class—and then outline the program and the jobs that will need to be done.

One group should be in charge of the artistic aspects—stage and costume design and decorations. A director and an announcer might be needed for a short skit. Some students should take care of the technical aspects— gathering and planning any props, costumes, or lighting needed. One group of students should work on the written material needed—a script, invitations, publicity posters, and so on. Costumes, an adjustable lamp as a stage light, and minimal scenery could be improvised. Be sure that everyone has some kind of role in the celebration.

Allow extra time for planning and rehearsing the celebration, and then have the class put on their performance for the invited guests.

EVALUATE

Student evaluation: Ask the students, "Which traditional celebrations are your favorites? Do you think it would be a good idea to have the class's celebration be an official one? Why or why not? Did you have any diffi- culties coordinating different groups' efforts when you planned your celebration? What were they?"

Teacher observation: Did students understand the theme of the story—that there are many, sometimes personal, reasons for celebrating? Did the students share their family celebrations? Did students invent creative new celebrations? Were students able to work together to create their own celebration?

CONNECTIONS

Social Studies: Have students explore celebrations around the world, such as New Year's Day, birthdays, harvest festivals, and masquerade days. Divide the class into groups and assign each group a particular kind of celebration to research. Ask students to find out how many cultures celebrate that particular occasion. They should investigate African, Asian, Southeast Asian, Hispanic, Native American, and European cultures. Have each group report back to the class.

RESOURCES

Baylor, Byrd. *I'm in Charge of Celebrations.* Macmillan, 1986.

Honey, Elizabeth, et al. *Festivals: Ideas from Around the World.* Delmar Publishers, 1988.

Introduction to Grade Five

The lessons in Grade 5 are sequential and cumulative. Review of sensory and emotional awareness, rhythm and movement, and oral communication is essential at every level, and the lessons for Grade 5 begin with an overview of these elements before going on to explore drama/theatre techniques and subject matter in depth. All areas of drama/theatre at this level become more sophisticated and complex than at earlier levels.

Students who have participated in the *Center Stage* curriculum at Grades 1–4 will need less review than those who have not, but it is not necessary to have studied drama in previous grades to participate in *Center Stage* at Grade 5.

The teacher may wish to survey the lower grade level materials to become familiar with the curriculum, whether or not students have previously been involved with *Center Stage*.

Expectancies for Grade 5 are that students will:

1. Grow in awareness of the senses and their relationship to the creative process.
2. Perceive rhythm and movement as the external expression of an inner idea or feeling.
3. Develop the voice as an instrument of communication.
4. React spontaneously and creatively to situations requiring problem solving.
5. Adapt materials for improvisation and recognize some of the basic elements of drama.
6. Gain some knowledge of the physical theatre.
7. Grow in critical evaluative skills, both in drama/theatre processes and in their own contributions and performances.
8. Continue to develop an appreciation of drama in the arts.
9. Grow in knowledge of their own cultural heritage and the heritage of others.

Contents of Grade Five

GRADE 5

Using the Senses

COMPONENT	Aesthetic Perception
SUBJECT	Sensory Awareness
OBJECTIVE	Students increase their perception and sensory awareness by imagining and pantomiming the lack of one of the senses.
MATERIALS	None required

Note: You may want to do this lesson in two sessions, one to act out the various activities, and the other to act out the activities without the use of a sense.

WARM UP

Ask the students to name the five senses. The responses should be touch, taste, smell, sight, and hearing. List them on the board. Say to the students, "Picture in your minds what it might be like if you had to give up one of your senses. Which one do you think you could do without?" Allow time for the students to think about the question; then call on a few volunteers to tell which sense they chose and explain why. What does each student think might be the results of the loss of that sense?

Ask the students to think about a number of everyday activities, such as eating or walking to school. What differences would it make in their actions if they did not have a particular sense? For example, ask, "What would it be like if you had to eat food without the sense of smell?" (If the students cannot imagine, suggest that at their next meal they hold their noses, take a bite, chew, and swallow to experience the feeling.) Call on a student to tell how not being able to hear might affect the way she or he would walk to school.

EXPLORE

Write the following list on the board, and have each student choose one of the actions from the list to pantomime before the rest of the class. As the student goes through the motions of the activity, he or she should think about which of the five senses are necessary to complete the action, and show how they are used.

1. looking through a door or window
2. opening a door
3. petting an animal
4. building a fire
5. drinking something
6. washing hands
7. wrapping or unwrapping a package
8. cooking food
9. answering the door or a telephone
10. painting a picture
11. looking for something
12. crossing the street

Following the acting out of each activity, ask the student which sense was the most important in performing the action. Why was it the most important? What other senses were used in the activity?

DEVELOP

Assign each student an everyday activity to perform, perhaps one of those already listed, and also assign each student one of the five senses to do without. Ask, "How would the lack of (a specific sense) change that activity? What would you have to do differently?" Give the students a few moments to think about their activities and how to complete them without one of their senses. Allow the students one at a time to pantomime their activities for the class. Ask each student, "How difficult was it to perform your action without using the sense of (the specific sense)? What did you have to do differently? Do you think you could get along without your sense of _____?"

EVALUATE

Student evaluation: Ask students, "What was the hardest part of pantomiming your activity without one of your senses? What was the easiest part?" Ask students to recall some positive aspects of other students' pantomimes that effectively conveyed both the activity and the lack of a particular sense.

Teacher observation: Do students seem to have a keener awareness of the function of each of the senses? Were students able to compensate for the loss of one sense by relying on another? Were they able to use problem-solving skills in planning a pantomime? Did all the students actively participate in this activity?

CONNECTIONS   *Social Studies:* Divide the class into groups. Have the groups discuss how animals might be trained to help people compensate for the loss of one or more senses. Have students list different skills that an animal must have and tasks that it must be able to perform. How might different animals be used for different disabilities? Have the groups make a chart with pictures of different animals that might be trained to help people, and a list of the tasks the animals could perform. Have each group share its chart with the class.

SPECIAL NEEDS   If a visually impaired, hearing impaired, or physically impaired (with tactile sensory loss) individual from the class feels comfortable doing so, ask that person to discuss how she or he carries out the actions in Develop as a "real life" example of coping with the loss of a sense, that is, vision, hearing, or touch.

RESOURCES   Brandt, Keith. *Five Senses.* Troll Associates, 1985.

Suzuki, David. *Looking at Senses.* John Wiley & Sons, Inc., 1991.

Van Der Meer, Ron, and Atie Van Der Meer. *Your Amazing Senses: Thirty-Six Games, Puzzles, and Tricks to Show How Your Senses Work.* Macmillan Children's Book Group, 1987.

Giving and Following Directions

COMPONENT   Aesthetic Perception

SUBJECT   Sensory Awareness

OBJECTIVE   Students increase their perception and sensory awareness by completing an activity depending on another person for the sense of sight.

MATERIALS   Classroom chairs

WARM UP

Place chairs randomly throughout an open space, so that the chairs form a maze. Divide the class into pairs; name one student in each pair A and one B. Have all the students stand on one side of the room. Tell A in one of the pairs to take B's hand and lead B, whose eyes are shut, through the maze of chairs. Demonstrate the path to follow. A must lead B through the chairs, giving verbal directions as they go, so that B does not touch any of the chairs. As one pair moves a few steps into the maze, allow another pair to begin.

After everyone has crossed the room through the maze of chairs, have the pairs switch roles, and have the B's lead the A's across the room so that they do not touch any of the chairs.

EXPLORE

Rearrange the chairs so that a new maze is formed. Again have one partner lead the other through the chairs, but this time tell the partners not to touch each other. Have the sighted partner stand very close to the nonsighted partner and give verbal directions to guide the partner through the maze of chairs. As soon as one pair is a few steps into the maze, allow the next pair to begin.

Both students will have to utilize a different set of skills to complete this activity. In the previous exercise students could rely both on hearing their partners' voices and touching their partners' hands, but for this variation they must rely on their communication and listening skills.

Once all of the pairs have completed the maze, have the partners switch roles to allow the other person the opportunity to experience the activity.

DEVELOP

Change the locations of the chairs in the open space. Make the maze wide enough so that the students following directions do not have to stand too close to each other. For this part of the activity, have five or six sets of partners face each other from opposite sides of the maze, the A's on one side, the B's on the other. Tell students that again, one member of the pair will direct the other through the chairs, but this time from a distance.

First, let the partners talk a little bit to get used to the sound of each other's voices, and make sure the partners know each other's names. Discuss what verbal directions will be necessary, such as *forward, stop, go, right*, and *left*. Remind students that *right* and *left* may be difficult, because when the students are facing each other, one's right will be the other's left!

Have all the A's shut their eyes. Have the B's verbally direct their partners through the maze of chairs, ending when the A partner is directly in front of the B partner so that they can touch.

There will be five or six people talking at the same time. Caution the students to speak in normal voices. The challenge is for the nonsighted person to concentrate on the partner's voice and instructions, blocking out all other commands. The sighted persons should make sure they are being understood, and give exact directions to bring their partners to them.

Have students switch roles and repeat the exercise. Continue the activity until all the students have had a chance to participate.

EVALUATE

Student evaluation: Ask students, "What was it like to rely on someone else to guide you through an unfamiliar environment? What was it like to be responsible for another person's safety? What did you learn from this activity about following directions? How could you use this experience in a dramatic presentation?"

Teacher observation: Were the students sensitive to the problems a nonsighted person has when they were trying to direct their partners through the chairs? Did all the pairs actively participate? Did individual students have difficulty concentrating on the partner's voice?

CONNECTIONS

Language Arts: Divide the class into groups. Have students work together to write directions that describe how to get from one school location to another. The directions should begin at a specified place and lead to a definite destination—for example, from the window to the cloak room to the swing set to the flag pole. Steps should include clues, number of paces, and directional information. Have groups exchange their sets of steps and see whether they can find each other's destinations.

SPECIAL NEEDS   These activities may make the visually impaired individual uneasy unless standard sighted guide and protective techniques are used. Ask your visually impaired student(s) for basic instruction in these techniques.

With eyes closed and the ability to read lips or see sign language removed, the hearing impaired will have difficulty with the Develop section of the lesson. Try designing a system of backtaps for communication with these students; for example, one tap on the right shoulder means a quick right turn, while steady pressure on the middle of the back means to keep going straight ahead.

Physically impaired students may require wide maneuvering spaces between chairs.

LESSON THREE

Recalling Sensory Experiences

COMPONENT | Aesthetic Perception
SUBJECT | Sensory Recall
OBJECTIVE | Students recall past sensory experiences to help them pantomime a particular weather condition.
MATERIALS | None required

WARM UP

Have the students sit either at their desks or in a circle. Ask whether anyone knows what it means to recall something that has happened to them. ("to call back to the mind, to recollect or remember") Ask, "Who can recall being out in some kind of unusual weather—either exceptionally violent or exceptionally beautiful? Were you in sunshine, wind, rain, a hurricane, snowstorm, hail, heat?" Ask the students what especially made the weather an unusual experience, or what made them remember it particularly. Call on several students to recall different experiences.

EXPLORE

Following students' responses, introduce the term *sensory recall,* and give an example of what it is. Define *sensory recall* as "the ability to remember, and almost feel again, the stimuli that accompanied a particular experience." With sensory recall one or more of the senses dominate the memory. An example would be remembering how it felt to walk barefoot through wet grass. The smell of the crushed grass might be the strongest remembered stimulus, or it might be the cool damp feeling to the feet.

Have the students move into an open space. Describe in detail a weather condition such as "cold and windy, with an icy rain that is coming down so hard that it is hard to see very far ahead," and ask students to remember a time when they experienced such a weather condition, and to convey that condition through movement and gestures.

Comment on various students' actions. For example, one student may enter the space and put out a hand to feel the raindrops. The student may then try to avoid getting soaked by putting an imaginary coat over his or her head. Ask the student how it felt to be wet. How could the idea of wind be conveyed? What could the student do to demonstrate the temperature as well as the rain? Ask similar questions of other students.

DEVELOP　　Continue this activity by giving each student the opportunity to choose another weather condition and demonstrate it. As each student presents a scene, emphasize the importance of being very detailed in each action. Ask the observing students for their impression of the weather condition being demonstrated, and what particular actions convey the weather. Encourage the students to make positive comments.

Use sensory recall as a vehicle to help with the dramatic process. Ask, "How were you feeling that day when you walked through the rain, or as you played in the snow, or as you sat in the shade in 100-degree weather? What details do you remember about that time? Where were you? Was anyone with you, or were you alone? How can you use the real occurrence to help with this imaginary situation?" As students recall more details, let them play their scenes again, adding the new details.

EVALUATE　　*Student evaluation:* In small groups or as a class, have students discuss other sensory situations that they can recall in specific detail. Ask, "Did you almost feel the sensations with your body as well as in your mind when you remembered the different kinds of weather?"

Teacher observation: Were the students able to recall sensory information to develop their scenes? Were the students able to convey the weather conditions in their presentations?

CONNECTIONS　　*Science:* Divide the class into groups. Have students in each group choose a meteorological phenomenon to study, such as a hurricane, blizzard, tornado, heat wave, or drought. Have students find out about the conditions that cause the weather pattern and share their information with the rest of the class.

Personifying Objects

COMPONENT	Aesthetic Perception
SUBJECT	Body Awareness
OBJECTIVE	Students visualize and pantomime inanimate objects to increase body awareness and dramatization skills.
MATERIALS	None required

WARM UP Ask, "Would anyone here like to be an ice cube? Why? Why not? What would it be like to be an ice cube? How could you show us, using your body only—no words, what it would be like to be an ice cube?" Allow several students to give their impressions of an ice cube. Ask the observing students to notice what postures and movements the performing students use to show the characteristics of an ice cube. In an open space, let all the students pantomime an ice cube, and then ask them to show how the ice cube would change if it were melting.

EXPLORE Continue this activity by challenging the students to become different objects. Tell them to see an object in their minds' eyes and to consider the size, shape, and weight of the object before becoming the object. Write a list of objects on the board to get students started:

a rag doll	a washing machine
a balloon	a cash register
a ball point pen	a pair of scissors
a spoon	a wet mop

DEVELOP Challenge the students further with, "What if the object you are portraying had feelings or emotions? How could you portray with your body the feelings of that object? Being careful not to bump into anyone, move about in a way that would show how that object feels. Have each student try pantomiming several objects. Additional objects could include:

a lawnmower	a drum	a lemon
a percolator	a turnstile	a light bulb
a popsicle	an eggbeater	a clock
a match	a pair of boots	a stick of butter
a willow tree	a CD player	a rock

an umbrella	a door	a rocking chair
an eraser	a bouncing ball	a teapot
a pillow	a window shade	toothpaste

As students move through the open space, ask questions of as many as possible. Have students describe their object and its imagined feelings, and their own movements. Stop the class's movements a few times during the exercise to point out some explicit and detailed movements of a particular student to the rest of the class. Ask students how practicing being an object might be useful to an actor.

EVALUATE

Student evaluation: Ask the students, "Is it easy to imagine objects having feelings? Why or why not? What was the most difficult object to pantomime? What was the easiest? Why? Did watching other students' movements give you ideas for adding details to your own movements?"

Teacher observation: Were the students able to use their bodies imaginatively in conveying the essences of the objects? Did their movements become more specific as they watched each other?

CONNECTIONS

Language Arts: Have students write riddles to describe ordinary objects, using the following formula: I am _____, I am _____, I am _____. What am I? Encourage students to be creative in thinking of and describing characteristics and features of each object. Have students present their riddles to the class.

Understanding the Emotions of Others

COMPONENT	Aesthetic Perception
SUBJECT	Emotional Awareness
OBJECTIVE	Students identify, respond to, and communicate different emotions.
MATERIALS	None required

WARM UP

Write "happy," "sad," and "angry" on the board. Ask the students how many other feelings, or emotions, they can name. Write their responses on the board. Ask how many of the students have felt each of the emotions on the list. Call out a few of the emotions students have named and ask them to show a face that corresponds with each emotion.

Tell the students that an actor must understand her or his own emotions in order to portray those feelings as a character in a play. The actor must be sensitive, too, to the emotions of other people. An actor cannot really "become" a character unless he or she understands the character's emotions and responses to others.

EXPLORE

Ask the students to close their eyes and see in their minds' eyes an object of their own that means something very special to them. Tell students to picture it in its surroundings—on a shelf, in a box, in the yard—wherever it belongs. Then ask the students to imagine that the object has been stolen; they are to picture the empty place where the object belongs.

After a moment, ask a few students how they felt when they imagined that their object was gone. Answers might include: a sick feeling in the stomach, bewilderment about how it could have disappeared, or anger at it being stolen. Comment that there can be a number of emotions in response to a given event.

Divide the class into pairs, assigning one student in each pair to be A and one B. A will describe to B his or her feelings on discovering the article gone. B's responsibility is to listen sympathetically and respond helpfully in some way to A's loss. B may respond with comfort, with words of advice on how to find it, with an offer to help find it, or in some other appropriate manner. Some students may be able to respond readily; some may have trouble being sympathetic.

Tell students that there is no right or wrong response; the object of the exercise is to become aware of their own and another's emotions. Ask the B students what emotions they felt while listening to A.

DEVELOP

Describe the following situation: A ruler of a country is awarding a high honor to a citizen who has completed a heroic deed—perhaps diverted a flood of water that would have destroyed all the homes in the country. The prime minister of that country is presenting the citizen to the ruler to receive the award.

Divide the class into groups of three. Each group is to plan a brief dramatization of the described situation, with each student playing one of the three characters. Tell students that as they play their characters, they are to choose a particular emotion to portray. It can be one of the emotions listed on the board or another selected by the student.

Allow the students time to plan and rehearse the dramatization, telling the other two in the group the emotions chosen. Then have the groups present their improvisations to the rest of the class. Ask the observing students whether they can identify the emotions portrayed.

EVALUATE

Student evaluation: Ask students, "Was it difficult to feel the imagined emotion? Why or why not? Which emotion was easiest to portray? Which was easiest to respond to? How does practicing showing different emotions help an actor in characterization?"

Teacher observation: Do the students seem to be more aware of the great range of emotions an actor portrays, and how important they are to creating a character? Were all the students willing to participate in the activity? If not, why not?

CONNECTIONS

Art: Have students use pens, pencils, crayons, or paint to make a picture of an emotion. Display students' finished artwork. Discuss the feeling that each picture evokes before revealing the emotion the artist had in mind.

SPECIAL NEEDS

Be prepared for resistant, emotional, or troubled responses from socially and emotionally impaired students. It may be difficult for them to deal with a dramatization of a particular emotion.

Recalling an Emotional Experience

COMPONENT	Aesthetic Perception
SUBJECT	Emotional Recall
OBJECTIVE	Students recall emotional experiences and communicate their emotions through speech and movement.
MATERIALS	None required

WARM UP
In Lesson 3, the students recalled and pantomimed particular sensations. Remind the students that to recall is to bring back into the mind, or remember. Call on selected students to recall a happy event. For example, ask, "Who can remember a birthday party or some other kind of celebration?" Ask those students what especially made the occasion a happy experience. Ask other students to recall times that were especially happy for them.

EXPLORE
Tell students that what they have been using is their emotional recall. Define *emotional recall* as "the ability to remember or bring back into the mind various feelings associated with certain situations." With emotional recall, the feelings dominate the memory. An example would be remembering the joy of winning a game, or pride in getting a good grade on a paper.

Ask students to choose a particular emotion associated with an experience they have had. Have students move into an open space and convey their chosen emotion through movement and gestures. Comment on various students' actions. For example, a student might stride around swiftly and shake a fist to demonstrate anger. Ask that student what the occasion was that made her or him feel angry. What else could the student do to express anger other than shaking a fist? Could the student have demonstrated anger without having felt it? Ask similar questions of other students.

DEVELOP
Tell the students that in drama/theatre the actor must display the emotions demanded by the role in the play. An actor does not really feel an emotion as he or she performs, but must remember it (have emotional recall), and demonstrate it as the character and script require. In order to portray an emotion, the actor must remember from experiences, from observation, and from what she or he has read. Then the actor must also add his or her own imagination.

Ask the students to remember in detail an emotional situation in which they were involved. What did their bodies do? What happened to their voices? What did they say? Give the students a few moments to plan a brief introduction to the situation, and to show the emotion by movement and speech. Call upon volunteers to present their situations. Ask the students who observed why each demonstration was effective, and to suggest other ways to show the emotion.

EVALUATE   *Student evaluation:* In small groups or as a class, have students discuss other emotional situations that they recall. Ask, "What happened in your body as well as in your mind when you recalled the emotion? When other students demonstrated their emotions, did you feel their emotions, too? How does this relate to acting?"

Teacher observation: Were the students able to recall emotional information to develop their improvisations? Were they able to detach themselves enough from the emotional recall to discuss their emotions objectively? Were the students able to relate emotional recall to the actor's task in a dramatic presentation?

CONNECTIONS   *Social Studies:* Have students practice reciting the Gettysburg Address, using appropriate emotions to convey the solemnity of the occasion and the tragedy of the circumstances.

SPECIAL NEEDS   Don't pressure socially and emotionally impaired students for responses. It may be difficult for them to deal with a dramatization of a particular emotion.

Developing a Character Role

COMPONENT	Creative Expression
SUBJECT	Characterization
OBJECTIVE	Students analyze their own behavior to increase their awareness of the process of characterization.
MATERIALS	Pencils, writing paper

WARM UP

Ask the students if they have observed some interesting people from real life, plays, movies, or TV. Allow selected students to describe the person they are thinking about. (If the persons are real persons whom other students know, tell students not to give their names.) Ask what special qualities make that person interesting or distinctive.

Tell the students that *characterization* is "the process of creating a believable person for a story or dramatization by imitating the physical, social, and psychological behavior of that person." In the theatre, an actor must learn as much as possible about the person she or he is to portray in order to "be" that person. The actor can learn about characterization by watching and studying the behavior patterns of others.

EXPLORE

Say, "By observing others we can learn a great deal about characters, how they walk and move, how they talk, and so on. We can also learn something from analyzing ourselves. If someone were observing your movements to imitate them, what would that person notice? How does your voice sound? In a story, what kind of character would you be? Describe yourself!"

Give the students a few minutes to think about what movements, facial expressions, and voice qualities of their own someone who was trying to characterize them might imitate. After a few minutes, call on volunteers to discuss themselves as characters. Encourage students to describe details of movement and voice quality. Do not allow other class members to contradict or argue with an individual student's self-perception.

DEVELOP

While the students are seated at their desks, tell them that they will have a chance to do some further self-analysis by writing down some of their preferences and beliefs. First, ask students to complete two sentences that begin, "I like...." Encourage students to think creatively about themselves and what kinds of people, objects, activities, and ideas they like. Give students ample time to think about and write their responses. Stress that the information is for each student's own personal use and will not be shared with the class unless they volunteer to share it themselves.

Continue by having students write two sentences that begin, "I don't like...." Allow writing time. Then ask students to write two sentences that begin, "I would like the world to be...." Again allow students time to write. Next, say, "Write two sentences that tell how you see yourself in your mind's eye." Give the students time to answer. The final writing assignment is for students to complete two sentences that begin, "I believe...." Allow writing time.

If students would like to share what they wrote, allow them to do so, and enjoy with them the uniqueness and diversity of their ideas. Students might feel comfortable sharing their self-analyses with a friend or in small groups. Also respect the need for privacy. Tell students that these writings are an exercise in characterization and are to be kept in their notebooks to refer to when they are developing a character role for an improvisation.

EVALUATE *Student evaluation:* Ask the students, "What kinds of details about your own behavior did you discover that you hadn't noticed before? Can you imagine yourself as a character in a dramatization? How could the information you wrote be used in developing details of a character's behavior?"

Teacher observation: Were the students able to analyze their own behavior? Of those writings that were shared, how detailed were students' descriptions? Did students seem to see the connection between analyzing their own behavior and analyzing the behavior of a character to be portrayed in a drama?

CONNECTIONS *Language Arts, Social Studies:* Have each student read a biography or autobiography. Then have each student prepare a first-person oral book report and give it to the class. Students may use simple props and costumes to portray the main character.

RESOURCES McCaslin, Nellie. *Creative Drama in the Classroom.* Longman, 1990.

Stanislavski, Constantin. *Building a Character.* Theatre Arts Books, 1977.

_____. *Creating a Role.* Theatre Arts Books, 1961.

Vocalizing for Meaning

COMPONENT	Aesthetic Perception
SUBJECT	Oral Communication
OBJECTIVE	Students practice various vocal exercises to increase their ability to convey meaning, both with and without words.
MATERIALS	Classroom reading material

Note: Consider using vocal exercises before any drama/theatre activity.

WARM UP

Have students sit in a circle. Ask, "How many of you have heard the saying that the voice is the actor's instrument?" Tell students that they can practice using their "instruments" to convey meaning with sound, but not words. Taking turns, each student should make a sound that mimics the sound of an animal. The sound that each person makes is to mean "no," "yes," or have the inflection of a question. Each animal should be different from the preceding animal.

For example, the first person mimics a horse. The group identifies that animal and the meaning of the sound. The next person cannot repeat a horse, but instead mimics a chicken. The group identifies that animal and the meaning of the sound. Continue around the circle until all students have had a chance to vocalize.

Tell students, "You have just practiced your instruments, keeping them in condition to perform. The actor needs to practice with the voice as well as with the body."

EXPLORE

Ask the students what they think *oral communication* means. The responses might include talking, yelling, cheering, sobbing, and whispering. *Oral communication* is defined as "the vocal or verbal sound conveying information." It can convey a mood, a feeling, or an idea.

Have students do a vocal exercise similar to the one in Warm Up, but this time ask students to make the sound of something manufactured instead of a natural sound. Start the exercise at a different point in the circle. The first person might make the sound of an electric drill, getting louder and stopping abruptly to mean "no!" The next student might choose to imitate an eggbeater, and raise the pitch of the sound at the end like a question, and so on around the circle.

Experiment with other vocal activities. You could ask students to imitate natural sounds in the environment, or sounds that change pitch. An example of a sound that changes pitch might be a motor that starts idling at a low pitch, and as it warms up, the sound gets higher and faster.

Let students offer their own ideas for vocalizing. Each person in the circle could make a vocal sound of his or her own choice and have the others guess the origin and meaning of the sound. The challenge is to make a different sound from the preceding one, and to convey meaning with the sound.

DEVELOP   Write on the board a sentence such as, "I want to go home now." Ask students to think of how many different ways this simple sentence can be said. Tell the students that actors can create different meanings with vocal sounds alone, but they can also use the voice to convey different meanings using the same words. The inflection, pitch, volume, and speed of a spoken line, as well as the words themselves, help determine what is meant.

Ask several students to say the sentence. Each student should try to convey a different meaning from the previous one. Compare the different ways the sentence was delivered.

Divide the class into small groups, and give each student an opportunity to read other materials aloud. Let students choose their own readings. Have them experiment with several ways to deliver their material, changing the volume, the speed, and the pitch of their words. Suggest that students vary the inflections at the ends of words and sentences. They could also try saying words and sentences differently from the way it might seem that they should be said. Ask the other students in the group to comment on the effect of each reading on the meaning of the words.

EVALUATE   *Student evaluation:* Ask the students, "What was your favorite vocal exercise? Why? Did you discover that your voice could do some things you hadn't tried before? What were they? What else do you think the voice could do? Why is the voice so important to an actor?"

Teacher observation: Were the students able to convey different meanings with the sentence, "I want to go home"? Did the students understand the benefit for the actor of doing the different vocal exercises? Taking varying reading abilities into account, did students choose interesting reading material to interpret?

CONNECTIONS   *Music:* Divide the class into groups. Have each group work together to create a rap song about school spirit, homework, recess, or another topic that relates to the school day. Ask students to discuss as a group the delivery of each line to convey a particular meaning. Have groups share their songs at a Rap Wrap-Up.

SPECIAL NEEDS   Hearing impaired students may actually be more aware of the different qualities of vocalization and how they affect meaning than hearing students, because of years of nonverbal vocalization and subsequent speech training. Be sure that the hearing impaired students make full use of their vocalizing techniques during this lesson, as well as sign language, facial expression, and body language.

Stretching the Imagination

COMPONENT	Aesthetic Perception
SUBJECT	Mental Imagery
OBJECTIVE	Students create mental pictures of past experiences and expand upon them to motivate dramatic movement and speech.
MATERIALS	None required

WARM UP   Say to the students, "We are going to play a game. When I say a word, I want you to see a picture of that object in your mind." Give the students a word such as *shoe.* Ask several students to share the pictures that come to their minds. Give students another word, such as *square.* Ask again, "What pictures come to mind?" Say another, more abstract word, such as *dream,* and ask for students' responses. Point out to students that they have been using their imaginations, and ask whether anyone can define *imagination.* Discuss students' answers. Accept all reasonable definitions, and add, if necessary, "the formation of a mental picture or image of objects or scenes not present to the senses."

EXPLORE   Ask, "How do actors use their imaginations to help them perform on the stage? How does imagination help the actor to believe something or to feel something more clearly?" (Often actors do not see complete pictures in their minds, but they add new ideas to round out the picture.) Comment or expand upon students' answers, and ask them to give examples.

DEVELOP   Point out that if actors are trying to form a picture of a whole scene rather than an object, the task can be difficult, and they may have to combine ideas from their own and others' experiences. For example, if an actor must portray a person lost in a freezing blizzard, she or he must form a mental picture of being cold and of being lost. If the actor has never been lost, she or he must imagine how it feels from reading stories or listening to others' experiences described.

Move the students to a large, open area. Tell them to close their eyes and imagine how it would feel to experience extreme thirst. Then have the students open their eyes and stand or move (being careful not to bump into each other) as someone would who was very thirsty.

Next ask students to think of one sentence that would help them express the feelings they are trying to show. Tell the students to imagine speaking the sentence to a partner. Give the students the opportunity to move and speak in a way that demonstrates the pictures they have in their minds. Stress that there is no right or wrong way to complete this exercise, but what is important is trying to reproduce clearly for someone else what is seen in the imagination.

EVALUATE

Student evaluation: Ask students, "Which was easier, to imagine an object or to imagine a feeling? Why? Did it make your mental picture clearer to express the feeling with words? How do you think an actor uses imagination to portray a character or an action?"

Teacher observation: Were the students able to translate their mental pictures into movement and speech? Did all the students participate? Did the movements and speech give you added insight about your students and their imaginations?

CONNECTIONS

Mathematics: Explain that there are many ways of forming a mental picture of numbers. For example, the number 20 might be 5×4, $100 \div 5$, $16 + 4$, or $30 - 10$. Give students several numbers and have them describe each one in as many different mathematical terms as they can.

Pantomiming in the Dark

COMPONENT	Aesthetic Perception
SUBJECT	Pantomime
OBJECTIVE	Students use pantomime to portray a described scene, and then pantomime a passage from children's literature.
MATERIALS	*The Hobbit,* by J.R.R. Tolkien

WARM UP

Define *pantomime* for the students as "movement without words that conveys an idea, an action, a character, and/or an emotion." A great portion of performance, whether in classroom improvisations or in a formal play, depends on pantomime. Ask the students to think for a moment about pantomiming the following scene. It may be performed at their seats. Students must plan the action from start to finish, show what is happening, and show how the character feels about it. Tell the students, "You are in a dark tunnel. Somewhere nearby, within reach, is a shelf where a candle can be found. Find the candle. Then search for the matches in your pocket, and light the candle. Think about what will happen next."

Give the students a moment to plan, and when you give the signal, have all of the students perform the pantomime. Ask, "Did you put the candle down when you hunted for the matches? Did you know where to pick it up again? How many of you lit the match first to help you find the candle? What did you do with the match after you lit the candle?"

Tell students that in order for pantomime to be successful, the action must be complete. For example, if one were to pantomime washing hands, the action would not be a simple washing motion, but should begin with the turning on of a faucet, wetting the hands, reaching for soap and using it, putting the soap back, rubbing the soapy hands, rinsing the hands, and turning off the faucet.

EXPLORE

Read from "Riddles in the Dark" in *The Hobbit*. Read the description of Bilbo in the tunnel from "When Bilbo opened his eyes, he wondered if he had, for it was just as dark as with them shut," through "So up he got and trotted along with his little sword in front of him, one hand feeling the wall, and his heart all of a patter and a pitter."

Say to the students, "Suppose this scene were part of a dramatization. There are some things you need to know about the action and the character. What is happening? How does Bilbo look? How is he feeling? Do his feelings change? How does Bilbo move? What kinds of gestures does he make?"

Move the students to an open space. Have them experiment with moving as Bilbo, trying out some of the action in the passage read. Remind students to make their pantomimes complete. Tell the students that sometimes, in order to call attention to a specific action, an actor might exaggerate it, or make it more pronounced than it would be in real life. Let students try this technique. Point out various motions that are effective as students perform the exercise.

DEVELOP   Remind the students that pantomime is action without words. Have students listen carefully and pantomime all the action as you reread the passage from *The Hobbit*. After reading the passage, ask the students whether having the story read as they performed helped them pantomime it. Have students tell what part of the action or emotion they think they did best. Ask various students to demonstrate parts of the action and emotion. Comment on the clarity of each pantomime. After each pantomime, ask the student if there is anything he or she would do differently in presenting it again.

EVALUATE   *Student evaluation:* Ask students, "How does pantomime help tell a story? In your own performance, which parts of Bilbo's actions or emotions were the most difficult to portray? Why? How does an actor use pantomime in drama/theatre?"

Teacher observation: Did the students seem to increase their awareness of the value of pantomime in telling a story? Were they able to understand and carry out a complete pantomime? Did all of the students participate?

CONNECTIONS   *Science:* Divide the class into pairs. Have students choose a famous scientist or scientific discovery. Have one student read a synopsis of the person or procedure as the other student pantomimes the story. Possibilities include Benjamin Franklin discovering electricity, Madame Curie working in her lab, Jonas Salk administering the polio vaccine, and so on.

RESOURCES   Straub, Cindie, and Matthew Straub. *Mime: Basics for Beginners.* Plays, Inc., 1984.

Tolkien, J.R.R. *The Hobbit.* Ballantine, 1986.

Improvising Original Stories

COMPONENT	Creative Expression
SUBJECT	The Five W's (*Who, What, Where, When, Why*)
OBJECTIVE	Students use given *who, what,* and *where* information to create original story improvisations.
MATERIALS	Three boxes, labeled "Who," "What," and "Where," each with about twenty 3-by-5-inch cards with one piece of information written on each one (The *who* cards describe the kind of person; the *what* cards describe the action, and the *where* cards describe the location.)

Note: This lesson could be extended over a number of days, if desired, so that the students have an ample amount of time for planning, rehearsing, and sharing their improvisations.

WARM UP Review with the students the five W's, or introduce the five W's if students are new to the CENTER STAGE curriculum.

Who refers to characterization—what a character thinks, feels, and acts; how the character moves; that person's background and outlook on life.

What refers to action—what is happening, what has led up to the present action, and what will be the results of the action. (The *what* of a story is also referred to as *plot*.)

Where refers to location—the immediate setting of the action (a park, a specific room, a cave) and sometimes the larger setting (a town, a forest, a factory).

When refers to time—the immediate time (early morning, the evening before the ball) and the era (during the late 19th century, a long time ago, 1925).

Why refers to cause—the reason behind the action, the motivation. It includes physical causes as well as emotional and intellectual events.

Tell the class that they will be working with the *who, what,* and *where.* Let each student choose one card from the "What" box, and practice pantomiming the simple action described on the card. For example: "You are a buying a melon," or "You are roller skating," or "You are cutting someone's hair."

Select two or three students to pantomime the *what* written on their cards for the class. Ask the viewing students to identify the action. Ask, "What was happening? Could you tell where the action was taking place or who was doing it? How could you tell?" Give each participating student the chance to discuss what he or she did in the improvisation.

EXPLORE

Group the students by pairs. This time each one of the pair will choose a card from a different box. Perhaps one student draws a *where* card, and the other draws a *who* card. The pair must then prepare an improvisation that involves both of them and uses the information from both cards as the basis for creating a story.

Following the planning and rehearsing, have pairs of students share their improvisations with the class. Evaluate each improvisation with such questions as, "What did you like about the presentation? Was the plot clear? How could the presenters improve the story? Was the pantomime clear? What actions identified the *who,* the *what,* and/or the *where?*"

DEVELOP

Redivide the class into groups of five or six students each. Have three people from each group select a card—one from each of the "Who," "What," and "Where" boxes. After choosing the cards, the three return to their group. Using the information on the cards, the group creates an original improvisation that includes all members of the group.

For example, the *who* card could say, "You are sky divers." The *where* card might say, "You are in a park." The *what* card could say, "You are trying to catch a thief." Suggest to the students that in their improvisations they might also think about incorporating the *when* and *why,* if it seems appropriate.

Following the planning, casting, and rehearsing, have the groups share their stories with the entire class. Evaluate each improvisation with such questions as those in the Explore section of this lesson.

EVALUATE

Student evaluation: Ask the students, "Were you able to use the *who, what,* and *where* information on the cards to create original stories? Why or why not? Were there any problems in trying to combine the information on your card with the information on someone else's card? If so, what were they?"

Teacher observation: Were students already familiar with the five W's? Were the students able to use the information on the cards imaginatively in creating stories? Were students able to work best as individuals, in pairs, or in groups? Why do you think so?

CONNECTIONS   *Art:* Have each student draw a comic strip depicting an event or mishap using only pictures, no words. The five W's should be readily identifiable. Share the strips in one of the following ways: have students explain their own strip to the group; have students trade strips at random and explain each other's strips to the group; or post each strip and have the class work together to suggest captions.

SPECIAL NEEDS   Pair your severely visually impaired students with helpful classmates who will describe to them the actions of those students who are pantomiming.

RESOURCES   *Center Stage Creative Dramatics Supplement.* (contains Five W's poster) Available from Dale Seymour Publications.

Variations on a Theme

COMPONENT	Creative Expression
SUBJECT	Improvisation
OBJECTIVE	Students work in pairs and in groups, using the idea of "Open Space," to improvise a story based on a suggested theme.
MATERIALS	None required

WARM UP

Ask students to think of a recent movie or television program that they have seen, and to identify its theme. (Lessons 17 and 18 of the Grade 4 CENTER STAGE curriculum provide an introduction to the study of *theme*.) The theme of a story or play is the central thought or idea of the story. It is not the same as the plot, or action of the story. Sometimes the theme is expressed as a statement about life (goodness is always rewarded, for example), and sometimes it is expressed in a general statement or word, such as *intolerance* or *loneliness*.

Tell students that they are going to need a theme for their activities in this lesson. Ask for theme suggestions, and list them on the board. Stress imaginative ideas, which could include "right makes might," "helping others," "old friends are the best friends," "achievement," or "vision."

EXPLORE

Introduce the students to "Open Space." "Open Space" is an area in the classroom or multipurpose room or on the stage that students are to enter with imaginative ideas for drama/theatre activities. Students may work as individuals, in pairs, or in groups, as the assignments require.

With the class, choose a theme from the list on the board, keeping in mind improvisations on a theme that might take place within the Open Space. Ask one student to enter the Open Space and begin pantomiming an activity that demonstrates the theme. If, for example, the theme is "helping others," the student may enter the Open Space, kneel down, and begin putting on the shoes of an imaginary toddler. The challenge to the other students is to identify the activity.

As soon as one student has identified the activity, that person may also enter the Open Space and join the first student in putting on a toddler's shoes. A conversation between the two, focusing on the activity, might develop. For now, limit the interaction to pairs.

GRADE 5

At the conclusion of the improvisation, ask the viewing students, "How did the improvisation demonstrate the theme? Was the pantomime detailed and clear? When (and if) the conversation developed, was it related to the action and the theme? What could be done to make the theme and action clearer, or to expand the idea of the scene?"

Repeat the activity, allowing other pairs of students to improvise a scene on the theme. Evaluate each improvisation with questions similar to those above.

DEVELOP

Allow more students to take part in the improvisation, as they plan ways to develop the original scene and theme with more action and more characters. This is a good time to remind students of the five W's, and to suggest that the students try to include them in their scene. Let the students experiment with the scene for a few minutes before stopping it. Ask the students to clarify the action and theme of their scene, and add a simple story line.

Allow students who have not yet participated in an improvisation to replay the scene in the Open Space. Suggest that students become more specific with characters, actions, and dialogue. Remind the students that concentrating on what is happening in the story and using imaginary objects will add dramatic impact, or make the scene more interesting and exciting to the viewers.

At the conclusion of the scene, ask the students how the second playing of the scene was different from the first. Ask the participating students, "Did focusing on the dramatic elements suggested for the second playing of the scene help you to play the scene?"

EVALUATE

Student evaluation: Have the students as a class discuss the improvisations done in pairs and as a group. Ask, "How were the scenes different? Which did you enjoy more? Why? Which was more challenging to perform? Why?"

Teacher observation: Did the students understand the concept of the "Open Space"? Could the students continue a scene begun by one student, increasing participation to include a group? Were the scenes presented creatively?

CONNECTIONS

Social Studies: Suggest to students that history is often divided by periods; for example, some periods in U.S. history are Colonial Times, the Revolutionary War, the Civil War, Reconstruction, Westward Movement, Gold Rush, World War I, and the Depression. Often a period is characterized by an underlying theme, such as hardship, expansion, retribution, or greed. Divide the class into groups and have each group explore information about a period in American history. Challenge students to identify an underlying theme for their period, and have them share it with the rest of the class.

SPECIAL NEEDS   Pair your severely visually impaired students with helpful classmates who will describe to them the actions of those students who are pantomiming.

RESOURCES   Spolin, Viola. *Improvisation for the Theatre: A Handbook of Teaching and Directing Techniques*. Northwestern University Press, 1983.

Commercials as Mini-Dramas

COMPONENT   Creative Expression

SUBJECT   Improvisation

OBJECTIVE   Students dramatize a current commercial, and then create their own imaginary product or service and improvise a commercial for it.

MATERIALS   None required

Note: This lesson may be divided into two parts. Divide it between the dramatization of the actual commercial and the development of the imaginary product commercial.

WARM UP   Explain to the students that commercials on television are mini-dramas. Most have a plot, with a beginning and a middle, and most have an end or a resolution of some kind. They generally have a purpose or message, one of which is to sell a product. The message could be stated as, "This product is better than any other product of its kind." Name a few of your own favorite commercials and briefly outline the beginnings, middles, and ends of them. Ask the students to name a few of their favorites, and to tell the plots.

EXPLORE   Divide the class into small groups. Each group must choose the current commercial that they like the best. Ask each group to tell the others in the class its favorite commercial, why it is the favorite, how the material is presented (with humor, beauty, volume, and so on), and what the purpose of the commercial is (to sell, to ask for something, to inform).

Ask students to think of how the five W's apply to the mini-dramas of commercials. Say, "If you were going to act out your commercial for the class, what would be needed? Who are the characters in the commercial? What needs to be said, and what could be shown through movement and gestures? What kind of space or set would be required? Would you need props and costumes to present the ideas in your commercial?" Let the students discuss ideas for dramatization in their groups.

DEVELOP   In groups, plan, cast, and rehearse the selected commercials. Allow each group to share its commercial with the class. Have students evaluate each presentation by the following criteria: Was the product or service clearly demonstrated? Were the beginning, middle, and end of the commercial well established? Did the commercial include all of the five W's, or were some not needed? Were the movements and gestures convincing? Were students' expressions and voices convincing? Did the actors utilize the space to the best advantage? These criteria can be written on the board to remind students to use them in evaluating the presentations.

After sharing and evaluating the dramatizations of current commercials, ask each group to choose an imaginary product and create a commercial that describes that new product. Encourage students to imagine unusual and different products and services. For example, a group might develop a commercial for a homework machine that does all of a student's homework in just five minutes or less with no errors.

Let the groups plan, cast, and rehearse the imaginary product commercial in the tradition of most commercials seen and heard. Share the improvisations with the entire class. Evaluate them according to the criteria used for the previous commercials.

EVALUATE   *Student evaluation:* Ask students, "Was it easier to dramatize a commercial you had already seen, or to dramatize one you created for an imaginary product? Why? Which was more fun to do? Which of the five W's did you successfully incorporate? Which commercials convinced you to buy the product?"

Teacher observation: Were students able to incorporate the five W's in their original commercial? Were the students imaginative in creating their products and commercials? Did they utilize a variety of ways to act out the mini-dramas?

CONNECTIONS   *Music:* Suggest that students in each group make up a jingle to advertise a product. Students may wish to sing about the product that they used for the commercial in the activity, or they may wish to choose something new. Plan a series of Station Breaks throughout the day, during which students may present their jingles.

Creating Stories from Objects

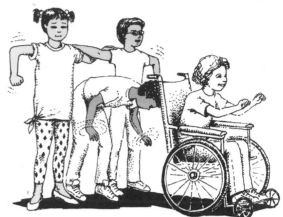

COMPONENT   Creative Expression

SUBJECT   Story Development

OBJECTIVE   Students work in groups to create and dramatize a story within a limited period of time, using given imaginary objects.

MATERIALS   None required

Note: Limiting the time allowed to create different objects is a motivational technique that forces quick decision making.

WARM UP

Remind students of their work in Lesson 4, when they "became" inanimate objects. Move the students to an open space. Challenge the students again to become various objects, such as a chair, a tree, a rock, or a stick, as you quickly call out the objects one by one.

Tell students that for the rest of this lesson, they are going to have to think fast to create the assigned objects. Their improvisations won't have to be polished or perfect, but they will have to make some quick decisions.

EXPLORE

Divide the students into groups of five or six, and give each group five seconds to create a boat, using everyone in the group. Have the students in each group look at themselves and remember their positions so that they can create a boat again later.

Continue by telling the class, "You have five seconds to make a group statue. Each person in your group must be positioned on a different level." When the statues are completed, tell the students to remember how they are positioned and what statue they have created.

Continue by saying, "Now you have five seconds to invent a machine that has never been seen before. Everyone in your group should be a moving part of the machine." When each group has put a "machine" together, tell the students to remember their positions and how they created their machine. Say, "When I count to three, I want you to make the boat that was your first creation. Go back to those exact positions you were in before." Also have students re-create their statues and machines.

DEVELOP

Have the students sit in their groups while you give directions for the rest of the activity. Review the five W's as they relate to drama/theatre (Lesson 11). Tell students that they are to create a story dramatization that involves a boat, a statue, and a machine. The story must have a definite beginning, middle, and end. Students will need to decide whether the dramatization will be verbal, nonverbal, or a combination of both. They could have a storyteller, for example, who tells the story while the other members of the group act it out, or they could create dialogue among the players.

Set a definite time limit—perhaps 20 minutes—to plan and rehearse. Caution students not to spend all their time creating the story, because they will also need to rehearse and share their story with the class. As students are working in their groups, remind them occasionally how much time is left for creating the stories and rehearsing, and then have them give their presentations.

Have the viewing students evaluate each dramatization. Did the group use the three objects in their story? Did the method chosen to tell the story seem appropriate? Was there a beginning, middle, and end to the story, and did the group use the five W's? In evaluating each presentation, be sure to note that time restrictions may have limited the full development of some of the story elements, and give each group credit for putting together a dramatization in a short period of time.

EVALUATE

Student evaluation: Ask the class to evaluate each group's ability to use the given objects imaginatively in a story. Compare the groups' different story lines using the same objects.

Teacher observation: How effective were the students in creating various objects using their bodies? Were the objects believable? Did the students use the five W's in their stories? Did being limited in time act as a stimulus to creative activity, or did it become a problem for some students?

CONNECTIONS

Language Arts: Have each student write a poem listing terms to describe an object or animal. Have students identify characteristics and traits, revealing the name of the object in the last line—for example: *Fuzz and whiskers, / Engine purrs, / Sly and lazy, / Downy fur. / Claws! Spit! Scat! / Cat!*

RESOURCES

Way, Brian. *Development Through Drama.* Humanities Press, 1967.

Creating Dialogue

COMPONENT	Aesthetic Valuing
SUBJECT	Dialogue/Characterization
OBJECTIVE	Students elaborate on given characters and create dialogue by making choices about how the characters would respond to each other.
MATERIALS	None required

WARM UP

Tell the students that you will set up a situation, and they are to think about what would happen next. Ask students to mentally complete the action in the story.

Say, "Suppose a mother and son are shopping in a department store. The boy sees a pair of jeans he likes and wants his mother to buy them. The mother sees how much they cost and thinks they are too expensive, so she says, '_____.'"

Tell the students that what the mother says determines the next words of the son. Ask what might be the son's reply if the mother said, "I can't afford them right now. Do you have enough money from your allowance to buy them?" Then ask what the reply might be if the mother said, "You are always whining. Do you expect me to buy you something every time we go to the store?"

Select two students and have them create a brief dialogue, developing one of the mother's responses. Stop the students after a few minutes, or at an appropriate point. Tell the class, "We have a beginning (the characters and the situation) of our story, and two possible middles (the mother's different responses). What is the resolution, or end of the story?" Let students offer several suggestions, depending on which of the mother's responses they use, and have the performing students bring the scene to a close by using one of the suggestions.

EXPLORE

Define *elaboration* as "working out further details with great care, or giving additional or fuller treatment to something." Elaboration in creating stories is developing or working out all the details that enrich the plot, develop the characters, and demonstrate the theme. For the story that was dramatized in the Warm Up, ask students to elaborate on the following:

1. Who are these people in our story? Describe them. Give them a history. For example, "The mother is a single parent, and her clothes are not expensive. She works to support her three children, and provides them with a home, nutritious food, and adequate clothing on a limited budget. The son is seven years old, and hasn't yet learned that he can't have everything he wants."

2. Given the description of the mother, what might be some of her different responses to the son? Tell the reason for each one.

3. How does the boy interact with his mother? Given a specific response from the mother, what will the son say back to her?

Select a different pair of students from the one that has already created a dialogue for the story, and ask the new pair to replay the scene based on the elaboration created by the class.

DEVELOP

Divide the class into pairs. The task of each pair is to establish characterizations and set up a simple scene in which one person responds to the other. One character should be the parent, the other a child. The scene should not be the one of the mother and son in the store, but some other situation involving parent and child. Ask the students to use their imaginations in deciding on the situation.

When the basic plot has been developed, the students should elaborate on it and on the characters and their responses to create a detailed scene. Remind the students that each choice made about what a person says or does determines what happens or is said next. Plan, rehearse, and share the scenes created by the pairs. Have the viewing students discuss the direction each scene takes, starting with the adult's response to the child.

EVALUATE

Student evaluation: Together as a class, compare all the different situations presented. Was there a similar theme running throughout the improvisations? Ask students whether they thought the dialogues were realistic, and why or why not. Ask, "How did elaborating on the details of story content and characters help you develop the characters' interaction?"

Teacher observation: Did the students understand how choices about situations and characters can affect the content of stories? Were the students able to work cooperatively in pairs to create simple two-person scenes? Did the students portray some creative outcomes to the adult-child situations?

CONNECTIONS *Mathematics:* Have pairs of students develop a dialogue between a child and a parent on the subject of allowance. The dialogue should include multiplication, division, addition, and subtraction. For example:

Dad: I am going to raise your allowance $2 per month, which is almost 50¢ a week.

Son: That's great, Dad. Added to the $10 I get already, I'll be getting $12.

LESSON SIXTEEN

Making Creative Choices

COMPONENT   Aesthetic Perception

SUBJECT   Improvisation

OBJECTIVE   Students use a given word to stimulate
                 mental images, then make choices
                 concerning those images to create a
                 story and dramatization.

MATERIALS   None required

WARM UP   Ask the students to close their eyes and see what picture comes to their
                 minds when you say the word *dreamland*. Give the students a minute;
                 then ask, "What is the most powerful and lasting image in your mind
                 when you think of dreamland?" List students' responses on the board, and
                 comment on the variety of the various images, and discuss similarities and
                 differences in what students saw.

EXPLORE   Together with the class, select one or more of the mental pictures sug-
                 gested by the students for dreamland, and brainstorm ways that a group
                 could use a particular image to create a story and a dramatization. What
                 would be the setting of the story? What action would occur, and what
                 characters would be taking part in the action? Would there be any dia-
                 logue, or would the story be in pantomime?

                 Point out that creative choice means all the decisions that one makes in
                 the creation of a dramatic work, not only in the story itself, but also in the
                 style and techniques of presenting the story. Ask, "How does making a
                 choice affect what happens in a story? How could those choices determine
                 the artistic quality of a dramatic work?"

DEVELOP   Divide the class into small groups. Explain to the students that they are to
                 create a story dramatization from another word, using the same technique
                 as they did to make decisions about a story for "dreamland." Give all the
                 groups the same word—a word such as *Interspace,* or *Rubberband Land,* or
                 Upsidedown World, or another that you think would inspire creativity.
                 Point out to the students that although they all have the same word from
                 which to create an improvisation, the choices that each group makes in
                 putting together its scene will make the scenes different.

Remind the students of the previous lesson, in which choices about characters and their interaction determined the events that happened next. In planning the scenes, the students are to consider carefully the choices they make in setting, characters, and action, and what the results of those choices will be. Following the planning, casting, and rehearsing of the scenes, have each group present its improvisation. Discuss what creative choices the students made, and how those choices affected their improvisations.

EVALUATE   *Student evaluation:* Have students compare the different improvisations in their small groups. Were the choices made by others similar to or different from their own? In what ways? If they were to make different choices for their own dramatization, what would the results be?

Teacher observation: Do students seem to understand what creative choice is? Were the students able to discuss the differences in the improvisations that were the results of creative choices?

CONNECTIONS   *Music, Language Arts:* Arrange to play a selection of instrumental music for students. Ask what mental pictures the music brings to mind, and have students write a story or poem that conveys the images of the music. Share students' writing as the music is played in the background.

Exploring Creativity

COMPONENT	Creative Expression
SUBJECT	Qualities of Creativity
OBJECTIVE	Students analyze the aspects of creativity and their relationship to drama/theatre.
MATERIALS	One copy for each student of the Qualities of Creativity list on page 123.

WARM UP

Say to the students, "Suppose there is a big cobweb on the ceiling. I don't have a broom or dustmop with a handle long enough to reach it, and I don't have a ladder to climb on. How can I get the cobweb down? How many ways, practical or fantastical, can you think of to help me solve my problem?"

Answers might range from climbing on the furniture to putting on a magic flying suit and flying up to reach it. Accept all the answers with positive comments as to their imaginative and/or practical value. Explain to the students that the ability to find solutions to problems is part of creativity.

EXPLORE

Ask the students, "What do you think creativity, or being creative, means?" Many of the answers will probably involve having new or original ideas. Say, "When I asked you how to get the cobweb off the ceiling, you thought of new and original ways to use objects, or some new method of solving the problem. You were showing your creativity."

Tell the students that there are certain traits or qualities that are associated with creativity. Give each student a copy of the list of qualities to read as you define them.

DEVELOP

Give the class a problem, such as, "Design a bird feeder that is attractive, makes the food available gradually, and keeps out squirrels and other animals." Then divide the class into five groups. Each group is to discuss the problem, and try to solve it using one or more of the qualities listed. The students might create an improvisation, a dialogue, a TV commercial, or some other method of presentation to illustrate the solution of the problem. Give the students time to discuss, plan, and rehearse their materials.

Share the improvisations with the class. After each presentation, ask, "What creative qualities were used to solve the problem? What technique (dramatization, pantomime, dialogue, lecture) was used to show the creative qualities? How did the demonstration help you to understand the qualities?" At the conclusion of all the presentations, ask the students, "Why is creativity important in drama/theatre? What difference would these qualities make in designing a set, or creating costumes?"

EVALUATE   *Student evaluation:* Ask the students, "Were you able to apply the creative qualities to the problem? How did the members of your group work together to be creative? Have you discovered creative qualities in yourself that you weren't aware that you have? How can you use these qualities in daily life?"

Teacher observation: Could the students understand each of the different qualities of creativity? Could you tell which of the five qualities seemed most familiar to the students? Did the students enjoy exploring creativity in themselves?

CONNECTIONS   *Social Studies:* Divide the class into groups. Have each group develop a program for recycling. Encourage students to use creativity in devising a program that people would want to use and that would be easy and cheap to use. Suggest that they brainstorm ideas for a community campaign to foster awareness and participation. Share each group's ideas with the rest of the class.

Qualities of Creativity

Objectivity   The ability to study a problem without prejudging, or making a decision too quickly.

A sense of aesthetics   A feeling for beauty, both external and internal.

An ability to frame unusual problems   Being able to enjoy the process of identifying the problem, examining it, and observing it, though not necessarily solving it; wanting to know how things work.

An ability to make unexpected connections   Looking at an object or a problem and making a connection to something else that most people would not.

An ability to use familiar information in new ways   Being able to adapt information, action, and thoughts, and use them in a different way than they have been used before.

COPYRIGHT © DALE SEYMOUR PUBLICATIONS

GRADE 5

Creating Improvisations from Real-Life Situations

COMPONENT	Creative Expression
SUBJECT	Improvisation
OBJECTIVE	Working in groups, students create an improvisation from their own observations of a real incident.
MATERIALS	None required

WARM UP Review themes (Lesson 12). Ask the students to define *theme* (the central thought or idea about life in an artwork), and to give examples. Ask the students to define *plot* (the action or story line of a play or story), and to give examples. Ask the students to recall the definition of *improvisation* (a response, or presentation composed or developed without previous study or preparation), and have them give examples from their own drama/ theatre activities. Ask the students where the ideas for the improvisations come from. Expect many different answers. Help students conclude that an improvisation can be motivated by a variety of sources.

EXPLORE If a student mentioned real life as a source, expand on that. If not, tell the students that one important source can be real-life situations. Events happen in our lives and the lives of others that provide interesting material for drama.

Say, "Think about a real situation that has happened in school recently that could be used to create an improvisation. Keep your idea to yourself for now. Think about who was involved. What actually happened? Can you remember the dialogue? Could the situation be developed into a dramatic event?" Stress to the students that the situation should be appropriate to share with others, and interesting enough to be used for a dramatization. Allow enough time for each student to select an event that could be an interesting story.

DEVELOP Divide the students into small groups of five or six students each. In their groups, have the students share their different ideas of real-life situations that happened at school. Following the sharing of the various ideas, each group is to choose one incident that all the members of the group would like to develop as a story. Tell students that they do not have to dramatize the incident exactly as it happened, if changing it would make a better story.

Have each group decide on the action, characters, dialogue, and setting. Allow enough time for planning and rehearsal. Come together as a class again, and let each group share its improvisation with the entire class. Evaluate each improvisation briefly with such questions as, "What was the theme of this improvisation? Was the story line clearly defined? Was the improvisation a repetition of the real-life situation, or were details added and changed to give the story a more dramatic interpretation?"

EVALUATE

Student evaluation: Have students, as a class, compare the themes and plots of each improvisation. Ask the students, "Was it difficult to dramatize a real-life situation? Why or why not? When using a real-life situation for dramatization, do you need to be accurate in its portrayal? Why or why not?"

Teacher observation: Did students cooperate within the groups to choose and dramatize a story? Were you familiar with the situations that the students chose to improvise? Were the groups able to change the real-life situations if necessary to make them suitable for dramatization?

CONNECTIONS

Social Studies: Divide the class into groups. Have each group choose a topic from the newspaper or from a magazine to dramatize for the rest of the class. Encourage students to include necessary background and facts that will enhance clarity and understanding. Suggest that students project possible outcomes if the events are unresolved. Have each group present its news story to the rest of the class.

RESOURCES

Dibell, Ansen. *Plot*. Writers Digest Books, 1988.

Using Literature for Dramatization

COMPONENT Historical and Cultural

SUBJECT Folklore

OBJECTIVE Students learn about different kinds of stories from world cultures, and research and dramatize a story from a culture different from their own.

MATERIALS One copy for each student of the list, Stories from Folklore, on page 128; anthologies and reference books

Note: This lesson may be presented in two sessions, the first for research and the second to present the story.

WARM UP Explain to the students that the literature they read is rich with stories from all cultures in the world. In each culture the stories make up the cultural tradition. The stories include fables, folk tales, fairy tales, legends, myths, and epics. Give each student a copy of the list on page 128 and briefly explain each kind of story. Ask the students if they can think of examples. You may wish to have the students write their responses on the board. Ask how many stories students know that are from a culture different from their own.

EXPLORE Divide the class into small groups. Provide several anthologies of folk tales, and have each group select a story that is part of the folklore of a culture different from their own. The group should decide what type of story it is from the list on the board, then research the story. Have students gather information about the culture from which the story came, and find out the location, customs, and history of the culture and of their story. Provide several reference books and resources in the classroom, or have students go to the school library, so that each group can prepare a presentation for the class. The group should decide how to present the background information about their story. This will be the introduction. Then the group should decide how to dramatize the story. Students could use choral speaking, hand puppets, shadow puppets, music and/or dancing, pantomime, and so on.

DEVELOP   Give each group time to prepare a presentation introducing their story, and to rehearse a dramatization of the story. The introduction should tell what type of story the group will dramatize, the country of origin, some customs of the people in that country, and the reasons for the story (if any). The same method of presentation may be used in the introduction as is used for the dramatization, or they may be presented differently. At the end of the presentations, compare the different kinds of folk stories chosen and the methods used to present them.

EVALUATE   *Student evaluation:* Ask the students, "What were some of the methods chosen to present the background information and dramatizations? Did they suit the stories? What did you learn about different countries and their cultural traditions?"

Teacher observation: Did the students understand the similarities and differences among the different kinds of folklore? How thoroughly did the students research their chosen stories? Were the students creative in their dramatizations? Did they try new methods of presentation?

CONNECTIONS   *Language Arts:* Present students with a selection of morals: "A fool and his money are soon parted," "All that glitters is not gold," "Never look a gift horse in the mouth," "Let sleeping dogs lie," and so on. Have each student choose a moral and write a fable to go with it. Suggest that students illustrate their fables, and display them on a bulletin board.

RESOURCES   Aesop. Joseph Jacobs, ed. *Fables of Aesop.* B. Franklin, 1970.

Asbjornsen, Peter Christen, and Jorgen Moe. *Norwegian Folk Tales.* Pantheon Books, 1982.

Briggs, Raymond. Virginia Haviland, ed. *The Fairy Tale Treasury.* Dell Publishing Company, 1986.

Dayrell, Elphinstone. *Why the Sun and Moon Live in the Sky.* Houghton Mifflin Company, 1990.

Gates, Doris. *Lord of the Sky: Zeus.* Puffin Books, 1982.

Hamilton, Edith. *Mythology.* Little, Brown, & Company, 1942.

Livo, Norma J., and Sandra A. Rietz. *Storytelling Folklore Sourcebook.* Libraries Unlimited, Inc., 1991.

Thistle, Louise. *Dramatizing Aesop's Fables.* Dale Seymour Publications, 1993.

Stories from Folklore

Fable A story that teaches a lesson, especially one in which animals act like people.

Folk tale Any story about a culture passed on from generation to generation. Myths, fairy tales, fables, and legends can also be folk tales.

Fairy tale A story, usually for children, about elves, hobgoblins, dragons, fairies, or other magical creatures.

Legend A greatly exaggerated story relating to the history of a culture, usually about people who really lived.

Myth A traditional story used by a culture to explain the unknown. Myths are often associated with religious beliefs.

Epic A long narrative poem, usually in a formal style that indicates historical importance, made up of traditional stories about a hero or group of heroes. An epic poem expresses the early ideals of the culture.

COPYRIGHT © DALE SEYMOUR PUBLICATIONS

Analyzing a Folk Tale

COMPONENT	Historical and Cultural
SUBJECT	Folklore/Story Components
OBJECTIVE	Students listen to a folk tale and improvise a scene that demonstrates one of the story components.
MATERIALS	None required

WARM UP   Review the definition of a folk tale (Lesson 19). A folk tale is any story that is culturally specific and has been passed on from generation to generation. Sometimes folk tales tell about people and animals with magic powers. Ask the students, "What folk tales do you know that tell of animals with magic powers?" Have the students give brief descriptions of the stories they name.

EXPLORE   Ask the students if anyone is familiar with the folk tale from Mexico, "The Horse of Seven Colors." If a student knows the story, ask the student to outline the plot briefly and tell what the theme is. Ask the student if there are any animals with magic powers in the story, and if so, what they are. If no one has heard the story, tell the students that as you read aloud the folk tale, they should think about what the plot and theme of the story are, and notice whether any animals have magic powers.

If necessary, review with students the story components of character, theme, plot, conflict, and resolution discussed in earlier lessons. Then read "The Horse of Seven Colors" provided in the Appendix of CENTER STAGE. Read with expression, varying your voice quality for the different characters, and being very dramatic at the climax of the story. Ask the students to answer the following questions about the story:

1. Who were the main characters in the story?
2. What is the theme of the story?
3. What is the plot of the story?
4. What are the major conflicts that need to be resolved in the story?
5. How are the conflicts resolved?

DEVELOP   Ask the students, "How did my voice convey meaning as I read the story? Did you notice any change in the volume, pitch, and tonal quality of my voice? Did I pause often? How was my voice different when I was reading the narrative from when I was reading dialogue? What happened to my voice at the climax, or most exciting part of the story? Did my voice change in any way?"

Divide the class into five groups. Assign to each group one of the following: the characters, the theme, the plot, the major conflict, and the resolution. Explain to the students that each group is to give a brief dramatization of a part of "The Horse of Seven Colors" that focuses on the assigned component. The components will overlap (characters will be in all of them, for example), but the main purpose of each group's scene will be to demonstrate the particular story element the group has been assigned. Each group will select one member to either explain the part of the story being dramatized, or to act as narrator for the action. There should be no attempt to dramatize the entire story. Allow the students to plan, cast, and rehearse their improvisations. Share the improvisations with the class.

EVALUATE   *Student evaluation:* Ask the students, "How did the improvisations demonstrate character, theme, plot, conflict, and resolution? Did having a narrator help in the improvisation? How? Is it possible to show just one component of a story? Why or why not?"

Teacher observation: Do the students understand the concepts of character, plot, theme, conflict, and resolution? Were they able to demonstrate the concepts in their brief improvisations? Were students able to connect your vocal techniques as a reader to the story components?

CONNECTIONS   *Social Studies:* Select a historical event from students' social studies curriculum. Possibilities include Paul Revere's ride, the landing of the Mayflower, the Battle of the Little Big Horn, and so on. Divide the class into five groups and assign a component—characters, theme, plot, conflict, or resolution—to each group. Have each group portray their component, and put the five together for an overall view of the event.

RESOURCES   *Center Stage: Creative Dramatics Supplement.* (contains an audiotape of "The Horse of Seven Colors") Available from Dale Seymour Publications.

Writing Haiku

COMPONENT	Historical and Cultural
SUBJECT	Haiku/Poetry
OBJECTIVE	Students learn about and write haiku, and improvise movement to this kind of poetry.
MATERIALS	*The Haiku Anthology,* by Cor Van Den Heuvel; writing paper and pencils

Note: This lesson could easily become two or more sessions in which the students: 1. read haiku, 2. write their own haiku, and 3. use haiku to create a movement improvisation with music.

WARM UP

Introduce haiku to the students by reading one or two of the haiku of Basho (1644–1694), one of the greatest haiku writers, and the poet who crystallized the style. Write them on the board or on a chart.

An old silent pond...
A frog jumps into the pond,
Splash! Silence again.

Mountain-rose petals
Falling, falling, falling now...
Waterfall music.

Tell students that the *hokku*—more commonly known as *haiku*—is a verse form that has been used by Japanese poets for hundreds of years. Originally the haiku was the first part of the *tanka*, a five-line poem, which was often written by two people as a literary game. One person wrote three lines, and then the other finished the poem with two more lines. The haiku, or first three lines, became popular as a separate form.

Explain that there are only seventeen syllables in the haiku; the first and third lines contain five syllables, the second line seven. Haiku poems record the essence of a keenly perceived moment linking people and nature.

EXPLORE

Point out that a haiku almost always tells the season, either directly or by inference. But there is also, in a good haiku, more than a mere picture of nature; there is an implied identity between two seemingly different things. Refer back to the haiku written on the board or chart.

GRADE 5

Read more haiku by Basho, and poems by other master haiku writers, such as Buson (1715–1883) and Issa (1763–1827) from *The Haiku Anthology*. Ask students how they think the poet links people and nature in each one. Have students identify the key words that give a hint about the season, and try to tell which two different things are being linked together.

Asleep in the sun
On the temple's silent bronze
Bell, a butterfly...

Buson

One man and one fly
Buzzing together alone
In a sunny room...

Issa

DEVELOP

Divide the class into pairs. Have each pair play a game of creating a haiku verse together. One person writes two lines, and the other writes one line. Have students select a topic in nature such as the sky, the ocean, an animal, and so on.

After a short period of writing time, have the students stop writing and create movements that express the images of the poems. The poems do not have to be complete or perfect, but the images in them should be developed enough so that they suggest movements for students to improvise. Allow the students to create their movement improvisations using music and/or speaking the poem in a variety of ways.

EVALUATE

Student evaluation: Ask students to evaluate their own poems and movement improvisation with their partners. Ask students to discuss what worked, and why. Was there something that didn't work? Why not? What was the best part of transforming the verse into movement?

Teacher observation: What were the students' reactions to haiku? Did the students understand how this kind of poetry presents occurrences in nature? Could students use haiku to motivate movement activities?

CONNECTIONS

Science, Language Arts: Have students research a scientific phenomenon, such as an earthquake, a volcano, a glacier, an avalanche, a meteor shower, or an eclipse. Using the formula for writing haiku (five syllables/ seven syllables/five syllables), have students write a haiku that describes their phenomenon. Have students share their science haiku with the class.

RESOURCES

Van Den Heuvel, Cor. *The Haiku Anthology: Haiku and Senryu in English.* Simon & Schuster, 1986.

Setting Up Conflict in Drama

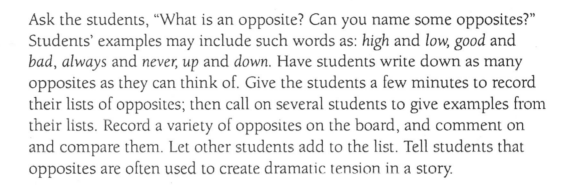

COMPONENT	Creative Expression
SUBJECT	Opposites/Conflict
OBJECTIVE	Students develop a dramatization from an original scenario.
MATERIALS	Writing paper and pencils

WARM UP

Ask the students, "What is an opposite? Can you name some opposites?" Students' examples may include such words as: *high* and *low, good* and *bad, always* and *never, up* and *down.* Have students write down as many opposites as they can think of. Give the students a few minutes to record their lists of opposites; then call on several students to give examples from their lists. Record a variety of opposites on the board, and comment on and compare them. Let other students add to the list. Tell students that opposites are often used to create dramatic tension in a story.

EXPLORE

Continue the exercise by saying, "If we were going to name some opposites that are traditionally used to create tension and set up conflicts in stories, what would they be?" Students may choose from the list on the board, or recall others. Examples could include love versus hate, good versus evil, life versus death, and so on.

Have each student choose a set of opposites from the list and write the beginning of a scenario, or plot outline, that would develop the opposites into the conflict in a story. An example (dishonest versus honest) might begin, "A young man has staked his claim on a piece of land that is rich in gold. A big company is illegally trying to take his claim away. As the scene opens, the crafty agent of the big company strikes up a conversation with the young man in the stagecoach. When he finds out that the young man does not have the title papers with him, the crafty agent sets fire to the land office to destroy the records." Allow enough time for students to write short scenarios.

DEVELOP

Have each student share with the class how he or she set up the conflict in a scene. Let the class select one of the ideas to be developed further.

GRADE 5

Divide the class into groups. Have each group create an improvisation from the chosen scenario by further developing the characters, setting, and dialogue, and giving the story an ending, or resolution. Let each group plan, cast, rehearse, and share their story with the class.

EVALUATE

Student evaluation: As a class, discuss each group's interpretation of the same conflict. Compare the settings, the characterizations, the dialogue, and the resolution of each group's presentation.

Teacher observation: Did each student write a short scenario? Did students use the idea of tension between opposites to set up a conflict? Could the groups work together to elaborate on the chosen scenario? Were the resolutions logically developed?

CONNECTIONS

Language Arts: Divide the class into groups. Explain to students that they are going to play an antonym game. Write a word on the chalkboard. Then give students two minutes to write down as many antonyms as they can. Have the students in each group play among themselves. When time is called, a student in the group should read his or her list. Words appearing on more than one list are crossed out. Other students in the group continue reading their lists until all of the duplicate words have been crossed out. Then two points are awarded for the original antonyms left in each student's list. Play a number of rounds, until one student in each group has reached a predetermined number of points.

RESOURCES

Hull, Raymond. *How to Write a Play.* Writers Digest Books, 1988.

Smiley, Sam. *Playwriting: The Structure of Action.* Prentice Hall, 1971.

Developing Story Outlines for Drama

COMPONENT	Creative Expression
SUBJECT	Creative Writing
OBJECTIVE	Students invent characters and conflicts to create and develop a story outline, and analyze its potential for dramatization.
MATERIALS	Writing paper and pencils

Note: Save the stories developed in this lesson for use in Lessons 24 and 30.

WARM UP
Ask the students how many have written any stories, poems, or plays of their own. Ask, "Where do your ideas come from?" Write students' responses about their sources on the board. Say, "In class we have used many sources for ideas in our improvisations. We have used stories and poetry; we have used words and places and objects. Today you can become your own source by writing a simple story outline which could be the basis for an improvisation." Ask a few students to describe stories they have created in the past.

EXPLORE
Tell the students, "As you invent your story, be as creative as possible. We'll follow the steps together, but each person will write a different story. We'll make an adventure out of writing!" Be sure that all the students have writing paper and pencils. Then say, "First of all, write down two names. They are to be the names of the characters in your improvisations. Write any kind of names you like; the characters can be persons, animals, and/ or imaginary beings."

Say, "Next, write down something that one of the characters wants very badly. It can be an object, or it can be something that the character wants to do or find or achieve." Continue, "Now write down something that is keeping that character from getting what she or he wants. Is it age? Is it distance? Is it people or things that interfere? Is it the character's conscience? Use your imagination to make up a reason, and write it down."

Conclude, "The final story element to write down is how the second character helps or hinders the first character. Think first whether the second character is a friend or enemy, then write a very simple statement describing the action that helps or hinders the character; for example, 'She gives her a magic cloak,' or 'The giant locks him up in a dungeon.' Use your imaginations!"

DEVELOP

When the students have completed their writing, ask selected students to read what they have written. After each reading, say, "We have the beginning and middle of a story. Can the members of the class suggest a resolution or ending?" Elicit two or three responses for each selection.

After each selection has been discussed, ask, "How could this exercise be turned into a story? How could it be turned into an improvisation? What more is needed to fill out the material for dramatization?" Expect answers such as, "Develop the characters"; "Put in more description"; "Make up a 'where' for the story."

If time allows, have the students work on their exercises to develop them more fully. Otherwise, suggest that the students make a few notes and put their story outlines away for use in a later lesson, or suggest that at another time the stories could be developed fully as a writing exercise.

EVALUATE

Student evaluation: Ask the students, "Did you try to think of something creative, unusual, or different to use in your story outline? Did your items in the outline relate to each other? Did hearing others' ideas give you some new ideas for your own story?"

Teacher observation: Were the students imaginative and creative in their stories? Did they understand the idea of using many different sources for dramatic material? Were the students able to help their classmates solve their story conflicts imaginatively?

CONNECTIONS

Mathematics: Have students provide numbers for the beginning, middle, and end of a math problem. Vary the operation for each problem. For example, the first student provides the beginning number: 20; the teacher provides the operation: division; the second student provides the middle number: 5; the class provides the solution: 4. You may also wish to scramble math problems and provide an operation and then have students identify the beginning, middle, and end: "5, 20, 4, division"; "35, 29, 6, addition"; and so on.

Analyzing and Writing Scripts

COMPONENT	Creative Expression
SUBJECT	Scripts
OBJECTIVE	Students use a scripted drama to become familiar with the format, and then write and read their own two-character scene.
MATERIALS	*Children's Plays for Creative Actors,* by Claire Boiko; students' story outlines from Lesson 23

Note: This lesson can be divided into a number of sessions to allow the students enough time to develop their scenes and to share those scenes with the entire class. Save the scripts for Lesson 30.

WARM UP Show the students a script written for two characters from a resource such as *Children's Plays for Creative Actors.* Point out the style of the written script; the name of the character always appears first, with that person's dialogue following. The descriptions of the setting, the action, and sometimes the actors' feelings are enclosed in parentheses and printed in italics.

Tell the story of the scene you are showing without telling how the conflict is resolved, and then select two volunteers to read a section of the dialogue. After the reading, ask the students who read how having the characters' parts written after their names affected their ability to play the scene. Did they feel restricted by the printed dialogue? Which do they prefer, a script or improvisational dialogue?

EXPLORE Explore the dramatic structure of the scene that was read. Ask students to describe the two characters in the scene and their feelings and motivations. Ask, "What is the setting? What are the characters doing in the scene? Can you tell what the conflict is between the two characters? How do you think the conflict will be resolved in this scene? How do you think the conflict will be resolved at the end of the story?"

DEVELOP Tell students that they will adapt their analysis of a script that has already been written to the writing of their own two-character scene. They may use the story outlines developed in Lesson 23, if desired, or you might want to give them a new situation, such as the following:

"Two characters are walking home late at night after seeing a movie, when one person sees a UFO. The other character doesn't believe it is a UFO, but rather an airplane in the distance."

Have students review their outlines from Lesson 23 to write a scripted scene, or ask them to develop the two new characters and conflict described above by writing a conversation between the characters. Students are to use the formal style, with the name of each character preceding that character's spoken words, and the action enclosed in parentheses. Students can use the written script as a model.

Allow enough time for the students to write their dialogues and then have each student choose a partner to help read his or her scene to the class. Choose one good example of a two-character scene and have the class develop the action and dialogue further. Ask, "How can the setting be shown in the dialogue? Is there any action that can help to indicate the setting?

"How can you show more of each character's traits, yet keep the original ideas of the story? Would expanding the characters' actions and dialogue help? Think about how the story might end. What would be the logical outcome based on what the characters said and did? How could this scene end?"

To get an objective view of her or his material, the writer may prefer to listen to other students read it. Select two students to read the script again and then briefly improvise the remainder of the scene with the outcome that the class decides is appropriate. Evaluate the dialogue (Does it seem realistic?) and rewrite various parts of the scene as a group. Replay the scene using two different actors.

Encourage the students to further develop their own scenes following the procedures used for the one scene done by the class. Find time, either in writing class or in another drama session, to go over the developed scenes.

EVALUATE

Student evaluation: Ask the students, "How is writing a scene different from improvising a scene? Why is it helpful to separate the dialogue and the action in a script? Do you prefer receiving suggestions to develop a scene, or do you prefer to develop the scene all on your own? Which technique works better for you, and why?"

Teacher observation: Were the students able to create dialogue between two characters in a written script? Were they able to expand a two-character scene further through action and dialogue? Could students use the written scene as a starting point to improvise an ending?

CONNECTIONS   *Science:* Have pairs of students work together to write a science dialogue. The dialogue may describe a scientific breakthrough, a natural phenomenon, or an ongoing experiment. Some pairs may wish to personify nature or present a first-person account, such as a dialogue between the heart and the lungs, between the earth and the moon, or between the ocean and the beach. Have the pairs present their dialogues to the class.

RESOURCES   Boiko, Claire. *Children's Plays for Creative Actors.* Plays, Inc., 1985

Hull, Raymond. *How to Write a Play.* Writers Digest Books, 1988.

Using Theatrical Terms

COMPONENT	Aesthetic Perception
SUBJECT	Drama/Theatre Vocabulary
OBJECTIVE	Students learn appropriate drama/theatre vocabulary, create a drama vocabulary list for their notebooks, and plan a project.
MATERIALS	Writing materials; illustrations from theatre sourcebooks; students' notebooks

WARM UP   Show students some illustrations from drama/theatre sourcebooks. Play a game with students by pointing to various illustrations of people and items for which there are drama/theatre terms, and ask students to name the terms. Try to find illustrations of different stages, sets, scripts, and people such as the lighting technician and the costume designer performing their jobs. Tell students that together they are going to develop a class vocabulary list of drama/theatre terms that they can add to their notebooks.

EXPLORE   Divide the class into small groups. Have the students in each group list as many words and their definitions that they can think of that are used in theatre or dramatic literature. Ask each group to report back to the class with their list of terms and their definitions. After reading and defining the terms, each group should turn in their list for you to compile a master vocabulary list for each student to keep in her or his notebook.

If the following terms are not on the list, add them, and define the ones that are new to any students.

Audience: At least one person, perhaps thousands, who observe and/or listen to a performance.

Dialogue: Words spoken by characters in a play.

Director: The person who integrates or coordinates an entire production. The director decides how the actors will speak their lines and move about the stage, and how the presentation will appear to the audience.

Performer: An actor or presenter of any kind of theatrical material or entertainment.

Script: The dialogue, descriptions of settings, and directions for a performance written down by the playwright.

Character: A person, animal, or other being in a story, scene, or play with specific distinguishing physical, mental, and emotional attributes.

Text: The content of a written script, or the agreed-upon structure of the dramatic material.

DEVELOP Divide the students into seven groups. Give each group one of the drama/theatre terms in the preceding list. Each group is to plan a project that will illustrate or demonstrate the given word. The project could be a brief improvisation, a poster, a model, an audiotape with sound effects, and so on. Give the students some time to plan their activities, and then share the projects with the class.

EVALUATE *Student evaluation:* Ask the students, "Were any of the drama/theatre terms new to you? Which ones do you yourself use in drama/theatre activities? Are there some that you use in everyday life? Which ones are they?"

Teacher observation: Were students able to create a sizeable list of drama/theatre terms? Were they able to associate the vocabulary words with actual experiences in drama/theatre? Did students record the list of terms and their definitions?

CONNECTIONS *Science:* Point out that all special fields have their own vocabularies. Have students create a science vocabulary notebook. Students may wish to divide the notebook into sections with terms for Earth Science, Physical Science, and Life Science. Encourage students to add to their notebooks for several weeks, jotting down words as they are encountered, before sharing them with the group.

RESOURCES Blum, Daniel. *A Pictorial History of the American Theatre 1860–1985.* Crown Publishers, 1986.

Bowman, Walter Parker, and Robert Hamilton Ball. *Theatre Language: A Dictionary.* Theatre Arts Books, 1976.

Brockett, Oscar G. *History of the Theatre.* Allyn & Bacon, Inc. 1990.

Huberman, Caryn, and JoAnne Wetzel. *Onstage Backstage.* Carolrhoda Books, 1987.

Dramatizing with Props

COMPONENT   Aesthetic Valuing

SUBJECT   Theatre Props

OBJECTIVE   Students read and analyze a scene for the kinds of stage properties that might be needed, and act out the scene using the props.

MATERIALS   *The Phantom Tollbooth,* a play by Susan Nanus from the original story by Norton Juster; items for use as props (see *Note*)

Note: Ahead of time, either collect or ask the students to bring to class on the day of this lesson 6–8 serving trays, 2 or 3 small flashlights, about 12 squares of fabric in assorted colors, 9 table settings (knife, fork, spoon, and plate), and a breadbasket.

WARM UP   Review with the students the definition of *properties,* or *props,* used in the theatre. *Personal props* are all those articles handled by the actor on the stage. *Stage props* are all those items on the stage that give atmosphere to and decorate the set, such as flowers, paintings, books, and so on. Stage props are usually set in place by someone from the stage crew, or persons who design and handle the scenery.

All the props are the responsibility of the property master, who is often called "Props." (In large productions there is usually a group of people called "the prop crew" who help the property master.) Ask the students to name some responsibilities of the property master, and list them on the board. The following is a formal list of the property master's duties, but it may be abridged for student use.

1. Learn what props are needed, and what qualities they must possess.

2. Make a list of the props.

3. Find or make (or be responsible for the finding and making of) the props.

4. Store and care for the props.

5. Put the props in their proper places on the stage before each performance, and see that each actor has his or her personal props (the ones carried with the actor) available and ready.

6. Collect and return the props to their storage places after each use.

7. See that the props are ready for the next usage.

8. See that the props are returned to the place or people they came from in good condition after the final performance.

EXPLORE

Read, or ask selected students to read, the banquet scene from Act I of *The Phantom Tollbooth,* starting with the announcement of the Page, "King Azaz the Unabridged is about to begin the Royal Banquet," through King Azaz's speech, "I was hoping no one would notice. It happens every time."

Have the class name the props necessary for the scene, and list them on the board. What props are named by the characters? What props are suggested? From the style of the play (fantastical, realistic, historical, for example), what do students think the props would look like? What qualities should each prop have—that is, what must the actor be able to do with it on stage?

DEVELOP

Appoint or ask for a volunteer to be the property master. Appoint or ask for a property crew. The crew will, under the supervision of the property master, assemble and lay out ready for use the properties necessary to the scene (those listed in the *Note* on page 142). If all the props are not available, use what you have and mime the rest.

Cast the scene. You will need Waiters, Guests, five Ministers, Humbug, Spelling Bee, King Azaz, and Milo. (Casting is easier if you cast the large groups first.)

Reread the scene to the students. Tell them they do not have to remember the lines as they are written, but they must know the story line so as to carry out the action. Students are to focus on the use of the props. Ask the property master to give out the props, and have the students play the scene.

Evaluate the dramatic action and students' use of the props. If time allows, replay the scene, again focusing on the use of the props, and re-evaluate the dramatic action.

EVALUATE

Student evaluation: Ask the students, "Did using and seeing the props help you play the scene? How? Why are props used in the theatre? What do they add to the scene? How can they help an actor? If you were to be the property master, what would be some of your responsibilities?"

Teacher observation: Did the students understand the value of props in theatre? Are they aware of the responsibilities of the property master? Do they understand why the style of the props should match the style of the production?

CONNECTIONS   *Mathematics:* List the following items on the chalkboard: 2 forks, 4 spoons, 6 knives, 11 bowls, 8 plates, 7 cups, 5 napkins, 16 slices of bread. Tell students that they are prop masters for a supper scene from "Snow-White and the Seven Dwarfs." Have students use mathematical operations to indicate how many more or fewer of each item they will need to provide a fork, spoon, knife, bowl, plate, cup, napkin, and two slices of bread for each of the eight characters. ($\times 4, \times 2, + 2, - 3, + 0, + 1, +3, \div 2$)

SPECIAL NEEDS   Have visually impaired students handle the props and explore their positions on the set once they have been placed. Also, it would be helpful to use some props that make sounds and some with bright, highly contrasting colors.

RESOURCES   Conaway, Judith. *Make Your Own Costumes and Disguises.* Troll Associates, 1987.

Holt, Michael. *Stage Design and Properties.* Schirmer Books, 1988.

Juster, Norton. *The Phantom Tollbooth.* Random House, 1961.

Nanus, Susan. *The Phantom Tollbooth.* (playscript) Samuel French, Inc., 1977.

Selecting Costumes for Characters

COMPONENT	Aesthetic Valuing
SUBJECT	Costumes/Careers
OBJECTIVE	Students learn about the role of the costumer in drama/theatre and improvise a scene to demonstrate an appropriate costume for a particular character.
MATERIALS	*Stage Costume Design,* by Douglas Russell; an assortment of costume pieces such as scarves, hats, flowers, sticks, capes and coats, and vests that help to define characters in a drama; different kinds of fabric, construction paper, scissors, stapler

WARM UP   Ask, "What are your favorite clothes?" Responses could include: party clothes, blue jeans and sweatshirt, bathrobe, swimsuit, running shoes, and so on. List the responses and ask the students to think about and comment on the individual differences in the responses. Ask, "What are the reasons different kinds of clothes are worn? How do clothes reflect an individual's personality?" Show the students some pictures of costume designs from *Stage Costume Design,* and tell the character for whom the designs were made. Lead students to the conclusion that clothes help to define a character.

EXPLORE   Find out what experiences students have had using costumes in theatre productions, and share with them any of the following information they don't know.

Define *costume* as anything an actor wears on stage. Costumes should be appropriate not only to the characters themselves, but to the style of the play. For example, if a play is a comedy, the costumes might be bright or even silly, but if the play is a tragedy, the costumes would probably look more serious.

In planning a costume appropriate for a particular character, the costumer must know the character's age, economic status, home, occupation, hobbies, and how the character looks at life. In short, the costumer must know the character.

The costumer works with a costume crew, and makes sure that the costumes are clean and in good repair, are in place for use in the play, and are stored properly. It is the actor's responsibility to return the costume to the costumer in good condition. The costumer must make costumes for an actor if no proper costume is available. Sometimes the costumer designs the costumes as well as makes them, but sometimes a different person works on the design. That person is called the "costume designer."

DEVELOP

Ask the students to think of a character in one of their improvisations, a character in literature, or an imaginary character. Provide a variety of costume pieces. Select three or four students to be the costumers.

Each student is to go to a costumer and describe the chosen character. The costumer will then look through the costume pieces and provide for the actor (student) a costume piece appropriate to that character. If there is not a costume piece available, the student may select another character, or wait until an appropriate piece is free, or together the two students can fashion a costume from fabric or construction paper. As soon as each student has a costume, he or she is to plan a scene, a pantomime, or some other device for demonstrating the costume and the character.

Allow students to present the scenes or actions that demonstrate their characters. After each presentation, ask the student to tell how the costume aided the characterization, whether it was comfortable, and how it affected movement. Also ask the costumer why that particular costume piece was selected.

EVALUATE

Student evaluation: Ask the students, "How did the costume piece help your characterization? Did the costume become part of the role you were playing? Did the costumes worn by other actors help you in your perceptions of the characters? Would you enjoy being the costumer in a dramatic production? Why or why not?"

Teacher observation: Were the students able to select appropriate costumes for their characters? Do they understand the task of the costumer? Are they aware that the costumes must not only suit the character, but also the style of the production?

CONNECTIONS   *Social Studies, Art:* Have each student choose an occupation, such as firefighting, nursing, cooking, gardening, or welding. Students should draw a picture showing the typical costume worn and props used by a person in that occupation. Suggest that students label any specialized equipment. Display the pictures on a bulletin board.

SPECIAL NEEDS   Describe the costume designs in *Stage Costume Design* to your severely visually impaired students. Also, have them try on and handle as many of the costume pieces as is feasible.

RESOURCES   *Center Stage Creative Dramatics Supplement.* (contains "Careers" poster) Available from Dale Seymour Publications.

Conaway, Judith. *Make Your Own Costumes and Disguises.* Troll Associates, 1987.

Cummings, Richard. *One Hundred One Costumes for All Ages, All Occasions.* Plays, Inc., 1987.

Russell, Douglas. *Stage Costume Design: Theory, Technique, and Style.* Prentice Hall, 1985.

GRADE 5

Evaluating a Performance

COMPONENT	Aesthetic Valuing
SUBJECT	Drama/Theatre Elements
OBJECTIVE	Students use drama/theatre elements to evaluate a performance.
MATERIALS	One copy for each student of the list of dramatic elements on page 150

Note: If possible, arrange for the students to view a live performance together either in school or in the community. If this is not possible, assign ahead of time, or tape for classroom viewing some worthwhile television drama (not a sitcom or action series). Give students the list of dramatic elements to use in their evaluations.

WARM UP   Following the viewing of the performance, discuss the students' general reactions to what they saw. What particular dramatic elements (the structure of the story, and how it was interpreted on stage) did students like? Why? What didn't they like? Why? What production elements (costumes, sets, lighting, sound effects, and so on) did they especially like or not like? Why? What would they like to have seen changed? Why?

EXPLORE   Ask students questions about specific production elements of the performance. For example, were the costumes appropriate to the style of the production? Were the costumes suited to the characters? Did the clothing that was worn affect you in any way? How?

How did the set help tell the story in the production? Were the set pieces appropriate to the action in the play? How did the set affect you as an audience member?

Did the lighting create a mood or atmosphere for you? How did the lighting in the production further the action of the story? Were you aware of the lighting while watching the performance, and did that affect you in any way?

DEVELOP

Divide the class into small groups and ask students to further evaluate the performance that they have seen, using the list of drama/theatre elements on page 150.

Ask the students in each group to come to a consensus on each question, and have someone in the group record the answers. Allow enough time so that all members of the groups can participate in the evaluation process. Then have one student in each group report to the entire class the consensus of the group's responses to the questions.

EVALUATE

Student evaluation: Ask the students, "How did the drama/theatre elements help you to evaluate the performance? What different aspects of the production would you notice that you hadn't noticed before, if you saw the performance again?"

Teacher observation: In what ways did the students' understanding of the elements of drama/theatre affect their viewing of the performance? Were the students able to evaluate each element separately and objectively?

CONNECTIONS

Social Studies: Divide the class into groups. Have students work together to design a scene for a historical event, such as the signing of the Declaration of Independence, the construction of the Brooklyn Bridge, or the opening of the Erie Canal. Suggest that students choose and research an event. Then have them sketch what the set would look like and indicate the kind of lighting, costumes, and props that they need to use in the scene. Have each group present its ideas to the class.

SPECIAL NEEDS

If the performance is a TV program, try to arrange for your severely visually impaired student(s) to watch it with several other students from the class. In this way the sighted students can describe and discuss the purely visual elements of the production.

RESOURCES

Barranger, Milly S. *Theatre: A Way of Seeing.* Wadsworth Publishing Co., 1991.

Levitt, Paul. *A Structural Approach to the Analyisis of Drama.* Mouton, 1971.

GRADE 5

Drama/Theatre Elements

Verbal and Nonverbal Communication Were the actors able to use words, movement, and gestures to convey meaning?

The Five W's Identify each of the five W's and tell how each was demonstrated in the production.

Beginning, Middle, and End of the Story How did the story begin? How was the action developed? How did the story end, or how was the conflict resolved?

Concentration of the Actors Were the actors able to concentrate on the play, its action, and their character portrayals, and not be distracted by the audience?

COPYRIGHT © DALE SEYMOUR PUBLICATIONS

Dramatizing Current Events

COMPONENT   Historical and Cultural

SUBJECT   Current Events/Dramatization

OBJECTIVE   Students research, form critical opinions on, and dramatize an issue from current events.

MATERIALS   Current newspapers and magazines; writing materials

Note: This lesson may be divided into two parts; the Warm Up and Explore sections may be one lesson; the Develop, another.

WARM UP   Remind students of the "Living Newspaper" lesson from Grade 4 of CENTER STAGE. The Living Newspaper was the Federal Theatre Project, the only federally funded theatre company in America. It lasted from October 1935 to July, 1939. The Living Newspaper dramatized and performed topics of current interest for audiences. Ask the students, "What are some possible themes, conflicts, or ideas you have read about recently in newspapers or magazines that could be used as subjects for creating dramatic works?"

List the students' suggestions. Their ideas may come from TV or radio news broadcasts, the daily newspaper, or current magazines. Suggest additional news stories, if necessary.

EXPLORE   In Grade 4 students dramatized a current news story, but at this level students will be expected to do more of their own research, and form an opinion on the issue, if that is appropriate.

Divide the class into small groups. Assign one topic suggested by the class to each group. Provide current newspapers and magazines so that the students in each group can research their topic. Each group should prepare a short analysis of the ideas and conflicts involved in their issue. For example, a current topic may be a recent debate in local government over whether taxes should be raised to pay for a new park. The group assigned this topic should find out as much about both sides of this issue as possible.

Ask each group to prepare its research in outline form, listing the people who are involved, the conflict, and arguments for and against the issue. If the group has its own point of view concerning the issue, then it should be included, as well as the facts. The group should make clear which information is opinion and which is fact. Each member of the group should be responsible for some aspect of the research, and one person can be the recorder.

DEVELOP

Have each group plan a dramatization of part or all of its specific issue. Ask students, "How could your research be condensed so that it is short and interesting enough to hold an audience's attention?" Have each group identify the characters, the conflict, the theme, and the outcome or projected outcome of their news story. If they want to sway their listeners' opinions, they might dramatize a possible negative outcome of the "wrong" actions taken. The group should choose their method of presentation—pantomime, narrated pantomime, dialogue, or combination—then plan and rehearse an improvisation that would demonstrate their issue and how the group members feel about the issue. They might dramatize two alternate solutions to their issue.

EVALUATE

Student evaluation: Ask students, "How difficult was it to adapt your topic to a dramatic presentation? Did you first identify the conflict and theme to help you? Do you think this method of informing the general public about current events would work today? Why or why not?"

Teacher observation: Were the students able to develop stories and dramatizations from current events? Were the groups able to choose the essential and interesting information from their research to present? Were they able to identify the dramatic elements—characters, conflict, theme—in stories from the daily newspaper?

CONNECTIONS

Mathematics: Have pairs of students work together to dramatize a story problem that the audience will solve at the end of the performance. Problems may be taken from students' math lessons, or students may write problems of their own. Students must be able to explain the problem and solution if the audience members cannot agree on the answer.

RESOURCES

Blum, Daniel. *A Pictorial History of the American Theatre 1860–1985.* Crown Publishers, 1986.

Celebration! World Puppetry

COMPONENT	Historical and Cultural
SUBJECT	Puppetry
OBJECTIVE	Students learn about puppetry as part of drama/theatre in world cultures, participate in making a simple puppet, and dramatize part of a script to demonstrate a particular kind of puppetry.
MATERIALS	*The Complete Book of Puppet Theatre,* by David Currell; other well-illustrated resource books; visual arts materials—paper, fabric, paper fasteners, cardboard, and so on—for making simple puppets and costumes; two-character script from Lesson 24

Note: Invite a puppeteer into the class to discuss and demonstrate puppetry from around the world. The school or city librarian, a local drama group, or perhaps the Chamber of Commerce might be able to help in locating a puppeteer. Be sure to tell the visitor ahead of time what kind of lesson you will be doing, and what kinds of artifacts to bring.

Plan to do this lesson in three sessions: the introduction to puppetry; further research, the making of the puppets, and rehearsal; and the presentations.

WARM UP

If possible, have a puppeteer discuss in detail the various uses of puppets throughout the world. Ask the artist to demonstrate how to use each of the three basic types of puppets:

1. Marionettes, or string puppets, operated from above by the moving of strings or wires.

2. Rod puppets, mounted on rods or sticks. Sometimes these are jointed, with separate rods to the hands or other body parts for individual control.

3. Hand puppets, manipulated by the hand within the puppet.

Have the puppeteer lead a discussion about the many different countries around the world that use puppets in their ceremonies and celebrations.

GRADE 5

Information covered should include the following: Puppets were used in religious rituals of Ancient Egypt, Greece, and Rome; they were used to perform entire operas in Salzburg, Austria; puppets form the core of the Japanese Bunraku theatre. Turkish shadow plays are full of comic puppets, and Java and Bali present elegant shadow plays with rod puppets. Thailand is also famous for its beautiful, costumed rod puppets, and marionettes are used by street performers in Delhi and Calcutta, India.

Show some illustrations from these and other countries that have used and still use puppets as part of their celebrations and ceremonies.

EXPLORE

Divide the class into pairs, and have each pair refer to their notebooks for the two-character scenes developed in Lesson 24. The pair of students is to choose one of their scripted scenes and make simple puppets representing the two characters.

From the material presented in Warm Up, have each pair choose a style of puppet and the country or culture that used such a puppet. Have the students do further research about the manner in which that country would present the puppets and then make a simple puppet. Students may use a hollowed-out styrofoam ball and a scarf; or cardboard, construction paper, and fasteners; or fabric and paper rolls; or tongue depressors, or other available materials.

Ask the visiting artist, if he or she is available, to help students with their selections and offer suggestions about construction.

DEVELOP

When the puppets have been completed, ask each pair to demonstrate their puppet characters. The first part of the presentation should tell something of the cultural background of the country that uses that type of puppet, and how it would be used there. The second part will be the scripted story as it was written, with each puppet representing one of the characters.

The puppet presentations can be developed into a performance for another class or for parents, if desired, or the puppets could be displayed at an open house, with each student pair standing by to explain and demonstrate the puppets for the visitors.

EVALUATE

Student evaluation: Ask students to recall the different styles of puppets they learned about, and the countries from which they came. How are some of the puppets from around the world alike? How are they different?

Ask students, "What do you think are the advantages and disadvantages of puppets as opposed to live actors in a dramatic performance?"

Teacher observation: Did the visiting artist seem to add to students' knowledge and enjoyment of puppetry? In your opinion, were the artifacts and information shared with the students helpful in increasing students' cultural awareness? Could students use what they learned to create their own puppet presentations?

CONNECTIONS   *Art:* Suggest that students research native costumes worldwide and choose one to create for their puppet, using the materials provided—paint, paper, fabric, string, yarn, and so on. The costumes may be as simple or as elaborate as students wish. Have students present their finished costumes along with the puppets when they are displayed, and give each student an opportunity to describe the country and dress he or she chose to depict.

RESOURCES   Currell, David. *The Complete Book of Puppet Theatre.* B & N Imports, 1986.

Marks, Burton, and Rita Marks. *Puppet Plays and Puppet-Making.* Plays, Inc., 1985.

Simmens, Rene. *The World of Puppets.* Elsevier Phaidon, 1975. (This book is out of print, but it is worth looking for at the library because of the many clear illustrations and photographs.)

Von Boehn, Max. (Josephone Nicoll, tr.) *Dolls and Puppets.* Cooper Square, 1966.

The Puppetry Store, A Service of Puppeteers of America Inc. (a good source of resources and artifacts) Send for catalog to 1525 24th Street S.E., Auburn, WA 98002-7837.

Simple Hand Puppet

1. Hollow out small portion of 3-inch styrofoam ball just big enough for forefinger.

2. Paste paper cutouts, yarn, feathers, beads, etc. on the ball for head features.

3. For costume, drape 10-inch square fabric or scarf over hand and secure it with a rubber band over thumb, around back of hand, and over little finger. Keep third and fourth fingers folded down.

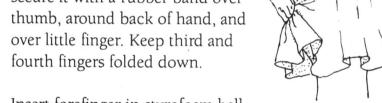

4. Insert forefinger in styrofoam ball.

COPYRIGHT © DALE SEYMOUR PUBLICATIONS

Introduction to Grade Six

The lessons in Grade 6 are sequential and cumulative. Techniques and subject matter at this level build on the knowledge the student has gained at previous levels and move students toward a competency in play production. In addition to the expectancies listed for Grade 5, which are valid for this level also, the expectancies at Grade 6 are that students will:

1. Be able to interpret a playscript.
2. Be able to make conscious decisions about staging and style, and be able to analyze individual elements in a dramatization in terms of the total effect.
3. Be able to analyze a play or dramatization and determine appropriate setting, lights, props, and costume requirements.
4. Develop a proficiency in basic acting skills, concentrating on objects and actions and the thoughts and emotions of characters.
5. Use the basic elements of formal acting: characterization, conflict, motivation, and setting.
6. Discover the connotative effects of movement, gesture, and vocal expression and their powers to move an audience.
7. Convey improvised and simple memorized speech and prose drama with vitality, clarity, and imagination.
8. Use objective thinking and knowledge of the theatre arts in viewing and evaluating the art form.

Contents of Grade Six

GRADE 6

Exercising the Imagination

COMPONENT	Aesthetic Perception
SUBJECT	Imagery
OBJECTIVE	Students visualize objects, scenes, and activities in their minds' eyes to increase their perception and sensory awareness.
MATERIALS	None required

WARM UP

Tell students that today they will do some of the exercises that professional theatre artists use to keep their artistic sensitivities sharpened. Say, "In theatre it is very important to be able to visualize, or imagine, or see in the mind's eye. Not only the actors, but the designers, the directors, and all the people involved in drama/theatre have to be sensitive to and aware of life around them in order for the theatre experience to have the greatest impact on the audience." Have students close their eyes, and tell them you will suggest an object in the environment that they should visualize. Say, "Visualize a tree, not just any tree, but a particular tree that you see in your mind's eye." Give the students a brief time to imagine, then ask, "How large is it? What color or colors are its leaves? What is the texture of the bark? What is the circumference of the trunk?" Continue asking students questions that will help them develop their visualizations. Then have them open their eyes. Ask, "Did you see a tree that really exists, one that you have seen, or did you see an imaginary tree?"

EXPLORE

Tell the students that you are going to name another object to visualize. Have them close their eyes. Say, "Just relax and let pictures form in your mind. This time visualize a room, one that you have never seen before. How big is the room? What color are the walls? What is on the walls? Are there pictures? If so, what do the pictures show? Look at the ceiling. How high is it? Is it decorated or plain? What is on the floor? Imagine walking on the floor and think about how it feels when you walk on it. Do you hear anything in the room? Look at the furnishings. What color are they? How big are they? Imagine yourself standing in the room, and look at the room as a whole."

Give the students a quiet moment to imagine their rooms. Then say, "Open your eyes. Can anyone tell me how imagining a room or a tree can help an actor, a director, or a set designer in the theatre?" Allow a few minutes for students to respond.

DEVELOP Explain to the students that the ability to relax and concentrate or focus the mind on an object or scene is an important aid to visualization. Tell students that you are going to lead them on an imaginary trip, during which they will experience various sensations. Stress to students that they should concentrate in order to visualize the scenes in their minds' eyes, and feel the sensations that you describe.

Before describing to students the various imaginary sensory experiences, allow them to relax and let the room become quiet. Students could be sitting at their desks or lying on their backs in an open space. Say, "Close your eyes and listen to all the sounds in the room." (Allow time between each set of instructions for students to visualize.) "Now listen to all the sounds outside this room."

The images you describe could be any combination of ideas and scenes that would stimulate and strengthen students' imaginative powers. Say, for example, "Imagine that you are sitting in a green field by yourself. Visualize the green grass and how it feels when you brush your hands against it. Hear the wind blowing softly. Clouds float above you, and flocks of birds come and go overhead. As you sit there, a beautiful cloud comes slowly toward you, surrounds you, and lifts you up gently into the warm sky..." and so on. Images could include all the scenes below as students float high up on the cloud. Invent whatever kinds of images seem appropriate for your students.

Adjust the exercise according to the maturity of your students and the length of time they are able to concentrate. Be as specific as possible in describing the sensory images, and avoid the temptation to let the exercise go on too long. End the exercise where it began, with the students listening to the sounds in the room.

EVALUATE *Student evaluation:* Give students an opportunity to discuss their images. Ask, "Were you able to visualize a scene? What did you see? How could this type of exercise help someone in drama/theatre? Could you do such an exercise by yourself? Why or why not? Why should we, or people in drama/theatre, practice strengthening our imaginative powers?"

Teacher observation: Did students seem to be concentrating as you described the images? Were they more able to relax and concentrate on the sensory images as the lesson progressed? Could students relate this exercise to training in drama/theatre?

CONNECTIONS   *Art:* Divide the class into groups. Have one student in each group describe an imaginary scene. As the first student describes the scene, each member of the group, including the one who is describing, draws the scene. Have each member contribute details in turn, which each person adds to his or her own drawing. When every student has had a chance to contribute details, have students share and compare their drawings and discuss their interpretations of the details.

SPECIAL NEEDS   Severely visually impaired students will have to describe a tree from their own tactile, olfactory, and auditory experiences. The value of this activity would be heightened for visually impaired students by preceding it with an actual tree-climbing session. Description of a room for both severely visually impaired and hearing impaired students will be limited to their own sensory experience. (This activity can serve as a good lesson for nonimpaired students to focus on the perspectives of those with impairments.) Socially and emotionally impaired individuals can benefit from the relaxing and mentally focusing aspects of these activities.

Sharpening Observation Skills

COMPONENT   Aesthetic Perception

SUBJECT   Point of View

OBJECTIVE   Students practice observing detail in both objects and actions, and analyze their own point of view for its effect on their observation.

MATERIALS   Small objects that can easily be covered or hidden or removed from the classroom

Note: For the Develop section you will need to prearrange for someone to enter the classroom on a certain cue, grab an object, shout, "I want that!" and then run out.

WARM UP

In Lesson 1, students practiced using their imaginations to increase their sensory awareness. Explain to the students that another skill that must be developed by all theatre artists is that of observation. Theatre people train themselves to observe detail carefully so that they can convey detail in a scene or character to the audience.

Show the students a specific object, such as a book, stapler, or box of thumbtacks, for about five seconds. Remove or cover the object; then ask a few students to describe in detail what they saw. Bring out the object again and let them check their recall. What conclusions can they draw?

EXPLORE

Explain that the location of the viewer—in front, to the side, near the object, or far from it—can affect the way the viewer perceives the object. Tell students that the location from which, or way in which an object or scene is observed is called "point of view."

Tell students that you are going to show them another object, and they should look at it as quickly and carefully as possible. Do so, repeating the procedure described in the Warm Up activity, but stand in the middle of the classroom, so that some students view the object from one side or the other, some view it from the front, and those in back of you can hardly see it at all. Then cover the object and ask students in several different locations to describe the object. Ask whether they think the point of view from which they saw the object made a difference in their observation. Lead students to conclude that to observe an object in as much detail as possible, it would help to see it from several points of view.

DEVELOP

Explain to students that just as their location can affect their observation, their physical and mental condition make a difference, too. The condition of the person's eyes, past experiences the person has had, and what the person expects to see all are part of someone's point of view.

As you are discussing point of view with the students, have someone who is not familiar to the students run into the room, grab an object, shout, "I want that!" and then run out of the room. Be sure that you and your accomplice agree on a cue, so that the event occurs unexpectedly for the students.

Calm the students, if necessary, and reassure them that the event was preplanned to test their observation skills. Then ask the students to write down the answers to the following questions:

1. Was the person male or female?

2. What was taken? Describe it.

3. Describe the person in detail: age, height, weight, hair color, skin tones, clothing.

4. What did the person say?

Review students' responses with the class, finding out how many students had the same observations. Ask, "How did the observations vary, depending on where the observers were sitting?"

Also ask the students to comment on their surprise, fear, or other emotions felt during and after the incident. How did those emotions affect what they observed? Ask students to tell how they think their observation was affected by their point of view.

Explain to the students that the theatre artist must be aware of both the location and the condition of the character she or he is portraying in order to convey that character's observations to an audience.

EVALUATE

Student evaluation: Ask the students, "Do you think that your ability to observe detail has increased? Were you able to identify your own point of view? How did it affect your observation? How does the actor use observation and point of view in the theatre?"

Teacher observation: Could the students identify the details of the preplanned incident? Did they understand the relationship of point of view to observation?

CONNECTIONS   *Mathematics:* Write a string of numbers on the chalkboard to establish a pattern. Then introduce an error, but continue using the original pattern. Have students study the numbers to identify the first wrong number that throws off the pattern. For example, in a +1, +5 pattern, a string of numbers with an error would be 1, 2, 7, 8, 13, 16, 21, 22, 27. The error was introduced with +3 (instead of +1) at number 16. Have students correct the error and rewrite the number string.

SPECIAL NEEDS   In Warm Up and Explore, use a highly reflective object such as a mirror, and have severely visually impaired students concentrate on any attributes they can perceive visually. Another possibility is to use an auditory stimulus, have those students describe it, and discuss what makes a difference in how it is heard; that is, the distance from sound, pitch, loudness, and so on. In Develop, when the unexpected person runs into the room, too many variables may quickly confuse the learning impaired student. Have those students concentrate on fewer factors.

Exploring Vocal Techniques

COMPONENT | Aesthetic Perception

SUBJECT | Theatre Vocabulary/Vocal Technique

OBJECTIVE | Students learn vocabulary terms related to the voice and practice vocal techniques to use their voices most effectively.

MATERIALS | Audiotapes of stories with several characters, or tapes of radio dramas; selected classroom materials for oral reading; one copy for each student of Vocal Techniques for Actors on page 170

Note: If possible, invite a voice specialist to the classroom to demonstrate for the students different vocal techniques, and to discuss the level of training professional performers must have.

WARM UP | Ask the students what an actor's voice reveals to the audience, besides the words of the playscript. Students should be able to respond that the actor's voice provides information about the character (age, education, strength, emotional condition), and that the voice gives special meaning to words and phrases (through vocal inflection).

Have students listen to an audiotape of a story with several different characters. Point out to the students the effectiveness with which the actors use their voices to convey characterizations and meanings. Tell the students that the training of the voice is an ongoing experience throughout a performer's life.

EXPLORE | Give each student a copy of Vocal Techniques for Actors on page 170. Discuss some of these terms and techniques that actors use to convey meaning and character to a listener. If a voice specialist can come to your classroom, ask that person to demonstrate each of these terms or techniques.

Ask a few volunteers to say a sentence such as, "Excuse me, please," varying volume, pitch, and articulation. Compare and comment on the different versions. Have students say their sentences again with very shallow breaths, then with deep breaths. What is the difference? (You or your guest may want to first demonstrate using these breathing techniques.)

DEVELOP

Explain to the students that they cannot speak without breathing. Proper breathing and breath control are essential to the effective use of the voice. Ask the students to sit up straight, grasp the edges of their seats firmly, take in as much air as possible without straining, and hold their breaths while you count to ten. Then tell them to relax and let all the air out of their lungs.

Point out that in public speaking of any kind (not only in acting, but also when giving classroom reports!), proper breathing gives the speaker plenty of reserve air so that she or he does not run out of breath. It also improves the quality of the speaking voice and the speaker's appearance. Again ask the students to hold on to the edges of their seats (this keeps the shoulders level) and to take in as much air as possible. Ask them to count together, using normal speaking voices, as far as possible without taking in another breath. Some students will be surprised at how high they can count!

Choose a paragraph from selected classroom reading materials. Have the students read through the paragraph silently and make a light pencil check at places where a breath can be taken. (These can be erased later.) A breath should be taken about every ten words or so. Ask selected students to read the paragraph aloud, in normal voices, concentrating on proper breathing. If time permits, let students work in pairs, reading to each other and experimenting with the best places in text to take breaths.

EVALUATE

Student evaluation: Ask the students, "How does proper breathing help a performer? In what other areas of life does proper breathing help? Name some vocal techniques that help convey meaning to a listener."

Teacher observation: Do the students understand how vocal techniques can affect meaning and expression in drama/theatre activities? Did the students become more aware of how breathing controls the voice?

CONNECTIONS

Social Studies: Choose a historical poem and have students practice delivering a stanza clearly, using appropriate volume, inflection, and emotion. Possibilities include "The Midnight Ride of Paul Revere," "The Charge of the Light Brigade," and "John Brown's Body."

SPECIAL NEEDS   Remember to substitute visual cues when necessary and possible for hearing impaired students; for instance, sign the phrase, "Excuse me, please," in different ways to convey different emotions.

RESOURCES   *Center Stage: Creative Dramatics Supplement.* (contains audiotapes of eight folk tales that could be models for vocal characterizations) Available from Dale Seymour Publications.

Laughlin, Mildred K., and Kathy H. Latrobe. *Social Studies Readers Theatre for Children.* Libraries Unlimited, Inc., 1991.

McGaw, Charles. J., and Gary Blake, *Acting is Believing: A Basic Method.* Holt, Rinehart and Winston, Inc. 1986.

Vocal Techniques for Actors

Volume The voice must be loud enough to be heard without difficulty; even quiet and intimate scenes must be louder than in a real-life situation.

Relaxation Actors must learn to relax when they speak so that their voices will not tire during a rehearsal or performance, and so that their voices will not be injured by straining.

Quality An actor's voice should be pleasant to listen to (unless the character requires an unpleasant voice) and capable of expressing various emotional states.

Articulation Actors must enunciate each word so that the words are clearly understood, even in passages requiring rapid speech.

Flexibility An actor must be able to portray many different kinds of characters by varying the volume, quality, and pitch of his or her voice.

Comfort Level The pitch of an actor's voice should be at a level that is comfortable for the speaker and pleasant to the listener.

COPYRIGHT © DALE SEYMOUR PUBLICATIONS

Conveying Meaning Through Vocal Techniques

COMPONENT	Aesthetic Perception
SUBJECT	Vocal Technique/Oral Communication
OBJECTIVE	Students practice breath control and relaxation techniques as they use their voices to convey meaning through the spoken word.
MATERIALS	A chart with lines of script from which students will read; see Explore (optional)

WARM UP

Repeat with the class the breathing exercises from Lesson 3. Explain to the students that if they talk with their jaws and lips nearly closed and the backs of their tongues humped (demonstrate), the sound that comes out will be harsh or flat or uninteresting. Have students try speaking like this, with exaggeration.

Now ask the students to yawn, and stop when their jaws are opened the widest. At that point, they should wiggle their jaws back and forth until they are no longer tense, but relaxed. Then have the students take in a deep breath and say a prolonged "aaah." Repeat the exercise, but instead of "ah," have students say, "What calm water!" prolonging the "ah" sounds. Remind students to keep their jaws relaxed.

EXPLORE

Write the lines of script printed below on the board, or show a prepared chart. Have each student select one of the lines of script to read aloud. Tell students not to worry about giving the line meaning, but to focus on keeping their jaws relaxed and using proper breathing techniques.

"Go home and don't come back. Can't you see His Majesty is here?"

"Haven't you been with me every moment, hunting out my old jewels?"

"No, no! You must surprise her when you come back a rich man!"

"Rather proclaim it that he which hath no stomach to this fight, let him depart."

"The evil that men do lives after them; the good is oft interred with their bones."

"She is so contrary and cross-grained that if she fell into a river, she'd float upstream!"

"Here I am running on and you not being served. I suppose you have all come for some gingerbread."

Help each student, as necessary, to breathe properly and relax as he or she reads the line.

DEVELOP

At this point, the students should be interested in reading the lines with some emotion. Review Lesson 3, which discussed vocal techniques for conveying meaning. Allow each student to read his or her line again, putting some emotion into it. After reading the line, each student should tell the class what emotion he or she added, and what words in the line suggested that emotion. Evaluate each student's breathing, relaxation, vocal quality, and so on, but make no critical judgments on the emotional interpretation, because at this point, especially with single lines, interpretation is still subjective.

EVALUATE

Student evaluation: Ask the students, "How did the breathing and relaxing exercises help you in the reading of the lines? How could such exercises help a performer in the theatre? Can you hear the differences in your own speech when you are relaxed and breathing properly? Can you hear differences in others' speech?"

Teacher observation: Are the students aware of the purpose of using good techniques in speaking, and of their value in the performing arts? Were students able to apply their knowledge of vocal techniques to the reading of specific lines?

CONNECTIONS

Social Studies: Divide the class into pairs of students. Have each pair choose a news story and script it for readers theatre. Emphasize the use of voice and interpretation to convey meaning and create settings and moods. Then have each pair present their script to the group.

Planning Movement Onstage

COMPONENT	Aesthetic Perception
SUBJECT	Stage Movement
OBJECTIVE	Students interpret a script for the movements made by the actors onstage.
MATERIALS	One copy for each student of the script of "When the Hare Brought the Sun" (pages 176–8) and the diagram of stage areas on page 56

WARM UP

Review Lesson 21, Grade 4, in which stage areas were defined. Provide each student with a copy of the diagram if students do not have it in their notebooks. Remind students that the stage areas are defined by the actor as she or he faces the audience. Explain that in theatre there are specific movements and movement patterns all theatre personnel must know. The patterns are created in reference to the stage areas. Draw a stage diagram on the board without the area labels and ask a student to come to the board and label each stage area.

EXPLORE

In an open space, have students outline a large rectangle to represent a stage. (Arrange chairs or put masking tape or chalk marks on the floor.) Point out to the students that in a dramatic production, no movement is made unless there is a reason (motivation) for it. Actors do not move aimlessly about the stage. Motivation usually comes from in the content of the line. For example, if the line is, "Isn't it a lovely day!" the actor might move to a window and look out.

Write the following terms and their definitions on the board and ask selected students to demonstrate each movement as it is discussed. (In Grade 4 students learned the term *cross*; these definitions are a further elaboration.)

Cross: any movement from one point to another. The director may say, "Cross from the chair to the window," or, "Cross from down right to left center."

Straight movement: a cross in a straight line. When motivations are strong and simple, the movements, or crosses, are straight. Usually straight movements are reserved for important moments.

Curved movement: a cross in a gentle curve. The curved cross is most commonly used. It has two advantages: It is more graceful and pleasing to the eye than a straight movement; and by choosing the appropriate curve, the actor can end the cross at any desired angle and body position. The curve may arch upstage or downstage.

Sideways movement: small arcs made with one or two sidewise steps. Whole circles are rare on stage, but small arcs are common. These movements show doubt or irresolution.

Have students draw and label an example of each movement on their diagram of stage areas.

DEVELOP

Divide the class into small groups, and give each group a copy of the script of "When the Hare Brought the Sun" (pages 176–8). Each group will collaborate to decide on the motivations for the stage movements necessary to the scene, and the movements themselves. Give the students time to plan; then ask each group to demonstrate their stage movements as they identify each part of the script in which the movement takes place. (Students need not actually play the parts.) Students should tell the class the motivation for each movement.

EVALUATE

Student evaluation: Ask the students, "What is motivation and how does it affect movement on the stage? Why must an actor understand the motivations in the lines? What were the differences in each group's presentation of the same script? Why is movement an important part of drama/theatre?"

Teacher observation: Were the students able to remember the "actor facing the audience" concept in planning stage movements? Do the students understand how motivation influences movement?

CONNECTIONS

Social Studies: Make a transparency of the stage areas and lay it over a map of North America (the audience is north). Play a game in which a leader "gets" the class to its destination by naming stage areas. (Each area should be contiguous to the one previously called out.) As the leader calls out each area, students may choose a place within that area to add to their itinerary. Have students keep notes and draw their routes with marking pen on the transparency at the end of the game.

SPECIAL NEEDS

Make sure to allow ample space for physically impaired students to maneuver in the stage areas. Severely visually impaired students will need extra practice time to familiarize themselves with the stage areas and any movement they need to make through them. Directions with multiple steps may be confusing for the learning impaired student. Work on only one or two directions at a time.

RESOURCES   Kamerman, Sylvia. *Dramatized Folk Tales of the World.* Plays, Inc., 1971. (This book is out of print, but is the source of the script "When the Hare Brought the Sun.")

When the Hare Brought the Sun

Characters

THREE STORYTELLERS	SUN GIRL	HEADMAN
MOON GIRL	STAGEHAND	HARE
CHIEF	PURSUERS	

(Before curtain rise: Three Storytellers remain seated. Second storyteller begins to beat drum.)

FIRST STORYTELLER: Listen!

SECOND STORYTELLER: Listen!

THIRD STORYTELLER: Listen to a continent.

FIRST STORYTELLER: Listen!

FIRST AND THIRD STORYTELLERS: Listen!

ALL: Listen to the rhythm. Boom, boom, boom, boom. Boomity boom boom, boom.

SECOND STORYTELLER: African beat! African beat! (First and Third Storytellers slap thighs.) Up through your feet! (All stamp feet.)

FIRST AND THIRD STORYTELLERS: Telling the folk tales…

SECOND STORYTELLER: Native, tribal folk tales…

ALL: Of—(pause, then shout) Africa! (Drum stops.)

SECOND STORYTELLER (rising):   I shall tell another story of the Hare. It is told among the tribes who live on the flat grasslands of the veld in Southern Africa. It is called, "When the Hare Brought the Sun." (Curtain opens.)

(Setting: bare stage)

(At curtain rise: Second Storyteller begins narration.)

SECOND STORYTELLER: In the early days when the earth had no sun or moon, the Hare took his musical instrument, called the mbira, and climbed up a giant spider web to visit the great country which was up there. (Hare enters, playing mbira, or another simple stringed instrument.) He came to the village, seeking shelter. (Stagehand carries on cutout of veld house, then exits.)

HARE (looking at house, then calling loudly):   Where is the chief?

HEADMAN (entering right):   I am the headman of this village. Why do you wish to see the chief?

HARE: I will play my instrument for him if he gives me shelter.

HEADMAN (calling off right):   Great chief, there is a hare who comes to our village playing the mbira. He seeks shelter

CHIEF: (entering right, to Hare): Play for me. (Hare plays instrument and dances.) You play well. I shall give you lodging in this house. (Chief points to house.)

HARE: Thank you. I have had a tiring journey. It will be good to rest. (Chief and Headman exit. Hare enters house.)

SECOND STORYTELLER: That evening the Hare looked out of his door and saw a girl sitting in front of two large pots. (Moon Girl enters right with a large red pot and a large yellow pot. She sits, and places the pots before her. Hare peers out of door and watches. Suddenly, Sun Girl enters, running, carrying a large red disc.)

SUN GIRL: I bring the sun back from our sky. (puts disc into red pot)

MOON GIRL: Then it is time for me to hang out the moon. (takes yellow disc from yellow pot and exits)

SUN GIRL: It is time for me to go to bed. (yawns and exits)

Hare (creeping out of house):   It would be a fine thing for my world below to have some of that sun. (He takes red disc from red pot and tears off a piece of it.) I'll climb back down the spider web to earth. (runs off right)

SECOND STORYTELLER: The next morning the two girls returned.

MOON GIRL (entering left with yellow disc):   It is time for me to rest. (puts yellow disc into yellow pot)

SUN GIRL: (entering): It is time for me to hang out the sun. (reaches into red pot) Something is wrong with the sun! (pulls out red disc) Look! Part of it is missing! Someone has stolen part of the sun! (Headman and Chief rush on from right.)

CHIEF: How dare anybody do such a thing?

HEADMAN: (looking at ground and pointing): It must have been the hare. These are his footprints.

CHIEF: We shall follow him. (Chief and Headman exit left, running. Sun Girl and Moon Girl follow, carrying pots. House is removed.)

SECOND STORYTELLER: The chief and his headman climbed down the great spider web to earth and called together the animals to pursue the Hare. (Hare enters left and runs across the stage in "slow motion." Chief, Headman, and Pursuers—other animals— enter left in single file and move after Hare, also in slow motion.) As the pursuers drew closer, the Hare threw the three-spiked devil thorn across his trail. (Hare pantomimes throwing thorns. Chief, Headman, and Pursuers cry out in pain as they step on thorns, rub feet or paws, and continue to track Hare.) The Hare pulled down huge vines to block his path. (Hare pantomimes pulling down vines, and others pantomime fighting through them.) The Hare caused a great rain to wash away his footprints. (Hare points to sky and others cover heads with hands, peering closer to ground.) The hare came to a stream. He lay down and turned into a log. (Hare lies down and remains motionless.)

CHIEF (stopping and looking around): I don't see the Hare's footprints anymore.

HEADMAN: Neither do I.

FIRST PURSUER (sniffing): We don't smell him, either.

CHIEF: I guess we've lost him. Come on, let's go home. (In single file, Chief, Headman, and Pursuers pretend to walk across "log" and exit. Hare jumps up and leaps for joy.)

SECOND STORYTELLER: So the Hare gave the sun to the earth, and we have had it ever since that day.

Physical Movements Onstage

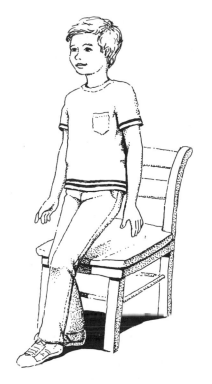

COMPONENT   Aesthetic Perception

SUBJECT   Body Control

OBJECTIVE   Students practice physical movements in relation to different situations and different characters.

MATERIALS   Classroom chairs

WARM UP   Tell the students that an actor onstage must constantly be aware of posture, and how posture portrays his or her character. Ask the students to stand, and to imagine that someone is pulling up on a string attached to the tops of their heads. Visualizing the tension will help pull students' spines straight, help their chests rise so that proper breathing becomes easier, and put their bodies in balance. Ask the students to take deep breaths while they are standing correctly.

Tell students that just as they learned the importance of motivation for large movements on the stage (see Lesson 5), they can learn to control some small body movements and positions in order to achieve a desired effect. These movements might be posture stances or arm gestures, to portray a character's abilities and attitudes.

Tell students that no movements in drama/theatre, no matter how small, are made without a reason, or motivation. Controlling the body and being able to position it perfectly are part of the performer's training.

EXPLORE   Actors use a variety of movement exercises and activities that help the body to relax and to respond on the stage in ways that seem realistic. The following exercise should increase students' confidence in their ability to sit down onstage without having to concentrate on the action.

Set a chair in a marked-out stage area. Have the students line up at either side of the stage; then one at a time, have them walk to the chair and sit down. Demonstrate the movement first, and then give the following directions as the first student practices the movement: "Take the first step with your upstage foot. [For some students this will be the left foot; for those on the opposite side of the stage, it will be the right foot. Demonstrate for students that the upstage foot is the one away from the audience.]

"Walk to the chair and turn so that you are facing out from it, ready to sit. Then place one foot a small step behind the other, so that the back of your leg just touches the edge of the chair. NEVER GLANCE BEHIND TO SEE WHETHER THE SEAT IS THERE; the back of your leg will tell you where the chair is! Next, keeping your back very straight, bend your knees. Let your weight rest on the front part of the seat of the chair. After your body is resting on the seat, you may shift back into a more comfortable position." Repeat the directions for each student if necessary.

After all the students have had an opportunity to practice sitting and to observe their classmates as they do the exercise, give directions for the reverse action: "To stand up, move your body forward to the edge of the chair. Put one foot ahead of the other. If the chair is not facing downstage, but is at an angle, put your upstage foot forward. Keeping your back straight, push hard with the foot nearest the chair. This action will bring your body to an upright position. Move away from the chair, using your upstage (forward) foot to take the first step. If the chair is facing downstage, put whichever foot you wish forward."

Students may wish to practice sitting and standing until they can do it easily without looking back at the seat.

DEVELOP

Move the students to an open space where there is ample room for them to move freely without touching one another. If a large space is not available, work with a small group of students while the rest of the class observes.

Ask students to walk, one at a time, from one end of the space to the other. Remind students of the posture exercise they did visualizing the imaginary string pulling on the tops of their heads. Students' arms should hang naturally without tension. Have the students consciously think about those parts of their bodies that may be tense, and try to relax those parts.

After all of the students have crossed the space, describe various situations that will motivate movement. For example, students are late for an appointment; they have a toothache; they are injured in some way; they are in love; they are afraid of something; they are a king or queen, a poor person with no place to go, a robber, or a soldier; they are very nervous, shy, or confident; they are playing a soccer game.

Have the observing students notice how their classmates adjust their body movements according to the various motivations. Compare these movements to those in Lesson 5, in which students' movements were motivated by a particular scene.

Ask the students to comment on the ways motivation changes an actor's style of movement, and how effective the students were in demonstrating the motivation.

If the class has been divided into groups for this exercise, continue with the second group.

EVALUATE   *Student evaluation:* Ask the students, "Why is it necessary to practice the correct movements for use on the stage? How could the sitting exercise help you in acting out a part? How does motivation influence the movement?"

Teacher observation: Did the students seem to increase their awareness of the necessity of body control for a performer? Did they come to the conclusion that forming correct physical habits makes performing easier for them, and makes the performance more professional?

CONNECTIONS   *Music:* Divide the class into small groups. Have each group choose a song and make up "video" choreography to accompany the lyrics. Have each group perform its song for the class.

SPECIAL NEEDS   Allow physically impaired students to work on whatever movements are possible for them. At the same time, encourage them to try movements of which they are capable, but do not usually do, such as transferring from a wheelchair to a chair.

Understanding and Expressing Emotions

COMPONENT	Creative Expression
SUBJECT	Emotional Awareness
OBJECTIVE	Students recall their own emotional experiences, explore ways to understand the thoughts and emotions of another person, and communicate emotions through drama.
MATERIALS	None required

WARM UP

Ask the students how they felt when they got up and thought about coming to school today. List the responses on the board. Students may answer that they were excited, bored, happy, angry, tired, worried, lazy, or impatient. Let at least half the class say how they felt. Then ask students if they can think of any way they might have changed how they felt.

Explain to students that just as performers constantly train their senses, their observational skills, and their bodies, they also train their emotions. Ask students to think of reasons that actors might want to train their emotions. Responses should include the reason that actors want to be in command of and understand their own emotions so that they can better understand and portray their characters.

EXPLORE

If it is appropriate, remind students that in Grades 4 and 5 they used improvisations to help them understand and demonstrate emotions. Tell them that the improvisation they will be doing now is the same technique actors use with one another to explore feelings.

Divide the class into pairs, and name one student in each pair A and the other B. Student A chooses a feeling he or she has had recently (it could be one of those on the board), and then describes the setting and the event that caused that feeling. Student A should also describe how she or he felt when the event first happened, how he or she behaved, and the results of the feeling and the behavior.

Student B listens carefully and thoughtfully to Student A, responds verbally as appropriate, and also tries to feel what Student A is feeling.

Bring the class together again, and ask all the A students these questions: "Was it easy or difficult to describe your feeling? Why? Did you have those feelings yourself again as you were describing them? Did feeling them again help you describe them? Why? How do you think your partner felt about your feelings?"

Ask all of the B students, "When your partner described the feeling, how did you respond? Could your partner make you feel the same way? Why or why not? Have you ever felt the emotions your partner described? Does feeling the same way help you to understand your partner better?"

Ask the class, "How does sharing an emotional experience affect the person who is telling it? The listener? How could either telling or listening to the experience help an actor portray a role?" (If desired, the exercise can be repeated with the students reversing the roles.)

DEVELOP

Remind students that the performer creating a characterization must understand and share the emotions of the character. Telling his or her own emotions, and listening to others tell about their emotions helps the actor explore the emotion itself.

Another way the performer portrays the emotions of a character is expressed in the saying, "If you think the character's thoughts, you will automatically feel the character's emotions." The lines of the play not only tell the story, but also give clues to what each character is thinking.

Explain to the students that once they know the thoughts of a character in a play, they will have clues to that person's emotions. Reread the scene from "When the Hare Brought the Sun" in which Sun Girl discovers that part of the sun is missing. Ask the students to pick out words in the lines that tell a character's thoughts. Encourage students to project how those thoughts are making the characters feel, and how the actors can use those thoughts in expressing the emotions of the characters so that the viewers can share them.

EVALUATE

Student evaluation: Ask students, "Did thinking about an event that caused a certain feeling help you to understand the feeling and share it? Did listening to someone tell about a feeling help you to understand and share it? Did understanding the thoughts of a character in a play help you to understand and share that person's emotion?"

Teacher observation: How well did students identify the thoughts and feelings of the characters in the play? Could they communicate particular emotions after identifying a character's thoughts?

CONNECTIONS *Language Arts:* Have students convey the emotion of one of the following characters from a familiar fairy tale—Hansel, Gretel, one of the three little pigs, one of Mufaro's beautiful daughters, the witch in "Snow White," Prince Charming in "Sleeping Beauty"—by being that character as they tell some of the story.

LESSON EIGHT

Dramatizing a Poem

COMPONENT   Creative Expression

SUBJECT   Poetry

OBJECTIVE   Students use poetry for dramatization and expressive movement.

MATERIALS   One copy for each student of the poem "Symmetry," (page 187), or another poem of your choice

       Note: The abstract visual images in "Symmetry" allow for a variety of interpretations.

WARM UP   Recall with students some of the sources they have used to create scenes and stories. Ideas may have come from objects, words, their own imaginations, newspaper articles, folk tales, and music. (See specific lessons in Grades 4 and 5 for more detail.)

       Review the techniques used to create improvisations from these ideas: establishing *who, what, where, when,* and *why;* establishing the conflict; and identifying the theme.

       Review the presentational procedure: planning, casting, rehearsing, performing, and evaluating.

       Remind the students of the purpose of movement in theatre: to demonstrate character, to express an idea, or to relate events.

       Ask the students what happens when rhythm is added to the movement. Answers might include dancing or marching. Perhaps the students remember using their bodies to make a machine, an activity in Grade 5 involving rhythmic movement.

EXPLORE   Choose a poem such as "Symmetry" (page 187) for dramatization.

       Define *symmetry* as "a regular balanced pattern, the same on one side as the other; a harmony of design." Read the poem to the students. Ask, "How do you think the definition of *symmetry* is carried out in the poem?" (Answers could relate to either the ideas—the comparison of the life cycle of an individual to the physical roundness of the earth—or the rhythm of

GRADE 6

the words—the way each line is balanced in two parts. There is much room for interpretation in this poem; accept many answers.)

Ask, "What images in the poem suggest movement? What kinds of movement—movement that creates geometric shapes with the body, or movement that interprets an idea—or both?" Have the students who reply volunteer to demonstrate the movement in an open space. Ask the students how the poem itself could be presented. They might suggest reading, choral speaking, or pantomiming or dancing to someone else's reading.

DEVELOP

Divide the class into groups of about six students. Tell them that their dramatizations must have two elements: the movement that interprets the images or the meaning of the poem, and the reading of the poem itself. They may be done separately or together—either everyone may be involved in both the movement and the reading of the poem, or part of the group may present the movement and the other part may present the poem. Allow time for planning and rehearsing. Then have each group present its dramatization of the poem to the class.

EVALUATE

Student evaluation: As a class, discuss the various choices that the groups made about presenting their work. How did the choices made affect their presentations? What were the differences and similarities in the groups' presentations?

Teacher observation: How did the students respond to the poem? Were the students able to use images from the poem to create a movement drama? How did students' choices affect their dramatizations?

CONNECTIONS

Science: Divide the class into groups. Have each group use movement and verse or choral reading to describe a scientific principle or event. Examples include the water cycle, the action of a glacier, an earthquake, a volcano, the heating of a liquid until it becomes a gas, gravity, magnetism, and so on.

SPECIAL NEEDS

Choose a poem with more concrete images for your mentally impaired students.

Symmetry

Sing a song of symmetry. Sing it me again.
Sing of earth every round, let symmetry begin.
Feather light in circle flight, on wing and feather down.
About the world in circle flight, complete your circle round.

Of birth I sing a circle song. Sing it me again.
Of mother love and father strong, let symmetry begin.
Life anew makes circle flight, on wing and feather down.
Old men die on windy nights. That makes your circle round.

(Author Unknown)

COPYRIGHT © DALE SEYMOUR PUBLICATIONS

LESSON NINE

Switching Antagonist and Protagonist

COMPONENT	Aesthetic Perception
SUBJECT	Theatre Vocabulary: Antagonist and Protagonist
OBJECTIVE	Students identify and use appropriate drama/theatre vocabulary and dramatize a familiar story in which antagonist and protagonist are reversed.
MATERIALS	None required; see *Note*

Note: An especially good example of role reversal is *The True Story of the Three Little Pigs,* by Jon Scieszka. If time allows, read it aloud during the Explore section of the lesson.

WARM UP   Ask the students if they have ever cheered "for" someone as they watched a play or read a story. Have they ever cheered "against" someone? What terms are usually used to describe these people? The students might answer *hero* and *villain*. (Both hero and villain can be either male or female.) Explain to the students that in drama/theatre, the hero and villain are sometimes called the *protagonist* and *antagonist*, respectively, although the terms are not completely interchangeable. Define the terms: write them on the board, and have students copy them for their notebooks.

Protagonist: the main character, who carries out the central thought, or theme of the story. The audience will usually have an emotional response in support of this character. (Sometimes there will be two or more main characters who are the protagonists, such as Hansel and Gretel, Romeo and Juliet, and the Bremen Town Musicians.)

Antagonist: the opponent of the main character in a story, who tries to keep the protagonist from reaching his or her goal. The audience will usually have an emotional response against this character.

Ask students for examples of a protagonist and an antagonist, such as the wolf and Little Red Riding Hood. Have the students identify the protagonists and antagonists in other stories.

EXPLORE   Ask, "What do you think would happen to a story if you switched the antagonist and protagonist? For example, what would happen in the story of Little Red Riding Hood if Little Red Riding Hood were the antagonist instead of the wolf?" Ask the students to make up some dialogue for the wolf and Little Red Riding Hood with their roles reversed.

If time allows, read *The True Story of the Three Little Pigs,* and discuss the differences between this story and the original "Three Little Pigs."

DEVELOP   Divide the class into groups of five or six. Have each group select a well-known children's story, such as "Jack and the Beanstalk," "Cinderella," "Snow White," "Three Billy Goats Gruff," or "Rumplestiltskin." Be sure that the stories chosen have identifiable heroes and villains.

The assignment for each group is to create a scene showing one part of the story in which the characters are reversed. The antagonist will become the protagonist, and vice versa. The groups are to improvise some dialogue and action that would change. Have the groups plan, cast, rehearse, and share their improvisations with the class.

EVALUATE   *Student evaluation:* Ask the students, "How did the action and dialogue of the characters in the stories change when the roles of antagonist and protagonist were reversed? Were you able to see a different point of view for each of the characters? Why or why not?"

Teacher observation: Do the students understand the role of antagonist and protagonist in drama? How well did the students change the roles of the characters? Did their improvisations demonstrate an understanding of the feelings of each character?

CONNECTIONS   *Art:* Have students create an abstract picture using only two complementary colors (red and green, purple and yellow, or orange and blue). Suggest that the subject of the picture be conflict or confrontation. Display finished pictures and discuss the moods they inspire.

RESOURCES   Ireland, Norma O., compiled by. *Index to Fairy Tales, 1973–77: Including Folklore, Legends and Myths in Collections.* Scarecrow Press, Inc., 1985.

Kamerman, Sylvia. *Dramatized Folktales of the World.* Plays, Inc.,1971. (This book is out of print, but may be found in your library.)

Scieszka, Jon. *The True Story of the Three Little Pigs.* Viking Children's Books, 1989.

Commedia dell'arte

COMPONENT   Historical and Cultural

SUBJECT   Theatre History

OBJECTIVE   Students investigate the commedia dell'arte style of drama/theatre, and improvise a scene in that style.

MATERIALS   Reference books with information about commedia dell'arte (see Resources)

Note: You may wish to split this lesson into two parts, between Explore and Develop, to allow time for students' research.

WARM UP   Divide the class into groups of about seven or eight, and tell students that they will be investigating a particular style of drama/theatre, called commedia dell'arte (co-MAY-deeuh dell AR-tay). Write the term on the board. Give students a list of specific questions for which they are to find the answers:

1. In what country did commedia dell'arte originate?

2. In what century was it established?

3. Name some of the characters that are almost always found in a commedia dell'arte play.

4. Describe the style of acting in commedia dell'arte.

Ask the groups to gather any additional information about commedia dell'arte that would help to identify it. Provide enough reference books, or send groups to the school library so that they can complete their research. Encourage groups to get as much information as they can, and to keep the information in their notebooks.

EXPLORE   Bring the groups back together to report on the information they found. They should have found out the following:

Commedia dell'arte originated in Italy in the sixteenth century. (Have students locate Italy on a world map.) This style of drama featured the same characters in every play:

the *young lovers,* who played the "normal" characters, against whom all the others looked exaggerated and foolish. The young lovers were depicted as witty, handsome, well-educated young men and women;

the *capitano* (cahp-ee-TAH-no), a braggart and coward, who wore a sword, cape, and feathered headdress;

a *pantalone* (pahn-tah-LO-nay), a middle-aged or elderly merchant, who wore a tight fitting red vest, red breeches and stockings, soft slippers, and a brown mask with a large hooked nose and gray beard; and

a *dottore* (do-TOR-ay), a doctor of law or medicine, who wore a long academic gown and cap. He showed off his learning, but was often tricked by others.

In addition, there were servant men and women. One of the most popular was *Arlechino* (ar-lay-KEE-no), Harlequin, who was a mixture of cunning and stupidity, and was an accomplished acrobat and dancer. His costume was originally patches, but developed into the diamond-shaped red, blue, and green pattern now associated with Harlequin. He wore a black half-mask, and carried a wooden sword.

Relate the following additional information about commedia dell'arte if students have not discovered it on their own:

Performances were improvisational, and performed by traveling companies of actors. Action was often exaggerated so that the audience would get the point. The accent in commedia was on visual performance. Speeches were added as an accompaniment to movement, gesture, and stage business.

The actors worked from a plot outline (scenario), on the basis of which they improvised dialogue and action. Most plots concerned love and intrigue, disguises, and deception. The scenarios were detailed. (For a scenario of a commedia dell'arte play, see the Crawford reference under Resources.)

DEVELOP

Point out to the students that two fundamental characteristics of commedia dell'arte are improvisation and stock characters. *Improvisation* ("to create a character or scene without a planned script") is a term with which students are already familiar. Tell them that *stock characters* are characters who are the same in every play or story. Have students add these two terms to their notes.

Tell students that they will have a chance to do an improvisation in the style of commedia dell'arte. As a class, agree on a plot outline, and then have students go back to their original groups. Let each student choose a stock character to portray (there can be two or three of almost any of the stock characters), and then have each group improvise a scene, using the agreed-upon plot. Remind students that their acting, except for the young lovers, should be exaggerated and silly rather than realistic.

Allow time for students to plan their scenes, and then have each group give their presentation. Compare the different versions of the same plot, and evaluate how well each group exaggerated their character roles.

EVALUATE   *Student evaluation:* Ask the students if they can give some examples of exaggerated characters in today's theatre. Who could be considered "normal," or serious characters? Did students enjoy playing exaggerated and silly roles? Do they know of any actors or groups who regularly perform improvisations?

Teacher observation: Could the students understand what "exaggerated" actions and characters are? Did the students follow what they knew about the commedia dell'arte tradition in planning their improvisation?

CONNECTIONS   *Social Studies:* Have students find out an interesting fact about Italy. Then have each student explain his or her fact in the persona of one of the stock characters featured in the commedia dell'arte.

RESOURCES   Crawford, Jerry L. *Acting: In Person and In Style.* William C. Brown Publishers, 1983.

Ducharte, Pierre Louis. *Italian Comedy: The Improvisation, Scenarios, Lives, Attributes, Portraits and Masks of the Illustrious Characters of Commedia Dell'arte.* Dover, 1965.

Smith, Winifred. *Commedia dell'arte.* Ayer Company Publishers, 1990.

Using Shakespearean Theatrical Devices

COMPONENT	Historical and Cultural
SUBJECT	Elizabethan Theatre
OBJECTIVE	Students learn about Shakespeare and the Elizabethan theatre, and experiment with some of Shakespeare's theatrical devices.
MATERIALS	A book of Shakespeare's plays; one copy for each student of the diagram of the Fortune Theatre on page 196

WARM UP

Ask the students how many of them have heard of William Shakespeare. List on the board any titles of Shakespeare's plays or poems, or quotations that students know. Write down any other information they have, and tell students that Shakespeare was a famous poet and playwright who lived from 1564 to 1616, during the time that his country, England, was a great sea-faring power.

Locate England on a map. Note that it is part of the island of Great Britain. Tell students that during Elizabethan times (1533–1603), England established a vast shipping trade and consequent riches for the country. As a result, people had more education as well as leisure time.

Education and leisure led to the growth of theatre. People loved to use and hear their growing vocabulary, and everyone, from the lowliest pie-sellers in the street to Queen Elizabeth, went to the theatre. Of course the street people sat or stood in the yard, while the lords and ladies and royalty sat in special boxes, but they all enjoyed the rich and elegant language, good stories, vigorous action, and complex characters that were presented.

EXPLORE

Ask the students if they might be able to think of some of the sources of ideas for plays in Elizabethan times—stories the people of that time might know. Answers could include: folk tales, history, commedia dell'arte, Greek and Roman myths and legends, events of the day, and old stories from literature. Shakespeare used themes common to all people: love, hate, revenge, power, enchantment, foolishness, magic, and adventure.

GRADE 6

Living on an island often influenced the content of Shakespeare's plays: several have island settings.

Give each student a copy of the diagram of the Fortune Theatre, which was a typical Elizabethan stage. Point out that it was a stage without curtains, except for a small area at the very back; performances were often held during the day so that special lighting was not needed; and settings were minimal.

Even though there might be no set or scenery, audiences always knew where and when the action was taking place. Ask the students how they think this might be accomplished. The answer lies in the first few lines of dialogue in each scene, wherein the characters gave clues to time and location. Read students this example from Act I, Scene I of "Hamlet," and ask them to listen for such clues:

BERNARDO: Who's there?...

FRANCISCO: You come most carefully upon your hour.

BERNARDO: 'Tis now struck twelve; get thee to bed, Francisco.
FRANCISCO: For this relief, much thanks; 'tis bitter cold, and I am sick at heart.

BERNARDO: Have you had a quiet guard?

FRANCISCO: Not a mouse stirring.

Ask the students where the scene might be taking place, who the people are, and what they might be doing. (The scene takes place at midnight outside the palace, and is the changing of the guard.)

Have students look at their stage diagram again, and note that different areas of the stage could be different settings, so that action could flow from one area to another, from one setting to another, by moving from one part of the stage to another without interruption. The audience could imagine the setting for the scene through the device of dialogue clues.

Explain, too, that Shakespeare could have vast armies marching about for his battles, or great crowds of people in scenes, simply by mentioning in the dialogue that thousands of people were passing by. Read students the Prologue from Henry V, in which the Chorus explains to the audience that they are to imagine the theatre pit as the vast fields of France, and that the theatre is full of soldiers (casques, meaning the soldiers' helmets). The Chorus says, "Think, when we talk of horses, that you see them/Printing their proud hoofs i' the receiving earth...."

DEVELOP   Have selected students read some of the first scene from Act III of "A Midsummer Night's Dream." Explain that the characters are buffoons, who are planning a play within a play, and discussing how the audience will react to their drama. Point out that the story they are portraying, "Pyramus and Thisbe," is from Greek lore, and would be well-known by the audience. Have students note that Quince's first lines give the setting and explain the situation.

Divide the class into groups. Each group is to choose a story from previous lessons, or from the class's readings, or to make up a story with a minimum of two, but preferably three brief scenes. The students are to use the Shakespearean dialogue devices mentioned: setting of time and place, identification of characters, indications of large numbers of people, and a continuous flow of action from one scene to another. Allow the groups time to plan and rehearse their scenes, and then have them present their improvisations to the class. With the class, evaluate each group's abilities to adapt the Shakespearean dialogue devices to their own dramatizations.

EVALUATE   *Student evaluation:* Ask the students, "Were you able to find ways for your characters to tell the place and time without directly saying the information? Could the action in your dramatization flow from one scene to another without interruption? Can you see a relation of this technique to motion pictures and television? What is the relationship?"

Teacher observation: Did students demonstrate knowledge of the information that had to be conveyed to audiences in the Elizabethan theatre? Did the students use dialogue in an imaginative way for their presentations?

CONNECTIONS   *Science:* Have students find out about an important scientist, scientific discovery, or scientific event. Then have students use Shakespeare's devices to create a dialogue that describes the person, circumstances, and date. Have each student present his or her Science Scene to the rest of the group.

RESOURCES   Birch, Beverly. *Shakespeare's Stories: Comedies.* Peter Bedrick Books, 1988.

_____ . *Shakespeare's Stories: Histories.* Peter Bedrick Books, 1988.

_____ . *Shakespeare's Stories: Tragedies.* Peter Bedrick Books, 1988.

Lamb, Charles. *Tales From Shakespeare.* Crown Publishers, 1988.

Mulherin, Jennifer. *Shakespeare for Everyone Series* (2 volumes). Silver Burdett, 1988.

GRADE 6

Plan of Fortune Theatre 1600

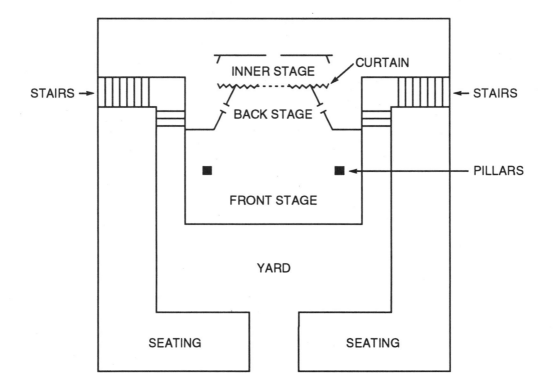

STAIRS →   INNER STAGE   CURTAIN   ← STAIRS

BACK STAGE

PILLARS

FRONT STAGE

YARD

SEATING   SEATING

COPYRIGHT © DALE SEYMOUR PUBLICATIONS

Dramatizing a Mexican Folk Tale

COMPONENT   Historical and Cultural

SUBJECT   Mexican Folklore

OBJECTIVE   Students research information about Mexican folklore, select a story from a particular category, and present an improvisation of that particular type of tale from Mexico.

MATERIALS   One copy for each student of the list on page 200 of the various kinds of Mexican folk tales; several anthologies of Mexican folk tales and reference books

Note: You may wish to divide this lesson into two parts, one for the research and one for the improvisation. Have students use the school or community library for their research.

WARM UP   Ask a student to point out on a map the border between Mexico and the United States. Note that the proximity of the two countries has given Americans an opportunity to experience Mexican culture through visual arts, music, and history. Mexican-Americans have a background from three cultures—Native American, Spanish, and Mexican—that they have brought with them to the United States.

Remind students that folklore has been passed down orally for hundreds of years. This lore includes religious stories, legends, whimsical anecdotes, and tall tales. If there are Mexican or Mexican-American students in the class, ask them to tell the class some of their traditions, customs, and stories. If you have no students with Mexican heritage, or if students feel hesitant about sharing, select information about Mexican folkways from the listed resources to discuss. Ask how those folkways are similar to or influence other cultures the students know.

EXPLORE   Read aloud a folk tale from one of the books listed in Resources, or another Mexican folk tale of your choice, and discuss the characters and settings with the students. Ask the students to identify the plot and the theme of the story.

Give each student a copy of the list on page 200 of the kinds of folk tales, and discuss them with the students. See whether they can categorize the story that was just read aloud. Ask, "What can you tell from this list about plot, theme, characters, and settings of the Mexican folk tales? Do you see any similarities between these stories and the folk tales of other cultures?"

DEVELOP   Divide the class into small groups, and assign to each group one of the types of folk tales in the Mexican culture. Tell the students that each group is to develop an improvisation from a story or poem that belongs to their assigned type of folk tale. Provide several of the listed resources for the students to research stories, poems, or dramas developed from folk tales that would be related to their assigned story type.

Allow the groups time to rehearse their improvisations; then share them with the class.

EVALUATE   *Student evaluation:* Ask the students, "Can you name specific stories from other cultures that fit into some of the categories of the Mexican stories? What are the similarities and differences in plots and themes between the Mexican stories you learned about and stories from other cultures?"

Teacher observation: Are the students able to relate the Mexican culture to their own? Were the dramatizations in keeping with the kinds of stories assigned? Do students have a respect for the cultures they have been studying, and a developing understanding of different peoples?

CONNECTIONS   *Mathematics:* Have students learn to count in Spanish and use the numbers to create addition and subtraction problems. One of your students or another teacher might help you teach students the Spanish number words if you do not know them. Challenge students to use the highest numbers they can name or to string together as many numbers as they can in a sentence! The following number sentences can be used: 2 + 3 = 5 is *dos y tres es cinco*; 5 - 3 = 2 is *cinco menos tres es dos.*

RESOURCES   Acuna, Rudolfo. *Occupied America: A History of Chicanos.* (third ed.) Harper & Row, 1988.

Anaya, Rodolfo A. *Legend of La Llorona.* Tonatiuh-Quinto Sol International Publications, 1984.

Baline, Peter. *The Flight of the Feathered Serpent.* Arcana Publishers, 1983.

Hughes, Jill. *Aztecs.* (rev. ed.) Watts, 1987.

Kamerman, Sylvia. *Dramatized Folk Tales of the World.* Plays, Inc., 1971. (This book recently went out of print, but you may be able to find it in your library.)

McKissack, Patricia. *Aztec Indians.* Childrens Book Press, 1985.

McLain, Gary. *The Indian Way.* John Muir Publications, 1990.

Montejo, Victor. *The Bird Who Cleans the World and Other Mayan Fables.* Curbstone Press, 1990.

Rohmer, Harriet. *The Legend of Food Mountain: La Montana del Alimento.* Childrens Book Press, 1982.

Steiner, Stan, and Luis Valdez, eds. *Aztlan: An Anthology of Mexican-American Literature.* Random House, 1972.

West, John O. *Mexican-American Folklore.* August House Publishers, 1988.

GRADE 6

Folk Tales of Mexico

Religious Stories   Most of these stories are about the Virgin of Guadalupe, patroness of Mexico. There are also stories about Juan Diego and his encounter with the Virgin of Guadalupe.

Supernatural Legends   Supernatural legends involve figures from another world. An example is the story of the ghostly woman named La Llorona (la yor-OH-na), the Weeping Woman, who wanders along canals and rivers crying for her missing children.

Treasure Tales   These stories are a natural outgrowth of the search for gold in Mexico.

Animal Tales and Fables   The reappearing character of a trickster exists in many cultures. In Mexican culture the trickster is the Coyote. The Coyote character is usually involved in some mischief, but is often outsmarted himself.

Compadres Tales   These stories involve two compadres (kom-PAH-drays), companions or friends. One is usually rich and the other poor.

Ordinary Folk Tales   These are sometimes called fairy tales, and usually involve three brothers, or three princesses, or three tasks to be performed. The stories often take place in a sort of magical never-never land.

COPYRIGHT © DALE SEYMOUR PUBLICATIONS

World Theatre: China

COMPONENT | Historical and Cultural

SUBJECT | Theatre of China

OBJECTIVE | Students learn about theatre in China during the Ming Dynasty, and create a dramatization using current topics that fit the Chinese theatrical classifications.

MATERIALS | Folded slips of paper, each with one of the eight classifications of Chinese theatre written on it; globe or world map

WARM UP

On a globe or large world map, have students locate the boundaries of China, and those of Mongolia and Tibet. Point out on the map the desert, plateaus, and mountains that surround China. Tell the students that China is the most populous country in the world and has 4,000 years of recorded history. It is also the country where silk, paper, the first printing press, gunpowder, porcelain, the first overhanging roof to keep out the sun's rays, and the great philosophies of Lao-Tzu and Confucius originated.

Tell students that China also has a well-developed theatre, but because of its geographical isolation from the rest of the world, and because the Chinese wanted to avoid contact with people from other countries, the style of theatre in China developed differently from Western theatre. Even so, the drama expressed the same themes and ideas of people everywhere. Ask students what some of those ideas and themes might be. List them on the board.

EXPLORE

Tell students that theatre especially flourished in China during the Ming Dynasty (1368-1644). It was a period of development of the arts, especially textiles, porcelain, and painting. More than 600 plays were produced during the Ming Dynasty. The plots and themes reflected everyday life at that time; ideas came from the experiences of all kinds of people.

During the Ming Dynasty, plays were classified or described as: Historical, Military, Civil (Political), Romantic, Criminal, Ethical, Fantastic, or Problem. Write these classifications on the board, and define any terms with which students are unfamiliar.

Ask the students to guess at the content of the plays in each of the classifications and give a possible example of each. For instance, an "Ethical" play would probably center around a moral decision of the time, such as working for your own good as opposed to working for the good of others.

DEVELOP   Ask the students, "What are some topics from today's society that could be used to develop plays that fit the eight classifications used in the Ming Dynasty? List some of students' suggestions on the board and compare them with the list of themes common to all cultures and the Ming Dynasty list.

Divide the class into eight groups. Have one person from each group come forward and choose a slip of paper with one of the classifications of Chinese plays written on it. Each group's task is to select a current topic that would fit the classification and convey it to an audience through the improvisation of a scene. The group may want to use an idea that was listed on the board and discussed, or think of another example from current events that would fit that classification.

Allow the groups enough time for planning, casting, and rehearsing. Then have them share their improvisations with the class. As each group shares its scene, the members of the audience can write down which classification they think the presentation fits. Allow all groups to perform before discussing the classifications. Then ask, "Where did the group get its idea? What classification was demonstrated? How was it demonstrated?"

EVALUATE   *Student evaluation:* Discuss with the class the universality of themes and topics in theatre. Ask the students, "How are the classifications of the Chinese theatre appropriate today? What did you learn from the improvisations of the other groups about how to convey a particular classification?"

Teacher observation: Could the students transfer many of the classifications of Chinese theatre to events happening in the world today? Did the improvisations stick to the classifications effectively? Do the students seem to be aware of the universality of themes, ideas, and topics in theatre?

CONNECTIONS   *Art:* Have students research design for Chinese textiles or porcelain and re-create them in designs of their own. Display students' art work.

SPECIAL NEEDS   Have a classmate quietly describe the pantomimes being performed to the severely visually impaired student so that he or she may participate.

RESOURCES   Scott, A.C. *The Theatre in Asia.* Macmillan, 1972. (This book is out of print, but may be in your library.)

World Theatre: Japan

COMPONENT	Historical and Cultural
SUBJECT	Japanese Noh Theatre
OBJECTIVE	Students study the stylized movements of Japanese Noh theatre and create a pantomime with similar, carefully controlled dance movements.
MATERIALS	Several reference books with pictures of Noh drama (see Resources)

Note: If a theatre historian is available, or someone knowledgeable about Japanese theatre, invite that person to the classroom to discuss the Noh play with students and how it relates to Japanese society.

WARM UP

In an open space, demonstrate and give directions for a set of movements, such as: "Raise your left arm half way into the air. Keeping your arm up, take very small steps as you turn completely around. Then walk forward, keeping your feet in a straight line, putting down toe, then heel, toe, heel, toe, heel." Be very precise in your movements as you demonstrate these three actions. Then ask for volunteers to repeat the three actions in succession without altering or adding to the movements.

Tell students that a Japanese drama form, called the Noh play, uses stylized movements such as the ones they just did to tell serious stories— both historical and legendary. Have a student locate Japan on a globe or large world map. Tell the students that Japan has a long tradition and history of theatre. Show students some pictures of Japanese theatre from reference books.

If someone knowledgeable about Noh Theatre is available, ask that person to give some of the background of Noh Theatre. If not, explain to the class that Noh Theatre was created in the 14th century, and is the oldest form of Japanese drama. The movements and gestures in Noh Theatre are highly controlled, and every movement has a meaning that adds to the development of the story. Actors use masks, and tell the story through dance, poetry, music, and mime. Only about one third of the play is speech. A chorus chants most of the important lines in the play. The language used in a Noh play is the language of the 14th century, which is hardly intelligible to audiences today. However, the Japanese recognize that this ancient, very beautiful, and traditional art form is worth preserving, and it is designated as a Japanese National Treasure.

EXPLORE

Point out to students that the most prominent feature of most Noh plays is dance. There are different dance forms for different kinds of characters, and each dance is divided into three or five sequences with intricate, highly conventionalized gestures and posturing. Tell students that learning all the dance movements takes many years and much practice, but they can try two of the movements typical of Noh dancing. One is the sliding step, with which actors move about the stage without raising their heels, lifting their toes only as they keep their feet parallel. Demonstrate this movement, and let students try it in an open space.

Another characteristic of Noh dancing is the stamping movement, in which the knee is lifted waist high and the foot brought down squarely on the ground with controlled precision. Show students this movement. Let them practice the stamping movement, and then combine it with the sliding movement in various patterns.

DEVELOP

Explain to the students that all the actors in Noh Theatre are men, even though some characters in the plays are women. Most Noh plays were performed in two parts. In the first part the main character tells his story. In the second part the main character returns as a deity, ghost, demon, or other character who has now become mentally unbalanced. Introduce two of the different kinds of Noh plays to students (if desired, have students copy these for their notebooks):

Waki (WAH - kee): A god appears in mortal form and tells the history of a particular place to another character. He appears again later in his own form and performs a dance.

Shura (SHOO - rah): A battle, symbolizing a conflict of good and bad in people's souls, takes place between a young villager and a ghost in full battle gear.

Divide students into pairs and ask them to work out dance movements that would demonstrate some kind of conflict between good and bad. They should focus on the two steps they have practiced, but may add other movements, each of which should be carefully thought out and performed.

Point out that since Noh actors use wooden masks with a single painted expression to represent their characters, the actors must concentrate on body movement to convey meaning. Ask the students to focus on body control, using only a single facial expression as they perform their movement sequence.

Have each pair share their movement sequence with the class, and tell the meaning of each of their movements.

EVALUATE   *Student evaluation:* Ask the students, "Could you keep a mask-like expression on your face? Did you use your body in a carefully controlled way? Could you convey meaning using body movements alone? Why or why not? Compare the body movements in Noh plays to some of your previous drama activities."

Teacher observation: Were students willing to try to imitate the Noh drama form? Could they convey meaning through highly stylized body movements? Could students relate the movements in Noh plays to some of their previous drama activities?

CONNECTIONS   *Science:* Divide the class into groups. Have each group explore a geographical or scientific phenomenon of the island chain of Japan (volcanoes, tidal waves, earthquakes, and so on). Display a large map of Japan so that students may refer to it as they make their presentations to the class.

SPECIAL NEEDS   During the lesson, ask a classmate to describe to the severely visually impaired student the body movements of students performing a scene.

RESOURCES   Berthold, Margot. *The History of World Theater, from the Beginning to the Baroque* (Vol. I.). Continuum, 1990.

Brockett, Oscar G. *The History of the Theatre.* Allyn & Bacon, Inc., 1968.

Keene, Donald, ed. *Twenty Plays of the Noh Theatre.* Columbia University Press, 1970.

Komparu, Kunio. *The Noh Theater: Principles and Perspectives.* Weatherhill, 1983.

Scott, A.C. *The Theatre in Asia.* Macmillan Publishing Co., 1972. (This book is out of print, but may be available in your library.)

Wickham, Glynne. *A History of the Theatre.* Cambridge University Press, 1985.

Russian Theatre and the Stanislavsky Method

COMPONENT	Historical and Cultural
SUBJECT	Stanislavsky and the Moscow Art Theater
OBJECTIVE	Students learn about Stanislavsky's place in drama history, and practice some of his Method acting exercises.
MATERIALS	None required

WARM UP

Ask students whether they would go to see a play for which the actors did not rehearse, the story was uninteresting, and the play began 45 minutes later than the advertised time. Let students discuss the effects of this kind of drama/theatre discipline on an audience. Explain that this was the state of drama/theatre in Russia in the late 1800s.

Tell students that in Russia, in 1897, a drama director and teacher, Constantin Stanislavsky, was disgusted with this lazy kind of behavior in the Russian theatre; so he, along with another Russian man, decided to form a new theatre in which every actor must be an artist. Write "Constantin Stanislavsky" and "Moscow Art Theater" on the board.

Some of Stanislavsky's rules for the Moscow Art Theater were:

1. Actors must study the inner lives of the characters as though they were real people, in order to give a truthful performance.

2. Everyone involved in a production—the actor, the scene designer, the costumer, and the stagehand—must concentrate on getting across to an audience the playwright's ideas.

3. Everyone involved in the production must be disciplined. Tardiness, laziness, tantrums, failure to learn parts, and repeating the same thing twice were not allowed.

Ask students which of those ideas are ones they have already learned in drama/theatre.

EXPLORE

Have a student locate Russia, and its capital, Moscow, on a map. Tell students that in the early 1900s the Moscow Art Theater soon became famous for realistic performances of plays by Chekov, Gorki, and other Russian playwrights.

Tell students that having the actor try to live the life of the character became known as the "Stanislavsky Method." The goal of the Method was to give as realistic a performance as possible. (Not all of what is now known as the Stanislavsky Method was actually developed by Stanislavsky. Many later dramatists studied Stanislavsky's original intent, then added other ideas to reach the same goal—to give as realistic a performance as possible.)

To get actors to think like the characters they were playing, Stanislavsky devised some exercises for them to do. One of Stanislavsky's exercises was for actors to justify in their minds every stage action they carried out. If, for example, a character sat, the actor had to have a reason for sitting.

Have students sit in order to rest. Then tell them to sit as though they were at a window, watching what is happening across the street. Then have them sit as though they were waiting for someone who was late. Let students think of some other reasons for sitting. Then have them act out the scenario and explain what they were thinking. Have the class analyze the movements and compare the different ways of sitting.

DEVELOP

Explain to students that another exercise for actors developed by Stanislavsky was the "magic if." Actors had to imagine what would happen if an unexpected event occurred, another character behaved in a particular way, or something magical or fantastical occurred. Then they had to dramatize the scene that they imagined.

Give students situations to act out. Say, for example, "You must be on time to school because the class is going on a field trip, and the bus will leave at 9:00. But when you get on your bicycle to ride to school, you notice that it has a flat tire, and by the time you fix it, you are late to school. What if the bus has left without you?" Ask for a volunteer to create a dialogue and actions to show what happens next.

Continue the activity by inventing other "what if...?" situations, real and fantastical, and asking for a volunteer to improvise what happens next. Ask students to compare this exercise with other activities they have done for drama/theatre this year or in other years. (The concept of the "magic if" was explored in Lesson 22, Grade 3 of CENTER STAGE.)

EVALUATE   *Student evaluation*: Ask the students, "What is the main idea of the Stanislavsky Method? In what country was it developed? Could you think of reasons for stage actions as you did them? Do you think trying to think or live like a particular character helps make dramatic action more realistic? Why or why not?"

Teacher observation: Could students do the two exercises presented to them as part of Method acting? Could students understand how Method acting could help them in some of their own drama activities?

CONNECTIONS   *Social Studies*: Divide the class into groups. Have each group use reference books to gather information about Russian culture, religion, history, or current events. Then have the groups share three or four interesting facts they learned about Russia and discuss what they discovered.

RESOURCES   Berthold, Margot. *The History of World Theater, from the Beginning to the Baroque* (Vol. I). Continuum Press, 1990.

Brockett, Oscar, G. *The History of the Theatre*. Boston: Allyn & Bacon, Inc., 1968.

Magarshack, David. *Stanislavsky: A Life*. Faber & Faber, 1988.

Moore, Sonia. *The Stanislavsky System: The Professional Training of an Actor* (2nd rev. ed.). Penguin Books, 1984.

Stanislavski, Constantin. *Building A Character*. Theatre Arts Books, 1977.

_____. *Creating a Role*. Theatre Arts Books, 1961.

Real People, Imagined Characters

COMPONENT	Aesthetic Perception
SUBJECT	Theatrical Roles
OBJECTIVE	Students recognize the difference between the role played by an actor and the actor as a real person.
MATERIALS	None required

WARM UP

Ask the students, "What is the difference between fiction and nonfiction?" Answers should indicate that fiction is developed from the imagination, and while it may seem real or true to life, it is not; it is invented. Examples of fictional literature include novels, short stories, and dramas.

Nonfiction is factual. Examples of nonfictional literature include biographies, newspaper articles, and historical accounts of events.

Ask, "Can real people and characters in a play have some of the same characteristics?" Let the responses lead to a discussion about the idea that both playwrights and novelists write some truths about people, but that the characters themselves are products of the playwright's or author's imagination.

Ask the students to name a few fictional characters from literature and compare them with real people.

EXPLORE

Ask the students if they have ever heard the saying, "Art imitates life." What does that saying mean to the students? Ask students to give examples of other art forms besides theatre in which life is imitated, represented, or copied. Have students describe television, film, and live theatre presentations with which they are familiar. How does each of these media represent real life? Which medium do students think is the most realistic, and why?

Ask the students what actors mean when they say, "Believe in the role and character you are portraying," "You must live and become the character," "You must be real as the character." Ask the class how actors portray a person that may be completely different from themselves. Is that possible? How? How do actors separate their own character traits from the traits that portray a character in a story?

DEVELOP   Ask the students how many of them expect actors they have seen on television to behave in real life like the TV characters they play. Ask, "If you see a very mean character in a stage production or on a film, do you believe that the actor portraying that character is also mean in real life? Why, or why not?"

Divide the class into pairs. Have each pair of students think of two characters that are opposite in some way, such as old/young, mean/kind, talkative/shy, or fast moving/slow moving. Each pair should improvise a short scene that allows their two characters to interact. Allow time for each pair to plan and play their scene.

Then ask each pair of students to discuss with each other how it felt to play their particular characters and what traits of the characters were also traits of the students themselves. If any pairs would like to share their scene with the class, allow them to do so. Ask the students whether they think it is easier to act out character traits that are most nearly like one's own.

Following the discussions, have the pairs reverse their roles. If one student played a mean character the first time, the second time he or she should be the kind character. Have students keep the same theme for their scene as the earlier improvisation. Again, ask pairs of students to discuss their scene in terms of the character traits that were like and unlike themselves. Select a few pairs to share their scenes, and let the class discuss whether the students seemed to be playing themselves.

Ask whether students have trouble adjusting to an actor as an older brother in a situation comedy one week, and then a young father in another program the next week. Also tell the students that sometimes different actors play the same character in a play on different nights. Ask, "Why does this work in theatre?"

EVALUATE   *Student evaluation:* Ask the students, "Were you able to switch roles to play, for example, both a kind and a mean character in the same scene? Why or why not? How do actors 'become' the characters they are playing? How do they separate themselves from their roles? How does an audience member, in viewing a performance by an actor, mentally separate the actor from the character? Should the viewer try to do this?"

Teacher observation: Were students able to understand the concept of separating themselves from the roles they play? Do the students have a better understanding of how actors create their roles? Do students seem able to view a theatrical piece as an art form rather than reality?

CONNECTIONS   *Mathematics:* Suggest a character type to students (grouchy sales clerk, strict teacher, child prodigy, English butler). Then have students think of a challenging math problem and use the voice, tone, and mannerisms of the character as they tell the problem to the class.

Developing a Character

COMPONENT   Creative Expression

SUBJECT   Character Studies

OBJECTIVE   Students use drama/theatre techniques they have learned to create a character, and then improvise interaction with other characters.

MATERIALS   None required

WARM UP   Ask students to name some of the techniques they have learned in previous drama lessons for creating characters. Answers should include observation of physical movement, listening to speech, thinking a character's thoughts so as to understand that person's emotions, and finding a feeling in oneself that corresponds to a feeling in the character. Students may also mention costumes, props, and understanding the background (history and experience) of the character. Write the students' responses on the board.

EXPLORE   Review with students the concept of stock characters, as it was introduced in Lesson 10 (commedia dell'arte). Remind students that stock characters are always the same, no matter which play they are in. Tell students that the best roles in theatre are those which seem unique; those to which the actors can give depth, or more than the obvious characteristics. A good actor will find ways to do this, no matter how small the role.

Explain to students that they are going to do an exercise to help in role development. Move them into an open space, and ask them to lie down, without touching each other, and relax and breathe correctly. (Relaxation and effective breathing are necessary elements of performance.) Students are to close their eyes and imagine an animal. Ask them to picture the animal in their mind's eye. Tell students that when the image is very clear and vivid, they are to rise and begin moving about in the manner of the animal selected. They should focus on rhythm of movement and facial expression.

Stop the exercise. Then ask the students to walk about as themselves, and gradually add elements of the animal to their own movements. Carry the exercise further by suggesting that each student think of a person who would have some of the attributes of that animal. For example, if a student has imagined and acted out a lazy cat, then the student is to think of someone he or she knows who moves like a lazy cat and seems to have the same kind of expression.

DEVELOP

Divide the class into groups of five or six. Each group is to imagine that they are all together in one of the following situations:

They are waiting in line at the post office.
They are waiting to be interviewed for a job.
They are attending a very polite tea party.
They are waiting to get into a rock concert.
They are drivers in a traffic jam.
They are stuck in an elevator.
They are soccer players waiting for an important game to begin.

Each student should think of the animal he or she selected to characterize in the previous exercise. His or her movement, facial expression, and temperament in the group scene will be based on that animal. In addition, the student should think of the age, the history and background, and emotions of the character in the particular situation. There need be no effort made in this exercise to develop a story. The focus of this exercise is to express a particular character in the group situation.

Explain to the students that their characters should interact; that is, they should respond to each other as well as to the situation. Give the students time to plan and develop the situation, and then present the characterizations to the class. Since there is little or no story development, stop each demonstration after a few moments if the students do not bring the activity to a natural close.

EVALUATE

Student evaluation: Ask the students, "What was the effect of using an animal as a basis for characterization? Was it easy or difficult to keep in mind all the elements of characterization as you performed your scene? Why? How did interacting with the other characters help you in your characterization?"

Teacher observation: Have the students become more aware of the complexities of characterization? Were they able to visualize an animal and transform it into a character? Did the interactions in the scenes reveal the characters?

CONNECTIONS   *Social Studies:* Have each student choose a world leader to research for a character study. Then have students present their leaders to the class, giving a thumbnail sketch of the personality, temperament, ideals, and philosophy of the person. Suggest that students act out the person they have chosen, using what they have learned to make the portrayal authentic.

RESOURCES   Crawford, Jerry L. *Acting: In Person and In Style.* William C. Brown Publishers, 1983.

Oral Communication: Readers Theatre

COMPONENT   Aesthetic Perception

SUBJECT   Readers Theatre

OBJECTIVE   Students learn what readers theatre is, practice reading some readers theatre scripts, and create a simple readers theatre script from a familiar story.

MATERIALS   *Social Studies Readers Theatre for Children,* by Mildred K. Laughlin and Kathy H. Latrobe; *Now Presenting: Classic Tales for Readers Theatre,* by Merrily P. Hansen; *Presenting Reader's Theatre,* by Caroline Feller Bauer

Note: This lesson may be done in two parts, if desired, with a break between the Explore and Develop sections.

WARM UP   Ask the students if any of them has ever read a story to a child with as much expression as possible, using different voices for different characters. Ask too, if students have had stories read to them that way. What made both experiences special? Could students imagine scenes more clearly, both as listeners and readers, when extra expression was put into the reading?

Introduce *readers theatre* as "a presentation by two or more people who read aloud a story in play form, interpreting the literary work in as lively a way as possible, without actually acting it out." Having each character's dialogue read by a different person helps the listener to form a picture of each character in his or her mind's eye and respond emotionally to what is read.

Ask the students what they think might be the differences between readers theatre and traditional theatre techniques. (Readers theatre uses voice and body tension for drama, rather than movement; the focus is on vocal interpretation; no costumes, make-up, scenery, or stage movement are used. Lines do not need to be memorized, but they are not improvised.)

Tell the students that performing readers theatre and concentrating on voice projection, appropriate inflection, diction, and accurate pronunciation of words can help sharpen their communication skills.

EXPLORE

Use selected scripts from the Resources to involve the students in stories adapted for readers theatre. Examples include: "The Secret Garden," by Frances Hodgson Burnett, "Alice's Adventures in Wonderland," by Lewis Carroll, and "The Nightingale," a Chinese folk tale adapted by Merrily P. Hansen.

Allow the students to choose speaking parts and read each script. Remind the students of the importance of proper vocal and breathing techniques (Lessons 3 and 4) as they are reading.

Readers' positions are also important in readers theatre. Readers may be standing or seated on stools or chairs. For some scripts, positioning the leading character in the center on a stool will indicate importance.

Remind students that they should focus on the portrayal of their character and that character's emotion. Diction, articulation, and voice projection are important, but for now have students concentrate on interpreting the story and conveying meaning. Once the students have completed the reading, comment on their effectiveness in conveying the idea of the story to the audience.

Give other students the opportunity to read the same script or another one in front of an audience. After they feel comfortable with the meaning of the story and the emotion of the characters, ask students to concentrate on good diction, articulation, and voice projection so that the audience will understand all the words. After several rehearsals, if desired, students could tape their readings for others to listen to.

DEVELOP

Identify with the students some of the literature they have enjoyed. From the stories they mention, choose a work that has conversation, either written or implied, to adapt for readers theatre. The entire work need not be adapted, but choose a section that demonstrates a particularly interesting part of the story, or several sections that can be edited, combined, or adapted to make a unified whole.

As a class, work together to create a simple script that can be read aloud using the readers theatre techniques. *Now Presenting: Classic Tales for Readers Theatre* outlines the steps to follow in adapting a story for readers theatre. For beginners, it may be easiest to read aloud a simple scene that involves both conversation and description. The description is read by a narrator, with the actors reading the characters' dialogue.

If the story is to be adapted, write the lines on a chart or on the board as the script is created. Then assign a student to each part, and have the group read the script aloud. Ask, "What needs cutting, expanding, or clarifying in the script?" Adjust the script and have students read it again. The readers should remember to stress characterization and emotional content as they read. Continue the reading and adapting process until a satisfactory script is created.

EVALUATE   *Student evaluation:* Ask the students, "What is readers theatre? What challenges are presented in trying to convey character and emotion through voice alone? What helps to convey the character? What helps to convey emotion?"

Teacher observation: Do the students understand the differences between readers theatre and traditional theatre? Were they able to use their voices alone to convey character and emotion? What advantages do you see in using readers theatre in the classroom?

CONNECTIONS   *Language Arts:* Divide the class into groups. Have each group decide on a novel to read. When the reading is complete, have the group members write a joint book report in script form and then present the characters, setting, and plot of the book, along with their individual recommendations, using the techniques of readers theatre.

RESOURCES   Bauer, Caroline Feller. *Presenting Reader's Theatre.* H.W. Wilson Company, 1987.

Hansen, Merrily P. *Now Presenting: Classic Tales for Readers Theatre.* (contains "The Nightingale") Addison-Wesley Publishing Company, 1992.

Laughlin, Mildred K., and Kathy H. Latrobe. *Social Studies Readers Theatre for Children.* Libraries Unlimited, Inc., 1991.

Playing Theatre Games

COMPONENT   Creative Expression

SUBJECT   Improvisation/Pantomime

OBJECTIVE   Students practice both nonverbal and verbal communication skills by learning and playing theatre games.

MATERIALS   None required

WARM UP   Review the term *improvisation* ("using movement and speech to create a character or object without a planned script"). Point out to the students that they have had many opportunities to improvise scenes. Ask the class, "Of all the improvisations you have done, which ones do you remember most vividly? Was it because they were very enjoyable, or because they were very difficult? What made them enjoyable (or difficult)?"

Tell students that they are going to participate in some new improvisational drama activities, called "theatre games." Describe theatre games as improvisational group activities with rules agreed upon by the group. Theatre games are frequently used by actors for warm up, motivation, and exploration of dramatic subtext. (*Subtext* is "the meaning underlying dialogue and stage directions in a dramatic script.") Ask students to describe any activities they have done in the past that fit the definition of theatre games. Why do those activities qualify as theatre games?

EXPLORE   Explain to students that before they play the theatre games they are going to practice some of the skills needed in the games. Review with the students *pantomime* (nonverbal communication), and ask for volunteers to pantomime various activities, such as climbing a mountain, fishing, bouncing a ball, and playing a video game. Remind students to make their actions specific and complete. Evaluate with the class how the actions were conveyed.

Then ask for two volunteers to act out (with dialogue) a two-character scene. The scene could be two people watching a ball game, cheering for opposite teams; two people going to a movie, each wanting to see a different one; a parent trying to get a child who wants to stay up to go to bed; and so on. Allow the pair a short time to organize their thoughts.

Remind them to include *who, what,* and *where* in their scene. Evaluate the scene with the class.

DEVELOP   Tell the students that they are going to learn how to play two theatre games—Imaginary Rooms and Freeze Tag. Then tell them the rules, and play each game.

Imaginary Rooms: This game requires the players to pay attention to detail as they use nonverbal communication to convey a specific action. The observers must also concentrate, so that they can re-create what they observe.

Have the class sit on the floor or in chairs. One student enters an open space and imagines being in a specific room—a bedroom, dining room, school room, hospital room, and so on. The student is to mime one activity only and then leave the open space and sit down.

A second student enters that same space. He or she begins in the exact position of the first actor, mimes the same action, and adds one specific action of his or her own. If the room is known, the second student might mime an action appropriate for that room. If the specific room is not obvious, the second student may add an action in a room that he or she imagines. Then the second student leaves the space and sits down.

A third student enters the same space, mimes the actions of the two preceding students, and adds another. The game continues until one person leaves out an action or mixes up the sequence. Tell the observers to signal when an action has been left out. At that point, stop the game, identify the missing action, discuss what room it might have been, and question all the players to see what rooms and actions they had in mind.

Play the game again with other students. Give students the challenge of adding on as many players as possible without making a mistake.

Freeze Tag: Have two students begin to improvise a given scene, perhaps one of those mentioned in Explore. After a short period of time, say, "Freeze." Point to another student from the class to come forward and take the place of one of the players in the scene. The third student then continues the game by changing the scene to a completely different activity. The person left onstage must adjust to the new story line of the incoming player.

For example, two students in a scene might be discussing whether to go to the movies or to the skating rink. After the story line is established and the two students are well into their discussion, say, "Freeze," and point to a student from the class. The third student might change the scene to a discussion between a principal and student about a fight that occurred on the school grounds. If the incoming student assumed the role of the principal, the other student would become the student in the school. The players continue to improvise the scene until they hear "Freeze," and then the next student changes the scene again. Continue until all the students have had an opportunity to participate.

EVALUATE *Student evaluation:* Ask the students, "Were you able to concentrate on the details pantomimed by others? Why or why not? Were you able to switch roles in the middle of an improvisation? Why or why not? How could each of these games help actors practice their communication skills?"

Teacher evaluation: Were the students able to pantomime an action specifically and completely? How well were students able to switch roles in the middle of a scene? How did the students show an understanding of the purpose of improvisation in the games?

CONNECTIONS *Physical Education:* On the playground, have students run, jump, hop, and skip within a confined area. When you blow your whistle, they are to freeze. Select one "statue" and describe its position or what it looks like to you. Then let students move, and when you blow your whistle again, have the student you selected go up to another statue and describe it. Continue the game as long as desired.

SPECIAL NEEDS Ask a classmate to describe to the severely visually impaired student the pantomime portions of the improvisations.

RESOURCES Spolin, Viola. *Improvisation for the Theatre: A Handbook of Teaching and Directing Techniques.* Northwestern University Press, 1963.

LESSON TWENTY

Assuming Responsibility in the Theatre

COMPONENT   Aesthetic Valuing

SUBJECT   Trust/Responsibility

OBJECTIVE   Students go through exercises that show the value of responsibility and trust.

MATERIALS   Several scarves or bandanas for blindfolds; classroom chairs; enough slips of paper for every student in the class—a few slips say "Wreck your group's drama by not doing your part, or by doing it badly," but most slips say "Remember to be specific and complete in your actions." (see Develop)

WARM UP   Ask the students for some examples of occasions in which they must be totally dependent on, or trust someone else. Examples might be as a passenger in an automobile, bus, or plane; being operated on in a hospital; or, as a baby, getting food and care from an adult.

Ask the students for some examples of situations in which everyone involved depends on each other, and each person must carry out a certain task so that the whole job gets done. Answers might include any kind of team sports or such activities as construction jobs, and of course, theatre. Ask the students, "How do trust and interdependence relate to drama/theatre? What do trust and interdependence mean in terms of personal responsibility?"

EXPLORE   Tell the students they are going to repeat an earlier trust exercise. Set up a number of chairs at random in an open space to create a maze. Divide the class into pairs, and name one student in each pair A and one student B. Do this exercise with only three or four pairs at a time.

Have students A stand on one side of the room, blindfolded. Students B stand on the other side of the room and verbally direct the partners through the chairs so that the blindfolded students do not bump into the chairs, but come safely to the other side. Then let the next group of pairs carry out the activity.

When all the A students have gone through the maze of chairs, have the students in each pair exchange places, and allow the B students to be blindfolded and go through the maze.

Ask the students, "What did it feel like to have to depend completely on your partner? What did it feel like to be responsible for the well-being of someone else?"

DEVELOP   Divide the class into small groups. Tell each group to improvise a scene in which they are building something: Noah's ark, a suspension bridge, a giant's castle, a delicate house of cards, a space shuttle, and so on. Each group is to plan carefully the sequence of events so that everyone's participation is necessary to the construction. Each person must have some very necessary task to perform. For example, if a throne is being built, perhaps one person is responsible for each leg of the chair.

As the groups are planning their dramatizations, walk around the room and give each student a slip of paper. Tell the students to read what is on the paper, then put it in their pockets without telling anyone what it says, but follow the directions on the paper during their group's presentation. The slip of paper will say, "Remember to be specific and complete in your actions," for all the students except one member of each group. That person's slip of paper will say, "Wreck your group's drama by not doing your part, or by doing it badly."

Each group will develop its dramatization as usual, but when the presentation is made, one student in each group will not do his or her job correctly. The student may choose not to do it, do it incorrectly, bring the wrong part of the construction material, take something away, take someone else's lines, or use another device to disrupt the flow of the dramatization.

Let the dramatization continue for a moment to see how the other students accommodate to the disruption. Then stop the dramatization. Ask the students what effect the failure of one student's responsibility had on the improvisation. How did the group compensate? Was it easy, hard, or impossible to finish the dramatization when one person failed in his or her responsibility? (Remind the class that the students who failed in their responsibility were only carrying out their part of an experiment.)

EVALUATE   *Student evaluation:* Ask the students, "How do trust and responsibility in the theatre relate to each other? How did you react when someone did not perform her or his task? Why are trust and responsibility important to the actors and the technical personnel in theatre? How are trust and responsibility important in your everyday lives?"

Teacher observation: Were the students willing to trust each other? Why or why not? How did students behave when one person ruined the group's dramatization? Did students understand how this experience relates to drama/theatre?

CONNECTIONS   *Social Studies:* Have students find out about safety policies in the school. You may wish to have the principal and/or a firefighter, police officer, or paramedic speak to the class. Discuss the responsibility involved in knowing and following school safety measures or emergency procedures to the letter.

SPECIAL NEEDS   This lesson provides a good opportunity for all students to benefit from the life experiences of special needs students as they relate their own feelings about dependence on others.

RESOURCES   Chekhov, Michael. *To the Actor.* Harper & Row Publishers, Inc., 1985.

Crawford, Jerry L. *Acting: In Person and In Style.* William C. Brown Publishers, 1980.

Spolin, Viola. *Improvisation for the Theatre: A Handbook of Teaching and Directing Techniques.* Northwestern University Press, 1963.

Way, Brian. *Development Through Drama.* Humanities Press, 1967.

Changing an Actor's Face

COMPONENT	Creative Expression
SUBJECT	Stage Make-Up
OBJECTIVE	Students observe a make-up demonstration to understand the purposes for make-up and learn how facial appearances are changed by make-up.
MATERIALS	Assorted new, unused make-up items, such as eyeliner, eyebrow pencil, rouge, lip color, cleansing cream, and facial tissues; photograph or picture of a face of a 20- to 40-year-old adult; photograph or picture of an elderly person

Note: If possible, invite a theatrical make-up artist into the classroom to do a demonstration for the students. This person could be a make-up specialist or a performer.

Extreme caution must be taken in using make-up with the students. Be sure to check for allergies or other problems which might prohibit the use of make-up on any of your students. All materials must be new and unused to prevent the spread of skin diseases.

WARM UP
Ask the students, "How many of you put on make-up for Halloween?" Have students describe how they used make-up. Ask the students who respond, "Why did you put on make-up?" Answers might include, "To look scary"; "To look like somebody or something else"; or "To change the way I look." Explain that changing a person's looks is one of the main reasons for wearing make-up in the theatre. Ask, "Can you think of any other reasons, besides the ones we have talked about, for an actor to wear make-up?" List the answers on the board. Students might say that make-up makes people look more attractive, or that audiences can see faces more clearly with make-up, or that make-up makes an actor feel more like a particular character.

EXPLORE
Hold up a photograph or a picture of an adult face. Ask a student in the back of the room to describe in as much detail as possible what she or he sees. Ask a student in the center of the room to add details to the first

description. Then ask someone close to the picture to add further detail. Point out to students that the closer one is to a face, the more detail one can see. Ask the students how this information might be important to an actor. Then point out that theatrical lighting tends to wash out or bleach color from the face, so that strong colors of make-up need to be used.

Show a photograph or picture of an elderly person. Ask, "What makes this face different from a young person's face?" Answers could include wrinkles, sagging muscles, faded skin color, and gray eyebrows or beard. Ask, "How do you think an actor could make his or her face look older?" The answers will probably be, "By painting lines on his or her face," and "By making the actor's eyebrows, beard, and/or mustache gray."

Explain to the students that shadow colors (darker tones of make-up) are used on the face to give the illusion of hollows, and lighter tones of make-up are used to make sections of the face stand out. With the proper use of dark and light make-up, the actor can appear to have sagging muscles, sunken eyes, and puffy or sunken flesh.

Have students refer to the list on the board, and summarize the purposes of stage make-up: to put back into the face (and sometimes hands and body) the elements which are erased or diminished by lights and distance, and to aid in characterization.

DEVELOP

If a make-up artist is available to come to the classroom, ask the artist to demonstrate on him- or herself a straight stage make-up. Define *straight make-up* as "make-up to show the actor as he or she normally appears; to define the features more clearly." If the visiting artist is an actor, ask him or her to show a make-up kit and its contents to the students, and describe the use or purpose of each item. Encourage the students to ask questions pertaining to the uses of make-up.

If a make-up artist is not available, bring to class new, unused items such as an eyebrow pencil or eyeliner, eyeshadow, lip color, and materials for removing it, such as cleansing cream and facial tissues. Demonstrate on only one student (for health purposes) the art of applying stage make-up.

Create a straight make-up, but apply the colors more heavily for stage use. With children, only the very lightest of make-up is used: eyebrow pencil to accent the eyebrows if necessary, a line across the eyelid to emphasize the eyes, perhaps a bit of eyeshadow, a touch of rouge if necessary, and a light application of lip color. (Note that black make-up or eyeliner is used only for special effects, not for normal, or straight make-up.)

After demonstrating the straight make-up, you might use a black eyeliner to make a spot on the end of the student's nose, and draw whiskers across the cheeks in imitation of a cat!

Suggest to the students that if they wish to try applying stage make-up to themselves, they should do so at home, with the parent's or guardian's permission.

EVALUATE   *Student evaluation:* Ask the students, "What is the purpose of stage make-up? How can stage make-up aid in characterization? What are some of the ways an actor can apply make-up to change his or her appearance?"

Teacher observation: Did the students understand the use of light and shadow in the application of make-up? Do they understand how make-up aids characterization? Did the students ask the visiting artist appropriate questions?

CONNECTIONS   *Art:* Have students use what they have learned about make-up application techniques to make "photo" albums containing drawings that highlight their past, present, and future lives. They should draw pictures of themselves from the time that they were born up to the present day. Then they should imagine themselves as they mature and draw pictures of themselves at 20, 40, and 60 years old.

SPECIAL NEEDS   A severely visually impaired student may understand the application of stage make-up if it is applied first to him or her. (You will need extra unused make-up to do this.) Allow the student to touch facial areas lightly with a few fingers to sense the texture and the amount and extent of its use.

RESOURCES   Buchman, Herman. *Stage Makeup.* Watson-Guptill, 1989.

Corson, Richard. *Stage Makeup* (7th ed.). Prentice Hall, 1986.

The Role of the Director

COMPONENT   Aesthetic Valuing

SUBJECT   Professional Theatre

OBJECTIVE   Students learn more about the role of the director in drama/theatre, and apply the director's tasks to a particular script.

MATERIALS   A copy for each student of "When the Hare Brought the Sun," pages 176–8 (students should have this in their notebooks from Lesson 5); videotape from the *Arts Abound Series: The Director,* by GPN

Note: You may want to divide this lesson into two parts, breaking it after Explore. If possible, arrange for a theatre director to visit the classroom.

WARM UP   Point out to students that in their improvisations they usually work together with other students, and each member of the group has equal responsibility for the presentation. Ask the students whether they have noticed that sometimes when they work in groups, one person takes charge, assuming a leadership role and making decisions. Elicit from students their reactions to such a situation. What are the advantages and disadvantages of having a leader? (An advantage would be that decisions and actions can be made and carried out faster; a disadvantage might be that the rest of the group doesn't feel involved or doesn't agree with decisions made.)

Review the role of the director in drama/theatre. Tell the students that the director brings all the technical and artistic elements together with the movement of the actors to tell the story the playwright intended.

Ask the students, "What are the parts of a theatre production that the director must be concerned with?" (The technical and artistic elements include lights, scenery, props, sets, and costumes. The director advises the actors on movement, voice projection, and interpretation of the script. The director makes sure everybody in a scene can be viewed by the audience, and suggests to the actors how the plot, characters, or actions can be communicated more clearly.)

Tell students that the director remains "outside" the production, trying to maintain an objective view of the dramatic production as a whole. The director must constantly evaluate and adjust his or her own decisions, so that the best combination of all the elements can be achieved.

Point out to the students that theatre is a group art; it requires the cooperation and collaboration of many people; but ultimately one person must have the responsibility for a performance. The director has this responsibility.

EXPLORE

Make sure that each student has a copy of "When the Hare Brought the Sun" (Lesson 5), and review it with them. Ask, "What would be a director's tasks for this drama?" Point out that the director must tell the actors to move on the stage in a way that would be appropriate to the mood and theme of the story, as well as to show the action. The director must also make certain that all the action is visible to the audience. If special effects with lights, scenery, props, sets, or costumes are to be used, the director plans for those.

Allow time for the students to study the script of "When the Hare Brought the Sun," and to draw on the script a sketch or diagram of the set, indicating where the actors stand and their movement patterns, as well as any significant gestures. Have students refer to their notebooks for the diagram of stage areas, and remind them of the directions for stage movement from Lesson 5.

Divide the class into groups. Have the students in each group compare their directions and discuss the similarities and differences in the decisions that each person made about the scene. Ask the students in each group to come to a general consensus about which plan or combination of plans would work best for that scene.

DEVELOP

Invite into the classroom a community theatre director to discuss his or her job in the theatre. Encourage the students to ask questions of the visiting director, and as a class, share the different groups' plans for the story of "When the Hare Brought the Sun." If a visiting director is not available, show the students the videotape of *The Director* from the *Arts Abound Series,* that describes what a director does in the theatre. Discuss it with the class, and let any of the groups adjust their plans for stage direction if they wish.

Have each group choose a director and then give its presentation of "When the Hare Brought the Sun," using the group's consensus plan for stage direction. Remind the students that although they collaborated on stage directions, they must ultimately do as the director tells them. Ask each director to explain how he or she made decisions.

EVALUATE

Student evaluation: As a class, discuss the students' perceptions about being a director. Which of the director's tasks did students find enjoyable, and why? Which tasks didn't they enjoy, and why not? What tasks were they unable to perform because of classroom limitations? For the students who were directed, how did having a director differ from developing a scene as an improvisation?

Teacher observation: Were the students able to understand the responsibilities and tasks of the director? Did the visiting director or videotape generate perceptive questions from the students? Did some students indicate interest in the role of director for themselves?

CONNECTIONS

Social Studies: Divide the class into groups. Have each group choose a news article to use as the basis for a skit. One person in the group should be the director, helping students interpret the tone of the article and act out the facts as objectively as possible. Have groups perform their skits and discuss them with the rest of the class.

RESOURCES

Arts Abound Series: The Director. Fifteen-minute videotape by Great Plains National, affiliated with the University of Nebraska-Lincoln, 1985.

Carra, Lawrence. *Controls in Play Directing.* Vantage Press, 1985.

Ross, Beverly B., and Jean P. Durgin. *Junior Broadway: How to Produce Musicals with Children 9-13.* McFarland and Company, 1983.

Identifying Technical Elements in a Drama

COMPONENT   Aesthetic Valuing

SUBJECT   Technical Theatre/Staffing

OBJECTIVE   Students learn or review the tasks of technical theatre personnel and plan the technical elements for a specific dramatic production.

MATERIALS   One copy for each student of the list of technical theatre staff on page 233; a script of the chosen play for each student

Note: This begins a series of lessons that concludes with the formal theatrical performance in Lesson 30. These lessons may take more than one classroom period. They do not necessarily follow the established Warm Up—Explore—Develop format, but rather explain a portion of the preparation for performance that will be ongoing for a few weeks. Choose a play from one of the collections listed in the Resources section or use another of your own choice for students to perform.

WARM UP   Give each student a copy of the list of technical personnel who are needed to staff a professional theatre (page 233), and review their tasks. Explain to students that they will be performing a play for an audience. Tell them the name of the play, and point out that as they prepare for a dramatic production, they will all be doing some of these technical theatre jobs.

EXPLORE   Ask the students to comment on the collaborative nature of theatre, or the interrelation of different elements of drama/theatre discipline. How do students think the various people needed for a production interact? (Have students refer to their lists, and think of the different tasks involved with the sets, lights, costumes, make-up, props, sound, and so on.) What are the individual responsibilities for a performance?

Provide each student with a copy of the play script that you have chosen, and discuss the story. Read the script as a class; identify from the list on page 233 the technical elements that will be needed for the production.

Have students check these elements off on their lists and keep the script in their notebooks to use for the remaining lessons.

DEVELOP Ask for volunteers to be part of each of the technical crews (the stage crew, the light crew, and so on) needed for the production. Make sure that each student in the class joins one of the technical groups. (By the time all the parts have been assigned, some students may be doing double duty, perhaps as performers and technical crew, or perhaps two different technical crew jobs.) Then have the students work together in their crews to identify and record the tasks that their group will need to do for the production of their play.

You may need to be the actual director of the production, but assign one, or possibly two or three students to be the student director(s), who will work closely with you and do as much of the directing as they are capable of doing. The director(s) should meet with all the crews and coordinate their work with the performers' work. If there will be many technical elements in the production, it may be necessary to have a technical director as well as a play director.

Identify a style (realistic, surrealistic, fantastical, etc.) as a starting point for the students.

Have each group review the technical elements identified in Explore, and then make a list of the materials that will be necessary for their particular crew to collect, make, borrow, or purchase. Have each group report the plan for its technical area to the class.

EVALUATE *Student evaluation:* As a class, discuss the personal responsibilities of belonging to a production crew. How does individual responsibility relate to the successful production of a play? How do the crews interrelate? What special abilities must a crew member possess?

Teacher observation: Were the students able to share and exchange ideas about production elements for the scenario? Were they able to identify the technical elements that will be needed in the production? Are they aware of individual responsibility as well as crew responsibility in producing a play?

CONNECTIONS *Social Studies:* Divide the class into four groups: a construction crew, a property crew, a wardrobe crew, and a paint crew. Have each crew describe and record what they will need to depict a scene from your state history. You designate the scene and provide information, but crews research what is needed to make their work authentic.

RESOURCES   Bellville, Cheryl W. *Theater Magic: Behind the Scenes at a Children's Theater.* Carolrhoda Books, 1986.

Boiko, Claire. *Children's Plays for Creative Actors.* Plays, Inc., 1985.

Harris, Aurand. (Coleman Jennings, ed.) *Six Plays for Children.* University of Texas Press, 1986.

Kamerman, Sylvia, ed. *Dramatized Folk Tales of the World.* Plays, Inc., 1971. (This book is out of print, but you may be able to find it in your library.)

_____. *Plays from Favorite Folktales.* Plays, Inc., 1987.

Thane, Adele. *Plays from Famous Stories and Fairy Tales.* Plays, Inc., 1983.

Ward, Winifred. *Stories to Dramatize.* Anchorage Press.

Technical Theatre Staff

Technical director   The person responsible for the coordination of all the technical elements in a theatrical production—lights, sets, sound, make-up, properties, and so on.

Construction crew   Those individuals who create the scenery/ sets for a given production. Scenery might include curtains, flats (pieces of scenery built on a flat frame), drops (pieces of scenery that are raised and lowered from above), and/or platforms.

Paint crew   The persons responsible for painting the scenery/ sets, and any other part of the stage area.

Stage crew   Those who are responsible for moving scenery or set pieces during the performance.

Property crew   Those persons responsible for personal properties (props that are carried on the actor's person and are used only by that actor), and stage properties (props that usually remain on the stage area, and that could be used by more than one actor).

Wardrobe crew   Those people responsible for making sure that the actors have the correct costumes, and who help with costume changes during the performance.

Make-up crew   Those persons who aid the actors, if necessary, in the use of cosmetics to change or emphasize facial features or other exposed surfaces of the body.

Lighting crew   Those persons responsible for the illumination of the stage by means of artificial lights, and who are also responsible for adjusting or changing the lights during a performance as necessary.

Sound crew   Those persons who are responsible for any music and actual or simulated sounds during the production.

COPYRIGHT © DALE SEYMOUR PUBLICATIONS

GRADE 6

Technical Script Analysis

COMPONENT   Aesthetic Valuing

SUBJECT   Technical Theatre/Scripts

OBJECTIVE   Students analyze the script for their dramatic presentation, identifying points in the production that will require the addition of a technical element.

MATERIALS   One copy per student of the production script (given out in Lesson 23)

Note: The scene used as a model in this lesson is from "In Search of the Theatre Family," a script developed by the author with fourth, fifth, and sixth grade students.

You will probably want to do this lesson in two sessions: one session for the groups to work separately on their own technical areas, and the other session to discuss and coordinate plans as a class.

WARM UP   Ask the director(s) to assemble all the technical crews established in Lesson 23 for a script analysis. Tell the students that a script analysis consists of identifying all the specific occurrences in the production that will need technical assistance. For example, when will the lights have to come on and go off? Will the furniture and/or set pieces have to be moved from one place on the stage to another, or removed completely from the stage area? Where do props for the actors have to be placed on the set so that they are in the right places for the action of the story?

The director(s) should have a script, and should indicate on that script, with the technical crews, what responsibility each crew will have. Introduce the word *cue* (the words or actions that occur immediately before something should be said or done in the play that alert the crew members to perform the task). The cue for the light crew is a word or action before the lights are turned on or off; for the stage crew, before a set piece is moved or the curtain pulled; and so on. As students make their analysis, have each technical crew identify all of its cues.

EXPLORE   Give students time to reread silently the script of the play that will be presented and to make notes for their crew's technical needs on their own copies of the script. Then have students meet with their groups to discuss the needs. As the crew members study the script, the director should describe the action so that the crews can visualize what needs to be done.

If a scripted play from theatre literature is used, suggestions for the technical needs will be written, usually in italics, to indicate what should be happening. These suggestions should be discussed and modified as appropriate.

Most of the work the technical crews are responsible for is done ahead of time, so that their work during the play does not interrupt the action. Decisions such as whether to use a microphone or music during the performance must be made ahead of time as well.

A microphone, or "mike," may not be necessary, if the presentation is to be made in a small room, or a mike might not be available. If one is used, however, the sound crew must know where the mike or mikes are going to be placed during the production. The sound crew must also know whether the mike is to be removed at any time, or will stay on the set during the entire production.

If music is to be used, the cue for the sound crew to begin the music must be established, as well as the volume and duration of the music. Ask the sound crew questions such as, "Does the music play throughout the scene; does it begin the scene, gradually fade away and go out completely; or does it play at the same level for the duration of the scene? What are the actors' cues for coming onstage? Will the music be the actors' cue, or will the students coming onstage be the music cue?"

The set crew will need to decide what set pieces, and/or backdrops, to construct for their setting. They will need to note any scene changes, and which pieces must be removed or added at particular times.

Be sure that each crew has considered the issues pertaining to its responsibilities, and encourage each group to make its own decisions.

The following script, "Icarus," is simply a model for you to see how to identify some of the technical elements that need to be addressed. Students will, of course, be working with the script for their own production. The text in brackets highlights the technical decisions that students must make.

Icarus

[Ahead of time, the prop crew will need to place feathers around the stage area where Icarus can pick them up; finished wings will also need to be placed out of sight of the audience where Daedalus can get them and attach them to himself and his son.

The lighting crew will need to set up a light system to be used at the beginning, and then mark places in the script where it is to be changed.

There may be background music as the students come onstage.

Spot lights could be put on the actor/speakers.]

STUDENT SPEAKER: It is to Athens at its height during the fifth century B.C. that we owe the development of the theatre as we enjoy it today. Drama then was performed not for private amusement, but for great public festivals. It was as if theatre was performed for the Greek gods' enjoyment.

STUDENT SPEAKER: Tragic dramatists did not invent stories and characters. Their dramas were based on myths and legends familiar to everyone. The stories were often about a proud person who thought that he or she controlled events. But the audience knew what would happen to the character, and also knew that it would happen in spite of what the character did. The story of Icarus could have been one of the myths performed.

[light entire stage area?]

CHARACTERS: Daedalus, Icarus, prisoners

[Costumers plan what the characters will wear.]

STUDENT SPEAKER: Daedalus (DED-a-lus) and his son Icarus (ICK-a-rus) find themselves prisoners on an island.

STUDENT SPEAKER: King Minos kept his prisoners on this island so that they could not escape.

DAEDALUS: Minos may control the land and sea, but be does not control the air. I will try to escape that way.

STUDENT SPEAKER: Daedalus told Icarus to gather up all the feathers he could find. You see, thousands of gulls soared constantly over the island. Icarus soon collected a huge pile of feathers. Daedalus then melted some wax and made a skeleton in the shape of a bird's wing.

[Props: simulated fire, pot for wax?]

STUDENT SPEAKER: Icarus played on the beach while his father made the wings. When the wings were finished, Daedalus fastened them to his shoulders and found himself lifted upwards, where he hung poised in the air. Filled with excitement, he made another pair of wings for his son. They were smaller than his own, but strong and beautiful.

[Prop crew and costumers here will need to decide how to fashion the wings and fasten them on the characters, and also how to create the illusion of Daedalus flying. Will he have to be lifted in some way, or go up a ramp, or lie on a darkened platform as he is flying?]

STUDENT SPEAKER: Finally one day, Daedalus fastened the wings on himself and Icarus. Daedalus told his son to watch the movements of the birds, how they soared and glided overhead. Icarus watched and was soon sure that he could fly. He fluttered his wings, and soared up like the birds. Then Daedalus called his son to his side.

[Prop crew will need to have finished wings hidden from the audience, but available for Daedalus to put on.]

DAEDALUS: No human being has ever traveled through the air before, and I want you to listen carefully to my instructions. Keep at a moderate height, for if you fly too high, the heat from the sun will melt the wax that holds your wings together.

STUDENT SPEAKER: The father and son prepared themselves, and were off. Icarus, beating his wings in joy, felt the thrill of the cool wind on his face. [sound of wind?] He flew higher and higher up into the blue sky, until he reached the clouds. His father saw him and called out in alarm. Daedalus tried to fly up to his son, but his wings would not carry him higher.

STUDENT SPEAKER: The sun beat down on the wings and softened the wax, but Icarus did not notice. Then the feathers dropped off his wings and he began to sink. Icarus cried out to his father, but his voice was submerged in the blue water of the sea, which has forever after been called by his name. [sound of splash?]

[Have the class analyze in this manner the entire script that they are going to produce.]

DEVELOP

Reconvene the class and have each group share its technical plans. Discuss the decisions that have been made, and allow the other groups to offer suggestions. Some adjustment of plans may be necessary so that crews do not interfere with each other if they are carrying out their tasks at the same time. Then let students work in crews again to mark their scripts with any added directions.

Once the technical analysis of the script has been completed, the technical aspects of the production should be incorporated into each rehearsal with the actors, so that the crews can familiarize themselves with other aspects of the production, and adjust their work as needed. Each crew should discuss and continue to develop further the technical needs of the production, and assign specific responsibilities to each member of the crew. (Some members of each crew will become actors with parts that will prevent them from carrying out crew responsibilities; their tasks can be reassigned later.)

EVALUATE

Student evaluation: Ask the students, "Did you consider all of the technical elements that would be needed for the script? Did you find suggestions from the other crews helpful? How did you interact with the other technical crews?"

Teacher observation: What, specifically, have the students learned about collaboration in drama/theatre activities? Were the students able to identify the different areas of responsibility, and are they able to solve the technical problems creatively within the scope of the production?

CONNECTIONS

Music: Divide the class into groups. Have students discuss the kinds of music they would use to convey certain feelings or to support particular settings. Provide tapes of different styles of music for students to listen to, and then have them select music for scenes such as the following: (1) It was a dark and stormy night. (2) Once upon a time there were three little pigs. (3) Halt! Who goes there? (4) And they lived happily ever after.

SPECIAL NEEDS

If some actors are in wheelchairs, or have other special needs, the stage crew should include in its plans whatever physical accommodations need to be made to the set.

RESOURCES

Cohen, Robert, and John Harrop. *Creative Play Direction.* Prentice Hall, 1984.

Franklin, Miriam A., and James G. Dixon, III. *Rehearsal: The Principles and Practice of Acting for the Stage.* Prentice Hall, 1983.

Lord, William H. *Stagecraft One: Your Introduction to Backstage Work.* W.H. Lord, 1979.

Auditioning

COMPONENT	Creative Expression
SUBJECT	Auditioning
OBJECTIVE	Students understand the purpose of an audition, and try out for parts in their performance.
MATERIALS	Students' copies of the playscript for their production (given to them in Lesson 23)

WARM UP   Ask the students, "How many of you have been in a formal play?" Ask those who have, "How did you get your role? Were you just told you had the part, or did you try out?" Ask a student who tried out to tell what happened. What was it like? How did it feel? Write *audition* on the board, and define it as "a trial performance given by a musician, actor, speaker, or other performer so that the *auditioner,* or person who decides, can judge voice qualities, overall abilities, performance, and stage presence, and then select the best actor or performer for the part."

EXPLORE   Explain that those students who want to will have a chance to audition for acting parts for their play. Tell the students that at an audition, the actors either read from the script the part for which they are auditioning, or they are asked to give a cold reading. Define *cold reading* as "reading a selection of dramatic literature without having seen that material so as to have been able to study it ahead of time."

Tell students that they may have a chance to do a cold reading later, but for their play auditions, they will be able to study the script ahead of time, and choose the part for which they want to audition.

Ask the students, "What personal qualities do you think a performer should possess in order to do well at an audition?" Answers should include the ability to stand in front of a group of people with calmness and dignity, and to have confidence in what one is going to do. Ask the students, "How do these qualities help in an audition? What effect will they have on the persons watching?"

Tell students that at an audition, actors are usually asked to state their names and tell the auditioner something about themselves. The auditioner

GRADE 6

might ask, "What do you do in your spare time?" Give the students an opportunity to practice such an experience. Have each student walk up to the front of the class, look at everyone in the class, give his or her name, and in two or three sentences, tell the class something he or she likes to do. Then the student is to walk back to his or her seat.

DEVELOP

Tell students that the next part of auditioning is the reading. Explain to the students that at an audition it is important to do one's very best work, because the auditioner is trying to choose the best performer from among several. If you wish, you may have students do a cold reading before their actual audition. Use a variety of theatrical literature, and give each student a different selection to read. All of the books listed under Resources have suitable readings. Poetry anthologies are also good sources of material.

Point out to students that this cold reading is just to get experience before the actual audition. Have each student enter the stage area, state his or her name, and then read the selection from theatrical literature. Allow as many students as possible the opportunity to do a cold reading.

Then explain that all students who want to may audition for parts in the play, and that you will make the decisions about who will play each role. Students should choose a character from their script that they would like to play. They should select a passage from the script that has several lines by that character, and practice different ways to deliver them. They may memorize the lines if they wish. Take the time to let every student who wants a part try out for it.

Evaluate positive aspects of each audition with the class, but do not allow the process to become a popularity contest. Once the parts have been assigned, give the actors a date by which they must have their lines memorized. Include this date in the rehearsal schedule (see Lesson 26).

EVALUATE

Student evaluation: Ask students, "How did you feel about auditioning? Was the experience exciting and challenging? How was the cold reading different from reading lines from a familiar script? Did knowing that others were also trying out for parts help you to relax? What are some anxieties that an actor would probably have about auditioning?"

Teacher observation: Did students understand the purpose of auditions? Were they able to put their best efforts into the readings? Were they able to keep their composure as they read?

CONNECTIONS   *Social Studies:* Have each student write a short campaign speech for a city, county, or state office. Have students focus on important issues that voters are facing. Speeches must be legible! Distribute the completed speeches at random and have students take turns at the Cold Read Campaign podium. Discuss speech-writers' ideas as well as speakers' effectiveness.

SPECIAL NEEDS   Dyslexic students may have difficulty in reading. Help them memorize the parts for which they wish to audition, or let them do an improvisation after hearing other students read.

RESOURCES   Boiko, Claire. *Children's Plays for Creative Actors.* Plays, Inc., 1985.

Harris, Aurand. (Coleman Jennings, ed.) *Six Plays for Children.* University of Texas Press, 1986.

Kamerman, Sylvia, ed. *Children's Plays from Favorite Stories.* Plays, Inc., 1985.

_____. *Dramatized Folk Tales of the World.* Plays, Inc., 1971. (This book is out of print, but you may be able to find it in your library.)

_____. *Plays from Favorite Folk Tales.* Plays, Inc., 1987.

Koch, Kenneth, and Kate Farrell. *Talking to the Sun: An Illustrated Anthology of Poems for Young People.* Henry Holt and Company, 1985.

Stanislavski, Constantin. (Hermine I. Popper, ed., Elizabeth R. Hapgood, tr.) *Creating a Role.* Theatre Arts Books, 1961.

Ward, Winifred. *Stories to Dramatize.* Anchorage Press.

Scheduling and Holding Rehearsals

COMPONENT	Aesthetic Valuing
SUBJECT	Drama Rehearsals
OBJECTIVE	Students learn how to schedule rehearsals, learn what kinds of rehearsals are necessary to put on a production, and practice for their performance.
MATERIALS	Production scripts; one copy of the completed schedule of rehearsals for each student

WARM UP

Together with the class, make a rehearsal schedule. Decide how many rehearsals there will be before the performance, and what part and/or parts of the play will be rehearsed each time. Have the student director(s) take notes or write the schedule on the board. (Use the form on page 245.) Start scheduling backward from the date of performance so that you will have enough time to rehearse all the scenes several times. For example, you may want to rehearse every Wednesday from 10:00 to 11:00, or every Tuesday and Friday from 1:00 to 2:00. You also want to use three rehearsal days for each scene; there are ten scenes. Start at the bottom of the chart with the performance and fill in dates and times, working up:

Rehearsals 22-24	Scene eight	(date)	(time)
Review rehearsal	Scene four	(date)	(time)
Rehearsals 25-27	Scene nine	(date)	(time)
Rehearsals 28-30	Scene ten	(date)	(time)
Technical Rehearsal		(date)	(time)
Dress Rehearsal		(date)	(time)
Polishing Rehearsal		(date)	(time)
Performance		(date)	(time)

Continue this process with the entire play. You may need to increase the number of rehearsals as you approach the performance date. Leave some space to write these in later. Include in your rehearsal schedule some review rehearsals so that the actors do not forget what has been done some time before. Have one of the student directors make a neat copy of the schedule, using as many pages of the prepared form as necessary, and duplicate it so that students have the schedule for their notebooks.

Have the student director(s) establish a schedule for each crew to coordinate with the rehearsals for the actors. Actors who have small parts may stay with the technical crews to which they were assigned in Lesson 24, and work with those groups except when they are onstage. Post all the schedules in a prominent place.

EXPLORE

Begin every rehearsal with a general warming up of the body and voice. Have the actors do movement, breathing, and vocal exercises so that they feel relaxed and ready to rehearse.

As the actors begin to rehearse their lines, they should experiment with movements, gestures, and delivery of their lines. Once both director and actors are satisfied with the way a scene is played, the actors repeat the scene that way each time, and the ideas in the scene are built upon, adapted, and refined in other scenes.

Each rehearsal should focus on a small part of the production. If, for example, a particular rehearsal is for Scene One, have the actors practice Scene One many times, both physically and vocally, until they are comfortable with their movements, their lines, and their relationship with the other actors in the scene.

The student director(s) should take notes about how the actors play their scenes, describing each scene in detail, so that the crews can modify and refine the technical aspects if necessary. The technical crews should then experiment with their tasks just as the actors have done.

DEVELOP

Rehearse each scene until it runs smoothly. Stress to the students the importance of repetition in drama/theatre. Each time a scene is repeated, the students may discover something completely different about the character, the setting, or the relationship of one character to another.

Stress the importance of concentration and discipline during rehearsals. Point out to students that if in rehearsals actors giggle, talk onstage, and so on, such behavior will probably happen during a performance. (Giggling usually comes from a lack of concentration. Give the students specific stage actions to work on, to keep them from becoming nervous, self-conscious, or frightened of the audience.) Tell students that talking offstage is not permitted at any time. Even though their scene is over and they are offstage, actors should respect the rights of the other actors and remain quiet.

Absences from rehearsal are very frustrating to the other players. Make sure that all the players understand that they are to miss rehearsal only if they are sick. If one actor is absent, a complete rehearsal cannot take place.

Remind students of the date by which the actors should know their lines. Forgetting lines is a fear that all actors experience. Usually thorough rehearsing will lower the fear of forgetting one's lines, but you may want to assign one student the job of prompter. A prompter is a person who holds a script, follows the lines and the action, and is ready to whisper the lines if an actor forgets them.

EVALUATE

Student evaluation: As the performance date approaches, periodically review the rehearsal schedule with the class. Do extra rehearsals need to be held, or could some be eliminated? After each rehearsal, discuss the play's progress with the class. What worked and what didn't work, and why? In what ways could the scene be improved? What should the players and crews work on at the next rehearsal?

Teacher observation: Were the students able to concentrate on their tasks for the day's rehearsal? Why or why not? In what ways have the students put their previous drama activities to use for this experience? Are all the students participating fully in the rehearsal?

CONNECTIONS

Social Studies, Mathematics: Have students plan the timetable for creating a festive dinner with soup, salad, bread, main dish, dessert, and beverage. This could be a traditional Thanksgiving dinner, or food typical of another culture. Students will need to consult cookbooks to estimate preparation times and find out cooking times. Students could also shop for all of the items needed and add up the cost of a holiday feast.

SPECIAL NEEDS

It is important that the socially and emotionally impaired student respect the rules of the stage and have consideration for the other actors. Discipline and concentration must be stressed. Emotional problems may reveal themselves during rehearsals and performances. Take special steps to build the self-esteem of these students and to have them relax. The movement exercises before the rehearsal or show should help.

RESOURCES

Cohen, Robert, and John Harrop. *Creative Play Direction.* Prentice Hall, 1984.

Franklin, Miriam A., and James G. Dixon, III. *Rehearsal: The Principles and Practice of Acting for the Stage.* Prentice Hall, 1983.

Rehearsal Schedule

Rehearsal	Scene	Date	Time
_____	_____	_____	_____
_____	_____	_____	_____
_____	_____	_____	_____
_____	_____	_____	_____
_____	_____	_____	_____
_____	_____	_____	_____
_____	_____	_____	_____
_____	_____	_____	_____
_____	_____	_____	_____
_____	_____	_____	_____
_____	_____	_____	_____
_____	_____	_____	_____
_____	_____	_____	_____
_____	_____	_____	_____
_____	_____	_____	_____
_____	_____	_____	_____
_____	_____	_____	_____
_____	_____	_____	_____
_____	_____	_____	_____
_____	_____	_____	_____
_____	_____	_____	_____
_____	_____	_____	_____

COPYRIGHT © DALE SEYMOUR PUBLICATIONS

Holding a Technical Rehearsal

COMPONENT   Aesthetic Valuing

SUBJECT   Technical Rehearsal

OBJECTIVE   Students rehearse the technical aspects of a dramatic production to be performed.

MATERIALS   Production scripts; the sets and sound and lighting equipment necessary to stage the planned performance

WARM UP

Before the technical run-through, the crews should be familiar with the actors' various entrances and exits during the performance. As soon as rehearsals start, the technical crews should watch the actors rehearse as much as possible, marking on their scripts the points in the performance at which they will need to perform a particular task. Following each rehearsal, each crew should review their technical plans and adjust them if necessary.

A technical rehearsal is customarily held just prior to the dress rehearsal. Before the technical rehearsal begins, have all of the technical personnel meet together, with their scripts, to discuss each of their responsibilities and the sequence of the technical needs for the performance. Have the student director(s) be in charge of this meeting. Tell the students to write everything down so that there will be no question about what technical elements are needed, or each person's responsibilities.

If some students are doing double duty, perhaps as performers and technical crew, or two different technical crew jobs, the director should make sure that the timing of the performance allows those students to carry out both tasks.

EXPLORE

Students should start using props and sets as soon as they are available, in order to be comfortable and familiar with them. Costumes are usually reserved for use at later rehearsals in order to preserve their freshness. However, if there is a costume that is difficult to move in, the actor should have ample opportunity to become accustomed to it.

Try out any unusual make-up during technical rehearsal to see the effect of lights on it, and to have the actor(s) become comfortable with it.

By the time the technical rehearsal takes place, the set crew has built the set, using background materials and whatever large set pieces are necessary to the production. The stage crew will be ready to arrange the set pieces as needed during the performance. In many productions the set crew and the stage crew are the same persons. (If the stage crew will be seen by the audience, you may want them to wear dark colors so to attract as little attention as possible.)

The property crew has assembled all the personal props needed for the production. The costume crew has assembled the different costume pieces the actors will wear. The lighting crew has identified the different moods of the production and has made arrangements for the appropriate lights. You may be fortunate enough to have a stage area with sophisticated lights; if not, the lighting may consist of a series of blackouts.

Have the student director(s) go through a checklist to see that each of the crews is ready with its materials or equipment.

DEVELOP

After the preparation and discussion, hold a technical rehearsal. The actors will rehearse, too, but this rehearsal focuses primarily on the technical aspects of the production. Start at the beginning of the play and go through the entire script, incorporating all the technical aspects of the production. Tell the actors to rehearse as if they were giving a performance, so that the technical crews get a realistic idea of what the timing of their tasks will be.

Let the actors practice their entrances and exits with the lighting, so that they know exactly where to move to be in or out of the light.

During the technical rehearsal, if something goes completely wrong, such as an important prop is missing from the stage, or the lights change on the wrong cue, stop the rehearsal. Repeat the sequence of actions until the technical element works smoothly. Then continue.

EVALUATE

Student evaluation: Ask the students, "Has each technical crew fulfilled its responsibilities? Are actors and technical crews cooperating as much as possible? How could this relationship be improved? What are some of the courtesies needed for a successful collaboration among all concerned?"

Teacher observation: Do the students understand their roles in putting on a performance? Are they able to fulfill their responsibilities? Can students apply what they learned about collaboration in previous drama activities to the cooperation necessary for a technical rehearsal?

CONNECTIONS   *Science:* Give students in groups an opportunity to identify and explore the many support teams involved behind the scenes of an operating room, a manufacturing plant (automobile, airplane, clothing, furniture, and so on), a space shuttle mission, or the construction of a building. Suggest that groups make flowcharts showing the people needed and the sequence of the process they researched.

RESOURCES   Cohen, Robert, and John Harrop. *Creative Play Direction.* Prentice Hall, 1984.

Franklin, Miriam A., and James G. Dixon, III. *Rehearsal: The Principles and Practice of Acting for the Stage.* Prentice Hall, 1983.

Holding a Dress Rehearsal

COMPONENT	Aesthetic Valuing
SUBJECT	Dress Rehearsal
OBJECTIVE	Students practice their dramatic production exactly as it is to be performed, with all the elements in place, to ensure a smooth performance.
MATERIALS	All the costumes, props, scenery, and technical equipment necessary to stage the production

WARM UP Bring the entire cast and crew together for a general warm-up activity. Have a student director lead the actors in a warm up that includes both physical and vocal exercises. It will help relax the crews to take part in these warm ups, too. The technical director should review with the crews the different technical aspects of the production, and be sure all the equipment is ready.

EXPLORE Dress rehearsal is an exciting event. It is run exactly as if it were a performance. The actors should perform in make-up and costumes, and the lights, props, set pieces, and scenery should all be in place.

Before starting the rehearsal, have the actors come onstage in their costumes and make-up to check the effects of the lighting to be used. Evaluate the costumes and make-up, making sure all the actors are dressed correctly for the performance.

The actors should also handle all the props, furniture, or other items that may not have been present in previous rehearsals, to familiarize themselves with anything that is new.

Tell the actors to make sure that all of their personal and set props are in the proper places. If a costume change is necessary, the actor should check to make sure that the wardrobe crew has put the costume in its proper place.

Although you may have allowed the cast and crew members to sit in the audience and watch previous rehearsals, for the dress rehearsal all the students should be in place as they would be for a performance. Only the director(s) and any people you have invited to act as audience should be out in front.

GRADE 6

If possible, ask selected adults and students to act as audience during the dress rehearsal, so that actors and crews can get a realistic idea of how an audience will respond during the play. Prepare the students for audience reactions—laughter, coughing, applause, or just general movement in the audience. New noises will occur at times the actors have not expected. If the audience laughs during the performance, tell the students that they should wait slightly before continuing, so that the next line after the laughter can be heard. They should not come out of character, however, nor let the audience know that they are reacting to audience noise.

DEVELOP

Have the director give the cue ("Action!") to begin the rehearsal. As the rehearsal proceeds, the director(s) should sit in the middle of the auditorium or viewing area to evaluate the total effect of the performance. The director(s) should take notes so that they can discuss any needed adjustments with the actors and technical people immediately following the dress rehearsal.

Don't stop the dress rehearsal unless it is absolutely necessary. Both actors and crews should have an opportunity to feel the production as a whole, and to time accurately their tasks during the performance.

Following the dress rehearsal, have the cast and crews sit in the audience to hear the director's *notes,* or comments. It is important for everyone to be present for notes, and to understand that this process is part of the evaluation. Remind students of the purpose of evaluation—to polish, adapt, or change the work so as to improve the performance.

EVALUATE

Student evaluation: Ask students to reflect on their roles in this production. Did they carry out their individual responsibilities for this rehearsal? Could their part of the performance have been improved? If so, how? Did all the members of cast and crews work together as well as they could? Could any part of the collaboration have been improved? If so, what? Was the rehearsal useful in refining the performance?

Teacher observation: Compare the students' knowledge and behavior in drama/theatre activities at the beginning of the year to their present knowledge and behavior. Have you recognized any growth? If so, in what areas? If not, why not? What skills and social responsibilities have students learned through their drama experience?

CONNECTIONS   *Art:* Have students or groups of students use crayons, paint, chalk, pens, and other materials to make publicity posters announcing the upcoming play. Posters should include the name of the production, the director, and the principal players, along with the day, time, and place of the performance. Display the posters in the classroom or corridor.

SPECIAL NEEDS   It is important that the socially and emotionally impaired student respect the rules of the stage and have consideration for the other actors. Discipline and concentration must be stressed. Emotional problems may reveal themselves during rehearsals and performances. Take special steps to build the self-esteem of students with emotional problems, and to have them relax. The movement exercises before the rehearsal or show should help.

RESOURCES   *Center Stage: Creative Dramatics Supplement.* (contains a blank "Now Presenting" poster that students can fill in with information about their play) Available from Dale Seymour Publications.

Polishing the Performance

COMPONENT	Aesthetic Valuing
SUBJECT	"Touch-Up" Rehearsal
OBJECTIVE	Students identify and adjust only those aspects of the production that need improvement before the performance.
MATERIALS	Any costumes, props, scenery, and technical equipment involved in the parts of the production being rehearsed

WARM UP

For this "touch-up" rehearsal you may or may not want to bring the entire cast and crew together. Determine from the notes that you and the student director(s) took during the dress rehearsal which actors and technical personnel are needed for this rehearsal. If there is more than one director, perhaps each can work with a separate group.

EXPLORE

Focus on specific parts of the performance that need further practice or clarification. Some movements or speeches may need more work; some entrances and exits may be confusing for a group of actors; or perhaps some of the transitions between scenes are difficult. Announce which sections of the production will be rehearsed, and in what order. Assign those who are not rehearsing a task related to the production, such as writing invitations to parents or writing a notice for the school newsletter.

DEVELOP

Rehearse again, several times if necessary, those sections of the production that need further work or adjustment. Impress on the actors and crew that they must note on their scripts any changes that are being made in the performance.

The director should also take notes to share with other cast and crew members, especially if any of the changes affect the tasks of someone who is not present.

EVALUATE

Student evaluation: Have the class discuss the changes made during this polishing rehearsal. Review each change and ask the students involved to tell how it will affect entrances, exits, and/or action in the performance.

Ask students to tell the purpose of this rehearsal, and whether they think it served its purpose.

Teacher observation: Did the polishing rehearsal clear up problem areas? Could students concentrate on the changes that were needed?

CONNECTIONS   *Language Arts:* Have students work together to make programs for the performance. The program should list all of the players and behind-the-scenes crew members. It may also include a brief biographical sketch of the playwright and the principal players.

Celebration!
The Performance

COMPONENT	Creative Expression
SUBJECT	Formal Theatre/Performance
OBJECTIVE	Students present their performance to a live audience.
MATERIALS	All the costumes, props, scenery, and technical equipment needed to stage the production

WARM UP

The great day has arrived! The day of the performance should truly be one of celebration for the students. They have worked hard, and their production will be the visible result of their efforts. The students will be excited, and their excitement can be channeled into helping them to give their best performances.

Explain to students that the theatre term for the time actors and crew are to be at the theatre space before the performance is the *call*. Give the cast a call that allows enough time for them to do a physical and vocal warm up. Actors should have time to dress, to put on their make-up, and to sit quietly for a few moments to concentrate on portraying their characters for the performance.

The technical crew should arrive early enough to check all their equipment to make sure that it is in place and ready to use.

Encourage the cast and crew as they prepare for their performance. Tell them that a tradition in theatre is to say, "Break a leg!" before actors go on stage, because it is considered unlucky to wish actors good luck.

EXPLORE

Everyone suffers from nerves before a performance. A certain amount of tension can be used as energy to give a good performance, but excess tension can be relieved somewhat. Some actors pace back and forth, or take deep breaths. Others say their lines over and over. You may wish to have student actors work in pairs, practicing their lines and their breathing together, and checking each other's make-up and costume.

Tell students that they, as actors and crews, are the only people who know whether a line is forgotten. Lines are forgotten in professional performances, too, but the only way an audience knows is if the actor stops performing. If a line is forgotten, tell students to pause and try to remember the line, make up a line that makes sense in the play, or wait for a prompter to whisper the line, but never come out of character. Students are to keep the performance going, no matter what. An actor may miss his or her entrance, lights may not go up or down at the proper time, a prop may break or be missing, or another actor may forget a line, but they should never bring attention to what has gone wrong. The show has to continue.

DEVELOP

Introduce the students' performance to the audience as the culmination of a year's work in drama/theatre activities. Mention the efforts of all the support people as well as the actors. Emphasize the collaboration that goes on in drama/theatre, and give full credit to the creative endeavors of the student actors and technicians.

As students give their performance, be ready to assist if help is truly needed, but it will be best if students can work out on their own any problems that arise. A challenge and a solution to a problem are part of students' growing experience, and having to solve a problem quickly in the middle of a performance is a necessary part of and an invaluable skill in a drama/theatre experience. Students' self-confidence will increase if they solve problems themselves.

SIT BACK AND ENJOY THE PERFORMANCE!

Immediately following the performance, give liberal praise to all involved for their efforts.

EVALUATE

Student evaluation: A day or two following the production, evaluate the performance with the class. If another performance is to be given, use the evaluation to make any necessary adjustments. Ask the students, "What did you like about the performance? Did anything happen during the performance that hadn't happened in rehearsal? How was it handled? Is there anything about your own performance that you would change? Did actors and crew collaborate to make the production run smoothly?"

Teacher observation: Were students prepared as well as possible for their performance? If not, why not? Were the students able to use what they have learned about drama/theatre in their performances? What learning experiences did the students have in putting on this production?

CONNECTIONS   *Language Arts:* Have students write a critical review of the performance for a newspaper or magazine. Have them include the strengths and weaknesses of the production. Encourage students to be objective in their appraisal, and suggest that they interview audience members for reactions to the performance.

RESOURCES   Cohen, Robert, and John Harrop. *Creative Play Direction.* Prentice Hall, 1984.

Franklin, Miriam A., and James G. Dixon, III. *Rehearsal: The Principles and Practice of Acting for the Stage.* Prentice Hall, 1983.

Huberman, Caryn, and JoAnne Wetzel. *Onstage Backstage.* Carolrhoda Books, 1987.

Glossary

Abstraction   A quality expressed separately from the actual person or thing that possesses it.

Act   To perform or play a role.

Acting   Playing a part in a drama. Acting is a cumulative and culminating experience involving sensory awareness, rhythm and movement, pantomime, oral communication, improvisation and playmaking. Acting is usually geared toward an audience.

Actor   A person who plays a role in a drama.

Aesthetics, a sense of   A feeling for beauty, both external and internal.

Antagonist   The opponent of the main character in a story, who tries to keep the protagonist from reaching his or her goal.

Arena stage   A stage with the audience seated on all four sides of the playing area.

Art disciplines   Music, Drama/Theatre, Dance, and the Visual Arts.

Audience   At least one person, perhaps thousands, who observe a player or players as they engage in an action that imitates life.

Audition   A trial performance given by a musician, actor, speaker, or other performer so that people can judge voice qualities, overall abilities, performance, and stage presence, and then select the best actor or performer for the part.

Backdrop   A curtain hung at the back of a stage area; often painted to be part of the scenery.

Call   The assigned time for cast and crew to be at the theatre before the performance.

Celebration   A public and formal ceremony to mark special occasions.

Center stage   The area right in the middle of the stage.

Ceremony   An act or series of acts performed in some regular order.

Character   A person, animal, or entity in a story, scene, or play with specific distinguishing physical, mental, and emotional attributes. Character portrayal is likely to be more complex and unpredictable than role portrayal.

Characterization   Imitating the individual and distinctive traits of a character in a play to portray that person or being to an audience; creating a believable person for a story or dramatization by imitating the physical, social, and psychological behavior of that person.

Choral reading   Reading or reciting a poem or piece of dramatic literature in unison with others.

Chorus   Performers who sang, danced, and recited narrative as a group in ancient Greek drama.

Climax   The turning point of the action in a story or play, in which some kind of change takes place that will bring about resolution of the plot.

Cold reading   Auditioning by reading a selection of dramatic literature without having seen that material so as to have been able to study it ahead of time.

Collaboration   Interrelation of different elements of drama/theatre discipline in creating an artwork.

Color   Visual sensation dependent on the reflection or absorption of light from a given surface.

Commedia dell'arte   A dramatic form that is improvisational and has the same characters, known as stock characters, in every play. It originated in Italy in the sixteenth century and was usually performed by traveling actors.

Common   Shared by all or many.

Communication   The process of interacting verbally or nonverbally with another person or persons to share meaning.

Concentration   Keeping one's mind and attention on one particular object, scene, or idea; concentration in drama/theatre is being able to focus attention in spite of audience or other distractions.

Conflict   The tension or struggle in a story or play between two or more characters, or between a character and some kind of force, or between two opposing ideas.

Contrast   To set in opposition for the purpose of comparing.

Costumer   The person who works with a costume crew to make sure that the costumes are clean and in good repair and are stored properly.

Costumes   Clothes that performers wear in a presentation.

Creative choice   The decisions that one makes in the creation of a dramatic work, not only in the story itself, but also in the style and techniques of presenting the story.

Creative dramatics   Drama as a learning tool, with the emphasis on the development of the individual through a problem-solving process. Creative dramatics can be extended to include formal performance.

Cross   A stage direction used to define the movement of an actor from one stage area to another.

Culture   All the traditions, customs, and history of a particular group of people.

Curved movement   A cross in a gentle curve.

Dance   An all-inclusive term referring to aesthetics of movement; physical movement with expressive intent, using rhythm and tempo.

Dialogue   The words spoken by the actors in a drama.

Director   In a theatrical presentation, the person who is responsible for bringing all the elements of the production together.

Downstage   The general area of a stage toward the audience.

Drama   A term used broadly to mean the reenactment of life situations. Drama does not require an audience.

Dress rehearsal   A rehearsal run exactly as if it were a performance, using costumes, make-up, props, costumes, lights, set pieces, and scenery.

Dynamics   The comparative loudness and softness in music or speech.

Elaboration   Working out further details with great care, or giving additional or fuller treatment to something.

Emotional recall   The ability to remember or bring back into the mind various feelings associated with certain situations.

Epic   A long narrative poem, usually in a formal style that indicates historical importance, made up of traditional stories about a hero or group of heroes. Epic poems are part of a culture's folklore.

Evaluation   Appraising personal efforts as well as reflecting on and making judgments about efforts of others.

Fable   A story that teaches a lesson, especially one in which animals act like people.

Fairy tale   A story about supernatural beings.

Fantasy   The use of imagination to create strange, unusual, or non-realistic characters or settings.

Film   The photographed performance usually shown in a movie theater (or from videotapes on the home VCR). It involves no audience/performer interaction.

Five senses   Any of the bodily faculties of perception or feeling (sight, sound, touch, smell, taste).

Five W's   *Who* refers to roles and characterizations. *What* refers to dramatic action. *Where* refers to setting, locale, environment. *When* refers to time in history, time of year, and time of day. *Why* refers to motivation.

Folklore   Customs, beliefs, stories, and sayings of a people handed down from generation to generation.

Folk tale   Any story about a culture passed on from generation to generation. Myths, fairy tales, fables, and legends can also be folk tales.

Gibberish   Meaningless sounds substituted for recognizable words.

Haiku   A verse form used by Japanese poets that records the essence of a keenly perceived moment linking people and nature. Haiku have exactly seventeen syllables; the first and third lines contain five syllables, the second line seven.

Hand puppet   A puppet manipulated by the hand within the puppet.

Hearing   The sensation of receiving information through the ears.

Hero   A person of distinguished courage or ability, admired for his or her good and brave deeds; in theatre, usually the protagonist.

"How and why" story   A story created by a particular culture to explain the cause of a natural phenomenon.

Human machine   Moving and connecting bodies in such a way that the shapes create a living machine with moving parts and sounds.

Imagery   Something perceived naturally and spontaneously by the senses.

Imagination   The power of forming mental pictures of objects or scenes not present to the senses. A mental image; a creation of the mind.

Imitate   To follow, as a pattern, model, or example; to copy.

Improvise   To act out without previous study or preparation. To act out without a script.

Inflection   A change in the tone or pitch of the voice.

Intent   The theme or message of a play.

Legend   A greatly exaggerated story relating to the history of a culture, usually about people who really lived. Legends have usually been embellished by the teller.

Line   In dramatic arts, the words spoken by one of the characters in a dramatic presentation; in visual arts, an identifiable path of a point moving in space that can vary in width, direction, and length.

Magic box   A device to stimulate imagination, of pretending to have in front of one an imaginary box, from which anything—an object, an idea, or a character to "put on"—may be taken.

Magic If   Drama/theatre term referring to "What would happen if...?"; releasing the imagination to create a story with limitless possibilities.

Marionette   Puppet worked by strings.

Mechanical sound   All those sounds made in the environment by manufactured objects.

Method acting   A system of acting developed by Constantin Stanislavsky, the founder of the Moscow Art Theater; a way of analyzing each phase of the actor's work to make it as realistic and efficient as possible.

Mind's eye   Imagination.

Moral   (adj.) Relating to the distinction between right and wrong. (n.) The lesson taught by a particular story.

Motivations   Those reasons or occurrences in a scene, story, or play that prompt a character to act and react in a certain way.

Music   The art discipline using voice and/or instruments for listening and performing pleasure that incorporates melody, tonal quality, rhythm, and tempo.

Myth   A story used to explain the unknown.

Natural sound   All those sounds in the environment made by things that exist in nature.

Noh play   An ancient Japanese art form, in which actors use masks, and tell a story through highly stylized dance steps. Noh drama combines dance, poetry, music, mime, and acting.

Nonverbal   Without words.

Notes   After a rehearsal, the director's specific suggestions to actors and crews for the improvement of the performance.

Objectivity   The ability to study a problem without prejudging or making a decision too quickly.

Observation   Noticing detail in what we see, hear, taste, smell, and feel.

Offstage   Off the acting area of the stage. Any part of the stage not enclosed by setting.

Open Space   A prescribed area with room for movement that students are to enter with imaginative ideas for drama/theatre activities.

Oral communication   The vocal or verbal sound conveying information.

Pantomime   Acting without words; using the body to express an idea, an emotion, or a character.

Perception   The process, act, or faculty of using the senses (sight, sound, touch, smell, taste, and kinesthesia) to gain information from the physical environment.

Performer   An actor or presenter of any kind of theatrical material or entertainment.

Pitch   Referring to the range of sound in music (high or low); sounds that can be repeated.

Play   A story written in dramatic form; that is, scripted, with dialogue and stage directions written out for the actors.

Playing area   A cleared space for dramatic activities without a designated place for the audience.

Playmaking   A term used to describe dramatic activities that lead to improvised drama with a beginning, middle, and end, employing the general form and some of the elements of theatre. The product may or may not be shared with others.

Playwright   The author of a dramatic work.

Plot   The "what happens" in a story as revealed through the action and dialogue of the characters. A plot has a beginning, which involves the setting, characters, and the problem they are facing; a middle, which tells how the characters work to solve the problem; and an ending, in which the problem is resolved.

Point of view   The location from which, or way in which an object or scene is observed.

Prop, or property   Any object used on the stage (excluding scenery, lights, and costumes) such as furniture, utensils, ornaments, and personal possessions. Personal props are those objects used by the actors onstage, and stage props are those items onstage that help create the setting.

Proscenium arch   A decorative arch that separates the stage from the audience.

Proscenium opening   The opening framed by the proscenium arch.

Proscenium stage   A stage with the audience seated on one side, usually directly in front of the playing area.

Protagonist   The main character, who carries out the central thought, or theme of the story.

Puppetry   The animation of artificial figures (not always, but often, doll-like figures), often jointed, by means of the hand, by a rod or rods, by strings, or by a combination of means.

Radio   A public broadcasting medium that is an auditory experience only. There is no audience interaction with the performers.

Readers theatre   A presentation by two or more people who read aloud a story in play form, interpreting the literary work in as lively a way as possible without actually acting it out. In readers theatre the focus is on vocal interpretation; no costumes, make-up, scenery, or stage movement are used. Lines do not need to be memorized, but they are not improvised.

Recall   To call back to the mind, to recollect or remember.

Rendering   A detailed drawing of the playing area.

Repetitive   Reoccurring.

Resolution   The final unfolding of the solution to the complications or conflicts in the plot of a story or play.

Rhythm   A regular pattern of sound, as in music and poetry, or of action as in dancing, measured by units of time. These pulses or beats can be organized in sets (meter) which move in twos or threes or multiples and combinations thereof.

Rod puppet   A puppet mounted on rods or sticks, sometimes jointed with separate rods to the hands or other body parts.

Role playing   Improvising movement and dialogue by putting oneself in another's place in a particular situation.

Scenario   A plot outline for a story or play.

Scene   A small part of a play or dramatized story. *Scene* often refers to the location of the story or play.

Scenery   Set pieces and backdrops that help the audience visualize the location of a dramatic performance.

Script   The written form of a dramatic performance; the dialogue, descriptions of settings, and directions for the actors written down by the playwright.

Seeing   The sensations perceived with the eyes.

Sensory awareness   Heightened perception of the physical sensations of touch, sight, hearing, taste, and smell; and of emotional states.

Sensory recall   The ability to remember various sensory experiences associated with persons, places or things; the ability to remember, and almost feel again, the stimuli that accompanied a particular experience.

Sequence   The order in which events happen or tasks are performed.

Set   All the scenery, backdrops, set pieces, and props used to create a stage environment for a dramatic performance; the performing area created by those elements.

Set pieces   The freestanding pieces of scenery within the stage environment for a dramatic performance.

Shadow play   A drama produced by placing a light source behind actors or puppets, so that the audience sees only their shadows on a screen.

Shape   A two-dimensional area or plane that may be organic or inorganic, free-form or geometric, open or closed, natural or manufactured. In dance and drama, *shape* can refer to the configuration of the body or the space in which the actors move.

Sideways movement Small arcs made with one or two sideways steps.

Smell Sensations perceived by the nose that distinguish odor.

Sound Vibrations in the air that stimulate the auditory nerves and produce the sensation of hearing.

Sound effects Sounds used to enhance a scene.

Sound voyage An imaginary trip taken with special attention paid to the sounds that identify the settings.

Stage left The area of the stage to the actor's left as the actor stands center stage and faces the audience.

Stage right The area of the stage to the actor's right as the actor stands center stage and faces the audience.

Story The narrative form of a series of events with an identifiable beginning, middle, and end, or plot.

Storyteller A person who uses the oral tradition to pass on information.

Straight make-up Make-up that shows the actor as he or she normally appears; used to define the features more clearly.

Structure The way the theme or message of a play is carried out in performance.

Subtext The meaning underlying dialogue and stage directions in a dramatic script.

Symbol That which stands for and represents something else.

Symmetry A regular balanced pattern, the same on one side as the other; a harmony of design.

Tactile Perceived by or related to the sense of touch.

Taste The sensations perceived by the tongue that distinguish flavor.

Technical rehearsal A rehearsal that focuses primarily on the technical aspects of the production.

Technique The physical skills essential to the performer; the integral training of the body.

Television (TV) The electronic public broadcast medium with live or prerecorded shows that is both an auditory and a visual experience. There is no audience/performer interaction.

Tempo   The rate of speed of a composition or section of music.

Text   In theatre, the content of a written script, or the agreed-upon structure of the dramatic material.

Texture   The surface quality of materials, either actual (tactile) or visual.

Theater   The place where a performance or show is held for an audience to see. It can be an outdoor setting as well as an enclosed building.

Theatre   All the collaborative activities needed to present a dramatic work to an audience.

Theme   The central thought, idea, or significance of action with which a play or story deals.

Thrust stage   A stage with the audience seated on three sides. The stage extends, or thrusts out into the audience space.

Time   Measurement of sound or movement involving breathing time, emotional time, and metric time (beat, pulse, accent, tempo, duration).

Touch-up, or polishing rehearsal   A rehearsal that focuses only on the specific parts of the performance that need further clarification or work.

Universal   Including all; present everywhere.

Upstage   The general area toward the back part of the stage.

Values   The social principles or standards held by an individual, class, or culture.

Villain   A scoundrel or a person devoted to wickedness or crime; in theatre, usually the antagonist.

Visual arts   Those creations that may still be viewed when the artist's work is finished.

Visualization   The formation of a mental image or picture; something in the mind's eye.

Wings   Either side of the stage out of sight of the audience.

Resources

CHILDREN'S LITERATURE

Aesop. (Joseph Jacobs, ed.) *Fables of Aesop*. B. Franklin, 1970.
These adaptations of 82 of Aesop's best-known fables include a brief history of the fables.

Anaya, Rodolfo A. *Legend of La Llorona*. Tonatiuh-Quinto Sol International, 1984.
"The Weeping Woman" searches for her lost children

Asbjornsen, Peter Christen, and Jorgen Moe. *Norwegian Folk Tales*. Pantheon Books, 1982.
This collection of Norwegian folktales contains an undertone of realism and folk humor.

Atkinson, Mary. *Maria Teresa*. Lollipop Power, 1979.
A young Chicana faces discrimination when she moves to a small midwestern town. She is helped by her puppet, *Monteja*.

Balin, Peter. *The Flight of the Feathered Serpent*. Arcana Publishers, 1983.
Mayan symbols and their meanings are explained.

Baylor, Byrd. *I'm in Charge of Celebrations*. Macmillan Publishing Company, Inc., 1986.
A dweller in the desert celebrates a triple rainbow, a chance encounter with a coyote, and other wonders of the wilderness.

Birch, Beverley. *Shakespeare's Stories: Comedies*. Peter Bedrick Books, 1990.
_____. *Shakespeare's Stories: Histories*. Peter Bedrick Books, 1990.
_____. *Shakespeare's Stories: Tragedies*. Peter Bedrick Books, 1990.
The author carefully follows the plots, and retains enough of the original text so that students experience Shakespeare's poetry.

Brandt, Keith. *Five Senses*. Troll Associates, 1985.
This simple explanation of the way our five senses work is appropriate for grades 3–6.

Briggs, Raymond. (Virginia Haviland, ed.) *The Fairy Tale Treasury*. Dell Publishing Company, 1986.
This is a collection of 32 of the world's best-loved fairy tales, including *The Emperor's New Clothes, The Frog Prince, Gone Is Gone,* and *The Sun and the Wind.*

Brown, Marcia. *Once a Mouse*. Charles Scribner's Sons, 1961.

_____. *Shadow*. Charles Scribner's Sons, 1982.

Carroll, Lewis. *Alice's Adventures in Wonderland and Through the Looking Glass*. Putnam Publishing Group, 1946–1963.
Alice meets a number of fantasy characters, who are sometimes delightful, sometimes exasperating. This edition of the classic story contains the full text and all the original illustrations. It also includes definitions of various words in "Jabberwocky."

Chase, Richard, ed. *The Jack Tales*. Houghton Mifflin Company, 1943.
These Anglo-American folktales are told in the dialect and style of the mountain country of North Carolina. They have humor, freshness, and a colorful American background.

Dayrell, Elphinstone. *Why the Sun and Moon Live in the Sky*. Houghton Mifflin Company, 1990.
In this old African folktale with beautifully detailed and stylized artwork, the storyteller explains how the Sun, the Moon, and the Water came to be where they are.

De Rico, Ul. *The Rainbow Goblins*. Thames and Hudson, 1978.
Seven goblins try to eat up all the colors of the rainbow. (This book is out of print, but the text is included in the Story Scripts in the Appendix of *Center Stage.*)

Dunnahoo, Terry. *Who Needs Espie Sanchez?* Dutton, 1977.
A young wealthy girl befriends Espie after both girls are involved in a terrible traffic accident.

Estes, Eleanor. *The Hundred Dresses*. Harcourt Brace Jovanovich, 1974.
Wanda said she had a hundred dresses at home, but her classsmates didn't believe her. They didn't realize her talent until after she moved away.

Goble, Paul. *The Girl Who Loved Wild Horses.* Bradbury Press, 1980.
The author tells in vivid illustrations as well as text the story of a Plains
Indian girl and her love of horses.

Grimm, Jacob, and Wilhelm Grimm. *The Fisherman and His Wife.*
Greeenwillow Books, 1978.
This familiar fairy tale recounts a story of greed similar to folk tales from
other cultures.

Hodges, Margaret. *St. George and the Dragon.* Little, Brown and Company,
Inc. 1984.
The author retells the story of how George slays the dreadful dragon that has
been terrorizing the countryside for years and brings peace and joy to the
land.

Holman, Felice. *Slake's Limbo.* Dial Books, 1975.
A fifteen-year-old boy makes some important discoveries about himself as
he learns to survive in the New York City subway system.

Janson, H.W., and Anthony F. Janson. *History of Art for Young People.*
Abrams, 1987.

Juster, Norton. *The Phantom Tollbooth.* Random House, 1961.
Milo is bored, but his fantasy journey to a strange land teaches him patience
and responsibility, as well as the importance of words and numbers.

Koch, Kenneth, and Kate Farrell. *Talking to the Sun: An Illustrated Anthology
of Poems for Young People.* Henry Holt & Company, 1985.
Poems are from different time periods and countries with illustrations from
the Metropolitan Museum of Art.

Konigsburg, E.L. *Jennifer, Hecate, Macbeth, William McKinley, and Me, Elizabeth.* Atheneum, 1967.
As she looks for a friend, Elizabeth finds one who is also a witch, and who
agrees to let Elizabeth be her apprentice.

Krumgold, Joseph. *And Now Miguel.* Crowell, 1953.
Miguel's wish—to go to the mountains with the men of his family and their
herds—comes true.

Lamb, Charles. *Tales from Shakespeare*. Crown Publishers, 1988.
Twenty of Shakespeare's best-known plays are retold, using the playwright's own words.

Lawrence, Jacob. *Harriet and the Promised Land*. Windmill, 1968.

Longfellow, Henry Wadsworth. *Paul Revere's Ride*. Greenwillow, 1985.

McLain, Gary. *The Indian Way*. John Muir Publications, 1990.
Stories and legends focus on how human beings must live in harmony with the earth.

Montejo, Victor. *The Bird Who Cleans the World and Other Mayan Fables*. Curbstone Press, 1990.
These fables and animal stories illustrate both differences and similarities between cultures, and reflect ancient wisdom.

Mulherin, Jennifer. *Shakespeare for Everyone Series* (2 Volumes). Silver Burdett Press, 1988.
Age appropriate materials (grades 5–12) of Shakespeare's work include "Hamlet," "Merchant of Venice," "Macbeth," "Midsummer Night's Dream," and "Romeo and Juliet."

Nanus, Susan. *The Phantom Tollbooth* (playscript). Samuel French, Inc., 1977.
The author adapts the well-known Juster story to be given as a drama.

Osborn, Steve. *Story Chest: Treasured Tales from Many Lands*. Addison-Wesley Publishing Company, 1991.
This set of stories contains "The Horse of Seven Colors," a folktale from Mexico about a young boy's adventure with a wizard and a magic horse that can fly; and "The Bunyip," an Australian tale about a mother bunyip's revenge for kidnapping her baby. Four copies of eight stories, a teacher's guide, and an audiotape are included in this package.

Raskin, Ellen. *Nothing Ever Happens on My Block*. Macmillan Children's Book Group, 1989.
As a child sits and complains about nothing ever happening on his block, he misses many fantastic adventures happening around him.

Rohmer, Harriet. *The Legend of Food Mountain: La Montana del Alimento.* Children's Book Press, 1982.
Written in English and Spanish, this is a retelling of an Aztec legend based on the Chimalpopactl codex. The god, Quetzalcoatl, creates man, but has nothing to feed him. A giant red ant appears and shows him the way to Food Mountain.

Scieszka, Jon. *The True Story of the Three Little Pigs.* Viking Children's Books, 1989.
The wolf gives his own outlandish version of what happened between him and the three little pigs.

Sendak, Maurice. *Where the Wild Things Are.* HarperCollins Children's Books, 1988.
A naughty little boy, sent to bed without his supper, sails to the land of the wild things where he becomes their king.

Suzuki, David, with Barbara Hehner. *Looking at Senses.* John Wiley & Sons, Inc., 1991.
How the sense organs work is simply explained, with projects for experimenting with each one. Activities that need adult supervision are marked with a special logo.

Tolkien, J.R.R. *The Hobbit.* Ballantine Books, Inc., 1986.
A well-to-do Hobbit lives comfortably until a wandering wizard chooses him to share in an adventure from which he may never return.

Van Der Meer, Ron, and Atie Van Der Meer. *Your Amazing Senses: Thirty-Six Games, Puzzles and Tricks to Show How Your Senses Work.* Macmillan Children's Book Group, 1987.

ADULT REFERENCES
Acuna, Rudolfo. *Occupied America: A History of Chicanos.* (third ed.) Harper & Row, 1988.

Adix, Vern. *Theatre Scenecraft.* Anchorage Press, 1981.
This "how-to" book tells how to construct stage settings and scenery.

Allensworth, Carl, et al. *The Complete Play Production Handbook Revised and Updated*. HarperCollins, 1982.
This book gives complete details concerning the production of a play, including tips on directing and technical elements.

Barranger, Milly S. *Theatre: A Way of Seeing*. Wadsworth Publishing Company, 1991.
The author communicates the excitement of live theatre, exploring the theatre from the audience's standpoint and giving the reader a guided tour of the vital elements in a dramatic production.

Bauer, Caroline Feller. *Presenting Reader's Theater*. H.W. Wilson Company, 1987.
Plays and poems are given in scripted form to read aloud.

Bellville, Cheryl W. *Theater Magic: Behind the Scenes at a Children's Theater*. Carolrhoda Books, 1986.
Follow the Children's Theatre Company as it produces a performance of "The Nightingale." The book describes how the play is planned, designed, cast, and rehearsed.

Benedetti, Robert. *Actor at Work*. Prentice Hall, 1990.
An in-depth look at the skill of acting shows how actors prepare for this profession.

Berthold, Margot. *The History of World Theater, Vol I: From the Beginning to the Baroque*. Continuum Press, 1990.
Theatrical traditions of many cultures, including those of Egypt, the Indo-Pacific, China, and Japan are explored in depth.

Blum, Daniel. *A Pictorial History of the American Theatre 1860–1985*. Crown Publishers, 1986.

Boiko, Claire. *Children's Plays for Creative Actors*. Plays, Inc., 1985.
These thirty-five one-act plays, mostly fantasies and comedies, are appropriate for holidays and other festive occasions.

Bowman, Walter Parker, and Robert Hamilton Ball. *Theatre Language, a Dictionary*. Theatre Arts Books, Inc., 1976.

Brandon, James R., ed. *On Thrones of Gold: Three Javanese Shadow Plays*. Harvard University Press, 1970.

Brockett, Oscar G. *History of the Theatre*. Allyn & Bacon, Inc., 1990. Criticism is included in this overview of theatre history.

Broman, Sven. *Chinese Shadow Theatre*. Coronet Books, 1981.

Brown, Rosellen. *The Whole Word Catalogue: A Handbook of Writing Ideas for Teachers*. Teachers and Writers Collaborative, 1975.

Buchman, Herman. *Stage Makeup*. Watson-Guptill, 1989.

Carra, Lawrence. *Controls in Play Directing*. Vantage Presss, 1985. A discussion of directing techniques for any form of theatre. Includes types of plays (comedy, farce, tragedy, etc.) and styles (naturalism, surrealism, etc.).

Center Stage: Creative Dramatics Supplement, © 1993. Planned to complement *Center Stage* lessons, this kit contains 2 audiotape cassettes of 4 folk tales each and scripts for the folk tales, a book of playscripts of some of Aesop's fables, and 4 posters. Available from Dale Seymour Publications.

Chase, Richard. *American Folk Tales and Songs*. Dover Publications, Inc., 1971.

Ciabotti, Patricia. *Gaming It Up with Shakespeare*. Creative Learning, 1980. This book offers text, analysis, and exercises to help students understand and enjoy the works of William Shakespeare.

Cohen, Robert, and John Harrop. *Creative Play Direction*. Prentice Hall, 1984. This easy-to-understand, hands-on book gives exercises and activities for acting, creating scripts, and blocking and lighting for the stage.

Conaway, Judith. *Make Your Own Costumes and Disguises*. Troll Associates, 1987.

Corson, Richard. *Stage Makeup* (7th ed.). Prentice Hall, 1986.

Craig, Edward G. *Toward a New Theatre, Forty Designs for Stage Scenes*. Ayer Company Publishers, Inc., 1913.

Crawford, Jerry L. *Acting: In Person and In Style.* William C. Brown Publishers, 1983.

This book contains everything the actor needs to know about voice control and speech. Scenes appropriate for an audition are included, as well as an in-depth look at the history of the theatre.

Cummings, Richard. *One Hundred One Costumes for All Ages, All Occasions.* Plays, Inc., 1987.

Currell, David. *The Complete Book of Puppet Theatre.* B & N Imports, 1986.

The history of puppetry is given, along with instructions for making various types of puppets, creating stage sets, and producing plays.

Dibell, Ansen. *Plot.* Writers Digest Books, 1988.

This easy-to-follow book concentrates on the plot construction techniques of fiction, drama, and novels.

Ducharte, Pierre Louis. *Italian Comedy: The Improvisation, Scenarios, Lives, Attributes, Portraits and Masks of the Illustrious Characters of Commedia Dell'arte.* Dover Publications, Inc., 1965.

Franklin, Miriam A., and James G. Dixon, III. *Rehearsal: The Principles and Practice of Acting for the Stage.* Prentice Hall, 1983.

This book contains practical information such as stage locations, stage diagrams, a glossary of stage terms, and what is involved in putting on a show.

Gates, Doris. *Lord of the Sky: Zeus.* Puffin Books, 1982.

A retelling of myths in which Zeus plays a part.

Grandstaff, Russell J. *Acting and Directing.* National Textbook, 1989.

An analysis of theater from the standpoint of the actor to the technical director.

Gullan, Marjorie. *Speech Choir.* Ayer Company Publishers, Inc., 1937.

Contains American poetry and English ballads for choral reading.

Hamilton, Edith. *Mythology.* Little, Brown, & Company, 1942.

This collection of stories about gods and heroes in mythology is a handy reference.

Hansen, Merrily P. *Now Presenting: Classic Tales for Readers Theatre*. Addison-Wesley Publishing Company, 1992.

Illustrated scripts for six plays are accompanied by teaching suggestions, simple costume patterns, and ideas for props.

Harris, Aurand. (Coleman Jennings, ed.) *Six Plays for Children*. University of Texas Press, 1986.

Holt, Michael. *Stage Design and Properties*. Schirmer Books, 1988.

This "how-to" book focuses on the role of the stage designer, explaining processes from set designing to scenery painting.

Honey, Elizabeth, et al. *Festivals: Ideas from Around the World*. Delmar Publishers, 1988.

Huberman, Caryn, and JoAnne Wetzel. *Onstage Backstage*. Carolrhoda Books, 1987.

Follow a ten-year-old actress and her association with a children's company preparing to perform Kipling's "Just So Stories."

Hughes, Jill. *Aztecs*. (rev. ed.) Watts, 1987.

This book traces the rise and fall of the Aztec Empire and explores its cultures and beliefs.

Hull, Raymond. *How to Write a Play*. Writers Digest Books, 1988.

This treatment of the fundamentals of play construction focuses on how to develop conflict through action and dialogue, and how to resolve the plot of a play.

Ireland, Norma O., compiled by. *Index to Fairy Tales, 1973–1977: Including Folklore, Legends, and Myths in Collection*. Faxon (Scarecrow Press, Inc.), 1985.

Useful reference series.

Janeczko, Paul. *Poetspeak: In Their Work, About Their Work*. Bradbury Press, 1983.

This work considers 62 active poets, and the reasons they write poetry. The poems, suitable for reading aloud, deal with a variety of social issues relevant to young people.

Johnstone, Keith. *Impro: Improvisation and the Theatre*. Theatre Arts Books, 1979.
Exercises and activities foster spontaneity and narrative skills through improvisations.

Joyce, Joy. *Me and More Shadows*. Joy-Co., 1981.

Kamerman, Sylvia E. *Dramatized Folk Tales of the World*. Plays, Inc., 1971.
(This book recently went out of print, but you may be able to find it in your library.) This work contains fifty royalty-free one-act dramatizations of stories from five continents.

_____. *Plays from Favorite Folk Tales*. Plays, Inc., 1987.
Fifty royalty-free plays for children in the lower and middle grades based on such folk and fairy tales as "Pandora's Box."

Keene, Donald, ed. *Twenty Plays of the No Theatre*. Columbia University Press, 1970.
These classic Japanese plays have been translated into English.

Komparu, Kunio. *The Noh Theater: Principles and Perspectives*. Weatherhill, Inc., 1983.

Laughlin, Mildred K., and Kathy H. Latrobe. *Social Studies Readers Theatre for Children*. Libraries Unlimited, Inc., 1991.
A collection of readers theatre scripts focuses on themes such as Colonial America, Settling the West, and A Divided Nation.

Levitt, Paul. A *Structural Approach to the Analysis of Drama*. Mouton, 1971.

Linklater, Kristin. *Freeing the Natural Voice*. Drama Books, 1976.
Exercises and activities are geared toward helping the student speak effectively in public and on the stage.

Livo, Norma J., and Sandra A. Rietz. *Storytelling Folklore Sourcebook*. Libraries Unlimited, Inc., 1991.
An overview of legends, riddles, costumes, customs, and folklore games of the world community.

Lonsdale, Bernard J., and Helen K. Mackintosh. *Children Experience Literature*. Random House Inc., 1973.
This overview gives a broad selection of children's literature and selected criticisms. It is a good source for educators involved in a curriculum development program.

Lord, William H. *Stagecraft One: Your Introduction to Backstage Work*. W.H. Lord, 1979.
This student handbook describes in detail all the work that goes on behind the scene of a play production, from scenery to props.

Machlin, Evangeline. *Speech for the Stage*. Theatre Arts, 1980.
Exercises and activities help improve acting ability.

Magarshack, David. *Stansislavsky: A Life*. Chanticleer Press, 1951.

Marks, Burton, and Rita Marks. *Puppet Plays and Puppet-Making*. Plays, Inc., 1985.
This collection of puppet plays also includes instructions for making puppets and costumes and tells how to produce a puppet show.

Martinez, J.D. *Combat Mime: A Non-Violent Approach to Stage Violence*. Nelson-Hall, Inc., 1982.
Techniques for acting out violence onstage without getting hurt are explained. Ways to fall, punching, and kicking are described and illustrated in this handbook.

McCaslin, Nellie. *Creative Drama in the Classroom*. Longman Publishing Group, 1990.
An activity book containing exercises to do with students in creative dramatics, with an overview of children's theatre.

McGaw, Charles J., and Gary Blake. *Acting Is Believing: A Basic Method*. Holt, Rinehart and Winston, Inc., 1986.
For those who wish to make acting a career, this book provides a readable guide to acting concepts, skills, and exercises. It also includes short plays.

McKissack, Patricia. *Aztec Indians*. Children's Book Press, 1985. This resource discusses the Aztec Indians, their history, religion, language, customs, and final days.

O'Connor, John, and Lorraine Brown, eds. *The Federal Theatre Project.* Heinemann Educational Books, Inc., 1986.
An overview of the times and operations of the Federal Theatre Project during the 1930s.

Parker, W. Oren, and R. Craig Wolf. *Scene Design and Stage Lighting.* Holt, Rinehart and Winston, 1990.
This is an up-to-date, sophisticated look at sets and lights for the stage.

Pellowski, Anne. *The Family Storytelling Handbook: How to Use Stories, Anecdotes, Rhymes, Handkerchiefs, Paper and Other Objects to Enrich Your Family Traditions.* Macmillan Children's Book Group, 1987.
Storytelling is treated as a form of family entertainment, and suggestions are given on how and when to tell stories.

Pilbrow, Richard. *Stage Lighting* (Illustrated). Applause Theatre Book Publishers, 1990.

The Puppetry Store, a service of Puppeteers of America, Inc. (a good source of resources and artifacts). Send for catalog to 1525 24th Street S.E., Auburn, WA 98002-7837.

Ross, Beverly B., and Jean P. Durgin. *Junior Broadway: How to Produce Musicals with Children 9 to 13.* McFarland and Company, 1983.
Musical revues and comedies to be staged with children include stage guides, plays, production notes, and directional notes.

Rugoff, Milton, ed. *A Harvest of World Folk Tales* (contains "Repaying Good with Evil"). The Viking Press, 1949.

Ruskin, Ariane. *Nineteenth Century Art.* McGraw Hill, 1968.

_____. *Seventeenth and Eighteenth Century Art.* McGraw Hill, 1969.

Russell, Douglas. *Stage Costume Design: Theory, Technique and Style.* Prentice Hall, 1985.
The author guides the reader toward a complete understanding of costume design, including changes that may have to take place between the original script and the production.

Scher, Anna, and Charles Verrall. *Another One Hundred Plus Ideas for Drama.* Heinemann Educational Books, Inc., 1987.

Scott, A. C. *The Theatre in Asia.* Macmillan Publishing Co., 1972.
The diversity of the theatrical art of Asian cultures is explored, along with the background and meaning of conventions which often seem remote and incomprehensible to the western viewer. (This book is out of print, but you may be able to find it in your library.)

Silverstein, Alvin, and Virginia Silverstein. *Wonders of Speech.* Morrow Junior Books, 1988.
This advanced approach to how children learn to speak discusses the many aspects of communication through speech.

Simmens, Rene. *The World of Puppets.* Elsevier Phaidon, 1975. (This book is out of print, but the many clear illustrations and photographs make it worth looking for in your library.)

Sklar, Daniel J. *Playmaking: Children Writing and Performing Their Own Plays.* Teachers and Writers Collaborative, 1990.

Smiley, Sam. *Playwriting: The Structure of Action.* Prentice Hall, 1971.

Smith, Winifred. *Commedia Dell'Arte.* Ayer Company Publishers, Inc., 1990.
This lively text presents the history of commedia dell'arte through illustrations and scenarios.

Spolin, Viola. *Improvisation for the Theatre: A Handbook of Teaching and Directing Techniques.* Northwestern University Press, 1983.
A sophisticated publication by a renowned author containing theatre games, improvisational exercises, and sensory awareness activities for drama students of all ages.

Stalberg, Roberta. *China's Puppets.* China Books & Periodicals, Inc., 1984.

Stanislavski, Constantin. *Building a Character.* Theatre Arts Books, 1977.
The great Russian teacher presents his sophisticated approach to method acting.

_____. Hermine I. Popper, ed. Elizabeth R. Hapgood, tr. *Creating a Role*. Theatre Arts Books, 1961.
The author outlines the process by which an actor creates a characterization. Narrative and exercises for actors are included.

Steiner, Stan, and Valdez, Luis, eds. *Aztlan: An Anthology of Mexican-American Literature*. Random House, 1972.

Straub, Cindie, and Matthew Straub. *Mime: Basics for Beginners*. Plays, Inc., 1984.

Thane, Adele. *Plays from Famous Stories and Fairy Tales*. Plays, Inc., 1983.
The twenty-eight short plays are based on works by Hans Christian Andersen and the Grimm Brothers.

Van Den Heuvel, Cor. *The Haiku Anthology: Haiku and Senryu in English*. Simon & Schuster, 1986.

Van Ness, Edward C., and Shita Prawirohardjo. *Javanese Wayang Kulit, An Introduction*. Oxford University Press, 1986.
Wayang Kulit (shadow plays with leather puppets) are beautifully illustrated in this book of plays, which also tells the history of the Javanese shadow play and how to construct the puppets.

Von Boehn, Max (Josephine Nicoll, tr.). *Dolls and Puppets*. Cooper Square, 1966.

Ward, Winifred. *Stories to Dramatize*. Anchorage Press.
These stories and scenes are appropriate for dramatizations by elementary school students.

Way, Brian. *Development Through Drama*. Humanities Press, 1967.
Practical activities and instructions involve children in the process of creating drama.

West, John O., *Mexican-American Folklore*. August House Publishers, 1988.
This anthology contains legends, songs, festivals, proverbs, crafts, and tales of saints and revolutionaries.

Wickham, Glynne. *A History of the Theatre*. Cambridge University Press, 1985.
Over 230 illustrations trace the changing directions of drama, ballet, opera, and spectacle in Asia and the West.

AUDIOTAPES

Living Sound Effects, Vols. 1, 3, 7. Bainbridge Entertainment Co. (recording of environmental sounds)

VIDEOTAPES

Arts Abound Series: The Director. Great Plains National: Affiliated with the University of Nebraska-Lincoln, 1985.

This 15-minute program explains the role of a director in a theatrical production.

Story Scripts

The Bunyip

Long, long ago, hundreds of men, women, and children lived in a camp at one end of a wide valley. They lived in huts made of grass and branches.

One day the young men of the camp went hunting for food. They walked down the valley, and they soon began to play games.

Some of them ran races. Others threw their spears as far as they could.

At last the young men reached a small lake near the other end of the valley. Bulrushes grew in the middle of the lake.

Now the young men knew that the roots of the bulrushes were good to eat, so they got ready to swim out and dig them up. But the youngest man said, "We are hunters. Why should we dig up bulrush roots? Let us catch fish and eels instead."

The other young men agreed. So they looked for bait to use on the ends of their fishing lines. Most of them found worms, but the youngest man was too lazy to look for worms. When no one was looking, he took a piece of meat from his pack and put it on the end of his fishing line.

The young men fished for a long time without catching any fish or eels. The sun began to sink, and it seemed that they would have to go home without catching anything.

Suddenly, the youngest man felt something pulling on his line. It was pulling so hard that it almost dragged him into the water. He cried out to the others for help. They ran to his side and helped him pull the line.

Bit by bit the young men pulled the line out of the water. But then they stepped back in fear. Instead of a fish or an eel, they had caught a strange creature. It had a long, flat tail and a smooth, round body.

The youngest man was not afraid. He grabbed the strange creature and threw it over his shoulders.

But the others would not touch it. They had never seen such a thing before, but they knew exactly what it was. It was the baby of a water monster called the Bunyip!

All of a sudden, the young men heard a loud wail coming from the lake. They turned and saw the giant mother Bunyip rising out of the water. Anger was flashing from her large yellow eyes. "Let it go! Let it go!" yelled the others to the youngest man. But he would not let go of the baby Bunyip.

"I caught it!" he yelled. "And I will keep it! You know that the mother cannot leave the lake!"

That was true. The mother Bunyip could not leave the water. As long as the young men stayed on land, they were safe.

And so the young men started back to the camp. Behind them they could hear the wails of the mother Bunyip, but they did not listen.

By this time the sun was setting. The valley was in shadows, but the tops of the hills were still bright. The young men were no longer afraid.

Just then, they heard a new sound behind them. It was the sound of rushing water.

The young men turned around and saw that the lake was growing bigger and bigger. The water was just a few feet away. They looked at each other and then began to run as fast as they could. The youngest man ran the fastest of all.

When the young men reached their camp, they turned around again. The water was still right behind them. All the men, women, and children in the camp were filled with fear.

At last the youngest man let go of the baby Bunyip, but the waters kept rising around him.

He yelled to the others, "We must climb to the tops of the trees! The water cannot reach us there!"

But even as the youngest man was speaking, he felt something cold touch his legs. He looked down and saw two webbed feet where his own feet should have been.

He put up his hands to cover his face, but they were now the tips of wings. And when he tried to speak, a strange noise came out of his throat, like nothing he had ever heard.

By now, the water had reached the youngest man's waist, and he began floating on it with ease. When he looked at his face in the water, he saw that he had become a black swan. Looking around, he saw other black swans floating on the rising waters of the lake.

Then he knew that all of the people in the camp had also become black swans. And to this day, they are different from other swans. Their voices sound like the cries and laughter of people.

As for the mother Bunyip, she carried her baby home, and the lake grew smaller again. It looks the same as it did before, but no one ever goes near it. It belongs to the Bunyips.

The Two Sisters

Once upon a time, a man named Moroko lived with his two daughters in a small village. The oldest daughter was named Zikazi, and the youngest, Zanyana. Both of them were old enough to be married.

One day Moroko walked to a nearby village, where a great chief lived. The people who lived there told Moroko that their chief was looking for a wife.

When Moroko got home, he asked his daughters, "Which one of you wishes to marry a chief?" "I do," said Zikazi. So Moroko said, "The great chief Makanda Mahlanu is looking for a wife. You must go to his village." Moroko then asked all his friends to walk with his daughter to the village of Makanda Mahlanu. But Zikazi would not let the people go with her.

"I will go by myself," she said.

"How can you say such a thing?" asked Moroko. "It is foolish to go by yourself." But Zikazi would not agree with her father's plan.

At last Moroko let his daughter do as she wished. She left their hut and walked alone on the path to the village of Makanda Mahlanu.

When Zikazi got tired, she sat down under a tree to rest. A boy who was herding goats came up to her.

The boy said, "I am very hungry. Will you give me some food?" "You are not worthy to speak to me!" answered Zikazi. "I will soon be the wife of a great chief, and I can't be troubled with you."

So the boy said, "Go on, then. You will see what will happen."

Zikazi went on her way again. Soon she met an old woman sitting by a big stone.

The old woman said, "You will meet trees that will laugh at you, but you must not laugh in return. Then you will come to a place where the path splits in two. If you take the wide path, you will be unlucky."

"You ugly thing!" answered Zikazi. "You are not worthy to speak to me. I will soon be the wife of a great chief, and I can't be troubled with you."

So the old woman said, "Go on, then. You will see what will happen."

Zikazi walked on. Soon she came to trees that laughed at her, and she laughed right back at them. When she came to the place where the path split in two, she took the wide path.

Then Zikazi came to a river and met a girl who was carrying water. The girl was the sister of Makanda Mahlanu.

The girl said, "Where are you going, my sister?"

"Do not call me your sister!" answered Zikazi. "You are not worthy to speak to me. I will soon be the wife of a great chief, and I can't be troubled with you."

And so Zikazi walked on. At last she reached the village of Makanda Mahlanu. The people asked her what she wanted. She said, "I have come to be the wife of your chief."

The people said, "Makanda Mahlanu is not at home. You must prepare millet bread for him. He will eat the bread when he returns to his hut this evening."

So the people gave Zikazi millet seeds to grind into flour. But Zikazi ground the millet badly, and the bread she made was not good to eat. Still she took the bread to Makanda Mahlanu's hut and waited for him to come home.

In the evening she heard the sound of a great wind. It was the sound made by Makanda Mahlanu as he came into the hut.

Suddenly, Zikazi began to shake with fear. Makanda Mahlanu was not a man! He was a big snake with five heads and large eyes!

Makanda Mahlanu asked Zikazi to bring the millet bread. He took a bite and spat it out. "Your bread is not good to eat," he said. "You shall not be my wife."

So Zikazi ran far away from the hut and was never seen again.

Time went by. One day Zanyana said to her father, "I also wish to be the wife of a chief."

Moroko answered, "Then you must go to the village of Makanda Mahlanu."

Moroko asked all his friends to walk with Zanyana to the village of Makanda Mahlanu. The girl was happy to walk with them.

"We will all walk to the village together," she said.

So they walked on the path to the village of Makanda Mahlanu.

When the people got tired, they sat down under a tree to rest. A boy who was herding goats came up to them.

The boy said to Zanyana, "I am very hungry. Will you give me some food?"

"Whatever we have is yours," she answered. The boy took food from Zanyana. Then he showed her the way.

The group walked on. Soon they met an old woman sitting by a big stone.

The old woman said, "You will meet trees that will laugh at you, but you must not laugh in return. Then you will come to a place where the path splits in two. If you take the wide path, you will be unlucky."

"We will take the narrow path," answered Zanyana.

Then the old woman showed her the way. The group walked on. They came to trees that laughed at them, but they did not laugh in return. When they came to the place where the path split in two, they took the narrow path.

Then the group came to a river and met a girl who was carrying water. The girl was the sister of Makanda Mahlanu.

The girl asked Zanyana, "Where are you going, my sister?"

"I am looking for the village of Makanda Mahlanu," answered Zanyana.

The girl said, "He is not at home, but his village is near." Then she showed Zanyana the way.

The group walked on, and they soon reached the village. Zanyana told the people that she had come to marry their chief. They gave her millet seeds to grind for bread. She ground the millet well, and the bread she made was good to eat.

Zanyana took the bread to the chief's hut and waited for him. In the evening she heard the wind made by Makanda Mahlanu. She was not frightened when she saw that he was a big snake with five heads and large eyes.

Makanda Mahlanu asked Zanyana to bring the millet bread. He took a bite. Then he said, "You shall be my wife."

And then a strange thing happened. Makanda Mahlanu changed into a man! Instead of five heads, he had only one. Instead of a snake's body, he had arms and legs. He came towards Zanyana and kissed her.

Zanyana and Makanda Mahlanu were married the next day, and they were happy forever after.

The Horse Of Seven Colors

Once upon a time, a poor boy named Juan went into a great forest to look for food. He soon became lost.

For days and days, Juan wandered under the tall and mighty trees. He ate what little food he could find during the day. At night he slept on the ground.

At last, Juan came to a huge castle in the middle of a grassy field. The castle door was wide open, but there was no sign of life.

Juan looked all around and then slowly walked in. He passed through room after room, but he saw no one. Then he came to a great hall where a warm fire was burning in the fireplace.

In the center of the hall stood a wooden table covered with wonderful food. Since Juan had found very little food that day, he sat right down and began to eat.

Juan ate and ate until he was quite full. As he was finishing the last bite, he heard footsteps behind him. He jumped to his feet and turned around. He found himself face to face with an old wizard.

"What are you doing in my castle?" growled the wizard.

"I was lost in the forest," Juan answered. "Then I found your castle."

"And why did you eat my food?" asked the wizard.

"I was very hungry," Juan said.

"Very well," answered the wizard. "You can stay and share my food, but only if you work for me." Happy to have food, Juan quickly agreed to the wizard's plan.

"This is what you must do," said the wizard. "You must keep the fire burning in this fireplace at all times. Every day you must feed my black horse. In return, I will give you all the food you can eat."

Juan did just as he was told. Every morning, he went into the forest to gather wood for the fire. Every afternoon, he went to the stable to feed the wizard's black horse.

One morning, Juan took a long walk in the forest before gathering any wood. When he returned to the great hall later that day, the fire had almost burned out. Beside the dying fire stood the angry wizard.

"I told you to keep this fire going at all times!" shouted the wizard, shaking his finger in Juan's face. "Bad things will happen to you if you ever let the fire go out!"

Quickly, Juan threw a log on the fire, which began to burn brightly again. But from then on, the boy lived in fear of the wizard. He did not dare go far away from the castle.

One afternoon, Juan went to the stable to feed the black horse. To his surprise, it began to speak.

"Listen carefully," said the horse. "Behind me is a magic pail filled with golden water. First dip your clothes in the water. Then throw the rest of the water over me."

Juan did just as he was told. He dipped his clothes in the water. Suddenly they turned golden. Then he threw the rest of the water over the horse. With wide eyes, Juan watched as the horse grew wings and its black hair became a coat of seven colors.

"Now jump on my back," said the horse. "We must fly away from the wizard's castle."

"But won't the wizard chase us?" asked Juan.

"No," answered the horse. "The wizard gets his power from the fire. That is why he ordered you to keep it burning. I have put the fire out now. We must get away before he can start it again."

Without another word, Juan jumped onto the back of the beautiful horse. Smoothly, the pair rose into the blue sky and flew away through the soft, white clouds.

Juan and the horse flew all day and all night, crossing a wide and mighty ocean. At last, they reached a great kingdom. They landed in a secret place not far from a splendid castle.

"That castle is the home of a king and his daughter, the princess," said the horse. "You must go there and do exactly as I tell you. But first you must hide your golden clothes."

The horse gave Juan some old clothes to wear and hid the shining, golden ones. Then he told the boy to ask for a job in the king's garden. The last order he gave to Juan was, "Bring food to me every day, and I will tell you what to do."

Juan did just as he was told. He went to the king's garden and asked the gardener for a job.

"You can pull weeds from the garden and sweep up the leaves," answered the gardener. "In return, I'll give you dinner every night."

So Juan set about his work. All day long, he pulled weeds and swept leaves. At night, he shared his dinner with the horse of seven colors. Sometimes Juan put on his golden clothes, just to see them glitter in the moonlight.

One day, Juan saw the princess walking in the garden. He knew at once that he wanted to marry her.

That night the horse said, "Tomorrow, many princes will come to the castle, hoping to marry the princess. They will stand in a row in the garden. Then the princess will throw a diamond apple in the air. It will fall at the feet of the prince she is to marry."

The horse went on. "When you are working in the garden tomorrow, slip in at the end of the row. The apple will fall at your feet."

The next day everything happened just as the horse had said. The princes stood in a row, and Juan slipped in at the end. The princess threw the diamond apple in the air, and it fell at Juan's feet.

The king and the princess then walked down the row to see where the apple had fallen. They stopped when they came to Juan. The princess knew at once that Juan was the one she wanted to marry.

The king was not pleased. "You are not a prince," he said to Juan. "You are only a gardener dressed in rags. But because the apple has fallen at your feet, I must let you marry my daughter. Prepare for the wedding."

Juan decided he would put on his shining golden clothes for the wedding. He ran to the secret place to dress in his beautiful clothes. Then he jumped onto the horse's back. Together the two rose into the sky and flew to the garden.

The princess and everyone around her stared in wonder at Juan's splendid golden clothes and his beautiful flying horse. Then the horse spoke, loud enough for all to hear.

"You were wise," he said to the princess. "Even though Juan was dressed in rags, you decided he was the one to be your prince."

So Juan and the princess were married that same day. And as the people in the kingdom looked on, the prince and his bride flew away on the wonderful horse of seven colors.

Johnnycake

Once upon a time an old man and an old woman lived on a small farm with their little boy. One morning the old woman made a flat, round cake called Johnnycake, and she put it in the oven to bake.

She said to the boy, "Now you watch Johnnycake while your father and I go out to work in the garden."

So the man and the woman went out to the garden and began to work with their hoes. The little boy stayed to watch the oven, but he didn't watch it all the time.

All of a sudden, he heard a noise. He looked up, and the oven door popped open, and out jumped Johnnycake! And Johnnycake rolled right out the door, and down the steps, and on to the road!

The little boy ran after Johnnycake as fast as he could, calling to his parents for help. So the man and the woman dropped their hoes, and all three people ran after Johnnycake. But they couldn't catch up with him, and they soon had to sit down to rest.

On rolled Johnnycake. By and by, he came to two workers who were digging a well. The workers called out, "Where are you going, Johnnycake?"

And Johnnycake said, "I've outrun an old man, and an old woman, and a little boy, and I can outrun you too-oo-oo!"

"You can, can you? We'll see about that!" said the two well-diggers. So they threw down their picks and ran after Johnnycake. But they couldn't catch up with him, and they soon had to sit down to rest.

On rolled Johnnycake. By and by, he came to two workers who were digging a ditch. The workers called out, "Where are you going, Johnnycake?"

And Johnnycake said, "I've outrun an old man, and an old woman, and a little boy, and two well-diggers, and I can outrun you too-oo-oo!"

"You can, can you? We'll see about that!" said the two ditch-diggers. So they threw down their spades and ran after Johnnycake. But they couldn't catch up with him, and they soon had to sit down to rest.

On rolled Johnnycake. By and by, he came to a bear who was climbing a tree. The bear called out, "Where are you going, Johnnycake?"

And Johnnycake said, "I've outrun an old man, and an old woman, and a little boy, and two well-diggers, and two ditch-diggers, and I can outrun you too-oo-oo!"

You can, can you? We'll see about that!" said the bear. So she jumped to the ground and ran after Johnnycake. But she couldn't catch up with him, and she soon had to sit down to rest.

On rolled Johnnycake. By and by, he came to a wolf who was resting under a bush. The wolf called out, "Where are you going, Johnnycake?"

And Johnnycake said, "I've outrun an old man, and an old woman, and a little boy, and two well-diggers, and two ditch-diggers, and a bear, and I can outrun you too-oo-oo!"

"You can, can you? We'll see about that!" said the wolf. So she jumped up and ran after Johnnycake. But she couldn't catch up with him, and she soon had to sit down to rest.

On rolled Johnnycake. By and by, he came to a fox who was sitting next to a fence. Without getting up, the fox asked, "Where are you going, Johnnycake?"

And Johnnycake said, "I've outrun an old man, and an old woman, and a little boy, and two well-diggers, and two ditch-diggers, and a bear, and a wolf, and I can outrun you too-oo-oo!"

But the fox pretended he couldn't hear. He said, "I can't quite hear you, Johnnycake. Won't you come a little closer?" And he turned his head to the side.

Johnnycake stopped and looked at the fox. He went a little closer and called out in a very loud voice, *"I've outrun an old man, and an old woman, and a little boy, and two well-diggers, and two ditch-diggers, and a bear, and a wolf, and I can outrun you too-oo-oo!"*

"I can't quite hear you. Won't you come a little closer?" said the fox. And he stretched out his neck and put one paw behind his ear.

Johnnycake came right up to the fox, and he screamed as loud as he could, *"I've outrun an old man, and an old woman, and a little boy, and two well-diggers, and two ditch-diggers, and a bear, and a wolf, and I can outrun you too-oo-oo!"*

"You can, can you?" said the fox. And he snapped up Johnnycake in his bright sharp teeth and he ate him all up!

The Rainbow Goblins

Once there was a land that lived in fear of seven goblins. They were called the Rainbow Goblins, and each had his own color, which was also his name: Red, Orange, Yellow, Green, Blue, Indigo, and Violet. Yellow, being the craftiest, was their chief. The goblins lived on color—they prowled the valleys and climbed the highest mountains looking for rainbows, and when they found one, they caught it in their lassoes, sucked the colors out of it, and filled their bellies with its bright liquid.

Only one place in the land had never known goblin-fear—the hidden valley called the Valley of the Rainbow, where the great arches of color were born. There the animals still lived in paradise.

But the Rainbow Goblins had heard tales of this Valley, and their mouths watered whenever they thought of the feast that awaited them there; and so they gathered up their lassoes and their pails and set off.

With great effort, the goblins made their way over the jagged piles of rock that guarded the entrance. When the climbing became difficult, Yellow roared: "Don't lose heart, comrades! Think of the delicious colors ahead!"

The sun had almost set by the time they reached their goal—the very meadow where the Rainbow sprang to life. Immediately beneath the meadow they found a cave. "We'll spend the night here," the Yellow Goblin commanded.

When the moon rose and saw them warming themselves around the fire they had lit, it shouted out in alarm: "The Rainbow Goblins are in the Valley!" The trees and the bushes took up the cry, and the flowers and the grasses and the animals and the waters passed it on, and by midnight the evil tidings had spread throughout the Valley.

The goblins could hardly contain their excitement. "Soon all the colors of the Rainbow will be ours," Yellow gloated. "We'll snatch it as it rises," said Green, "when the colors are still fresh and creamy." The Blue Goblin cackled, "Look at the roots dangling from the walls. They're straining to hear our plans. A lot of good it will do them, or their friend the Rainbow."

Finally, exhausted by their scheming, the goblins fell asleep. Outside, the moon shone on the mirror-like surface of the water, and its magical light was reflected into the cave.

Then all seven goblins had a wonderful dream—the same wonderful dream about the paradise of Rainbowland, where all you had to do was lie on your back and open your mouth and the most succulent colors dripped down your throat.

The dream went on and on, the greedy goblins drank and drank, and at dawn, just as their bellies were about to burst, they were awakened by a distant clap of thunder.

The goblins sprang to their feet and rushed to the mouth of the cave. "A storm, a storm!" Red shouted. "Look how the wind is driving it toward us!" Orange cried.

And all the goblins danced and pranced about in glee, for they knew that after the wildest morning thunderstorm comes the most beautiful rainbow.

Yellow was so proud of his plan of attack that he went over it again, while each goblin tested his lasso. "Red, don't forget that you must seize the left flank." "And I move in on the right," the Violet Goblin burst out excitedly. Before the last roll of thunder had faded from the Valley the goblins took up their pails and lassoes and marched single file out of the cave.

The sight that greeted them when they reached the meadow took their breath away. The rising arch of the Rainbow, so rich with color and promise, almost blinded them. Trembling with excitement, Yellow finally managed to give the signal to attack.

The goblins swung their lassoes around and around, and hurled them into the sky. But in that same instant the Rainbow vanished, as if it had been swallowed up by the earth. The goblins were dumbfounded. Nothing like this had ever happened to them before. They stared up at their empty outstretched lassoes . . . which a second later snapped back at them. Indigo wept, Blue cursed, Yellow stumbled, Orange cried out, "Treachery!" Violet tumbled to the grass, Red raged; but the more they thrashed about, the more tangled up they became in their own lassoes, until they had snarled themselves into a grunting, groaning mass of goblins on the ground.

As they lay there helplessly, a flood of color poured forth from all the flowers of the meadow. "The flowers," screamed the Blue Goblin, "the flowers!" He had suddenly remembered the dangling roots he had made fun of in the cave. Through their roots the flowers had heard the goblins' plans, and they had devised a counterplan to save the Rainbow. The moment the attack was launched, the flowers had drained the colors of the Rainbow into their petals, and as soon as the goblins became ensnared in their own lassoes, the petals had let loose the deluge.

So the goblins drowned in the colors they had come to steal, and no one in the Valley wept for them.

The Rainbow itself was reborn more magnificently than ever. Out of gratitude, it lifted up the flowers that had saved it and transformed them into glittering dragonflies and butterflies and splendidly plumed birds.

But since that time the Rainbow has become more cautious. Now when it arches across the sky it is careful not to touch the earth anywhere. No matter how you try to sneak up on it, you can never come to the place where it begins or ends.

Scope and Sequence

Subject	Grades K–1	Grade 2	Grade 3
	Students will		
Sensory Awareness	Identify and describe objects with the senses; Create a scene about sensory qualities	Imagine and identify sensory experiences	Imagine, describe, and dramatize sensory experiences
Emotional Awareness	Identify, respond to, and communicate emotions	Transform ideas, feelings, and values into artistic forms through improvisation	Identify and modify the emotional content of a story
Sound/ Voice/ Language/ Communication	Identify and create sounds with voice and/or movement	Create and record radio drama	Transform single word into idea for dramatic action; Express a single word in several ways
Discipline			Work with others to create a "body machine"; Recognize the value of collaboration in theatre

Subject	Grade 4	Grade 5	Grade 6
	Students will		
Sensory Awareness	Use sensory experiences to identify objects; Notice how sounds convey images; Strengthen observation skills with sensory experiences; Use sensory recall to improvise a scene	Use sensory recall to develop a pantomime; Imagine performing an activity without one of the senses; Depend on another for the sense of sight	Visualize objects, scenes, and activities to increase sensory awareness; Recognize how point of view affects observations
Emotional Awareness	Experience how color affects moods; Identify emotions expressed in poetry	Identify, visualize, and respond to emotions; Use emotional recall to act out an emotional situation; Analyze emotions of characters in a play or story	Recognize how emotions affect observations; Analyze thoughts and words to understand and express a character's emotions
Sound/ Voice/ Language/ Communication	Imitate the voice inflections of others; Use gibberish to give directions; Use sounds to convey images; Create sound effects to bring to mind a scene	Give directions to someone who cannot see; Portray emotions through speech; Use vocal exercises to increase the ability to convey meaning	Learn vocal techniques for drama; Use imagery to motivate dialogue; Learn technical terms related to the voice; Play a verbal communication game
Discipline	Practice concentration by focusing on reading aloud while being distracted; Work in a group to do improvisation, choral reading	Work with a group to create a story within a limited time; Concentrate on verbal direction; Recognize the need for collaboration in theatre	Practice concentration to visualize a scene; Recognize interdependence of theatrical personnel; Assume responsibility in theatrical production

Subject	Grades K–1	Grade 2	Grade 3
	Students will		
Rhythm and Movement	Respond physically to rhythmic patterns and moods in music; Use movement to solve problems; Use movement and music to explore characters; Use poetry to improvise movement	Respond in diverse ways to rhythmic patterns; Use movement to express feelings and explore characterization; Use movement to interpret poetry	Respond in diverse ways to rhythmic patterns; Dramatize stories from interpretive response to musical selections
Body Awareness	Use "living statues" to create a story	Practice body movement in response to rhythm and with imaginary objects; Mirror another's body movements; Use movement to convey meaning	Practice body movement in response to rhythm; Create a "machine" with others, using their bodies; Use movement to convey meaning
Pantomime	Use the body to express ideas, emotions, and characters	Imagine objects and stimuli in acting out a scene; Create a story by pantomiming specific actions; Solve problems through pantomime	Develop a pantomime from one word; Pantomime using an imaginary object; Pantomime as part of dramatic action in a story

Subject	Grade 4	Grade 5	Grade 6
	Students will		
Rhythm and Movement	Move like animals; Move in slow motion; Portray emotions and moods with movements; Observe and imitate body movements and gestures	Use body language to portray emotions; Move in the manner of a described character; Create movements suggested by haiku images; Move in open space; Use mental pictures to motivate movement	Use a script to motivate movement; Learn terms for stage movement; Use body control to portray characters and refine stage movements; Use movement to interpret a poem; Study the controlled movements of Noh Theatre
Body Awareness	Move in the manner of a particular animal; Use slow, controlled motions; Notice how body language shows emotions	Use body movements to portray an inanimate object; Use body movements to show emotions; Analyze body movements of characters	Practice good breathing and posture for body control; Recognize how physical condition affects observations; Practice controlled movements of Noh Theatre
Pantomime	Develop a pantomime using sensory recall; Pantomime using sensory details of an experience; Pantomime a character doing an activity in slow motion	Develop a pantomime using sensory recall; Pantomime an activity using only four of the five senses; Pantomime a weather condition; Pantomime an inanimate object; Pantomime a scene from the Hobbit	Use pantomime to develop an idea in the manner of a Noh play; Pantomime using Method acting; Play Imaginary Rooms to practice nonverbal communication

Subject	Grades K–1	Grade 2	Grade 3
	Students will		
Storytelling	Discover similarities and differences in stories; Identify the moral in a story; Learn about historical role of storyteller	Study oral and written traditions of American folklore	Investigate oral traditions of ways stories have been passed on; Listen to African stories
Story Elements	Recognize the *What* in a story; Portray more than one character in a story; Identify and act out the five W's in a story	Identify the *What, When, Who, Why,* and *Where* as basic story elements	Create and dramatize stories using the five W's
Improvisation	Use imagined objects to create a scene; Act out parts of a folk tale; Use poetry to improvise movement activities	Improvise facial expressions and postures; Improvise a scene with specific characters	With others, create with their bodies an imaginary machine; Create drama with imaginary objects; Improvise a scene with an object as a prop; Analyze a "What if...?" story and dramatize it

Subject	Grade 4	Grade 5	Grade 6
	Students will		
Storytelling	Create a story based on a sequence of events; Explore storytelling through shadow plays; Explore common themes in folklore	Create dialogue for a story; Choose dramatic presentation for a story from another culture; Invent characters and conflicts to create and develop a story	Dramatize a Mexican folk tale; Dramatize a familiar story reversing protagonist and antagonist; Use readers theatre for telling stories
Story Elements	Recognize beginning, middle, and end to a story; Use the five W's to create a story and then add events to the story; Create an outline for a story	Create a story using five W's and three given objects; Identify characters, theme, plot, conflict, and resolution in a story; Use opposites to develop conflict in a story	Understand roles of protagonist and antagonist in story; Analyze a current topic and create a dramatization that fits one of the classifications of Chinese Theatre
Improvisation	Use emotional theme of a poem for improvisation; Improvise imagined characters; Do improvisations in different types of playing areas; Use sound effects as motivation for an improvisation	Develop improvisation based on a given *Who, What,* and *Where*; Create TV commercials; Become aware of creative choices in developing an improvisation; Improvise using an actual incident for a theme or plot; Improvise using a folk tale as a basis	Develop protagonist and antagonist characters; Improvise a scene in the commedia dell'arte style; Improvise a scene in the style of Shakespeare; Improvise a scene based on a Mexican folk tale; Improvise using the controlled movement of Noh theatre; Play *Freeze Tag* to practice verbal communication

Subject	Grades K–1	Grade 2	Grade 3
	Students will		
Folklore/ Cultural Awareness	Compare stories from different cultures with similar themes; Dramatize a Native American story; Participate in drama activities from various cultural celebrations	Recognize common themes from diverse cultures; Investigate fables, folk tales, myths, legends, and fairy tales; Read and dramatize a Native American myth; Create a legendary story; Dramatize a story from another culture	Compare "How and Why" stories; Investigate African stories; Become more aware of the diversity of American culture; Listen to and dramatize particular events in American history
Perception/ Art Appreciation	Use visual arts pieces and physical selves to create designs; Compare different moods and settings used in children's literature	Imagine objects or animals in specific environments; Interpret images in poetry	Analyze parts of visual and dramatic art to understand the whole; Identify, describe, and participate in drama, visual arts, dance, and music activities

Subject	Grade 4	Grade 5	Grade 6
	Students will		
Folklore/ Cultural Awareness	Study historical and cultural themes of good and evil; Study shadow puppetry and its origins in Asia; Use choral speaking to learn about the Greek theatre	Study and compare folklore from different cultures; Use a folk tale as a basis for an improvisation; Study and write haiku; Study how puppets are used around the world	Study history, vocabulary, and structure of commedia dell'arte; Study Elizabethan times and Shakespearean theatre; Learn the different types of Mexican folk tales; Learn about theatre in China during the Ming Dynasty; Study Japanese Noh Theatre; Learn about Stanislavsky and the Moscow Art Theater
Perception/ Art Appreciation	Use poetry to understand emotions; Use Lewis Carroll's "Jabberwocky" as a basis for characterization; Identify themes in literature by studying well-known stories	Use literature for establishing character images; Use the Hobbit by J.R.R. Tolkien as motivation for a pantomime	Study pattern and rhythm in poetry to create an improvisation; Study harmony of dance, poetry, music, mime, and acting in Noh Theatre

Subject	Grades K–1	Grade 2	Grade 3
	Students will		
Evaluation	Learn meaning of evaluation and its relationship to a story and to an audience	Use objective criteria in evaluating story performance	Analyze a performance in terms of props, sets, and costumes; Use *intent* and *structure* to evaluate a theatrical work
Problem Solving	Enact stories requiring problem solving	Explore real and imagined situations that require problem solving	Analyze the parts of a story and create different endings; Use "What if...?" situation to create stories
Characterization	Interpret meaning and movement qualities of story characters; Portray more than one character in a story	Improvise a scene with specific characters; Create characters and stories using costumes and props	Dramatize actions, ideas, and emotions by creating specific characters

Subject	Grade 4	Grade 5	Grade 6
	Students will		
Evaluation	Evaluate characterizations, movements, emotional validity, voice quality, and adaptability of stories for themes or plays; Use drama/theatre vocabulary and ethical standards to analyze a dramatic performance	Evaluate characterizations, movements, emotional validity, voice quality, and adaptability of stories for themes or plays; Evaluate drama/theatre elements in an actual performance	Evaluate characterizations, movements, emotional validity, voice quality, and adaptability of stories for themes or plays; Evaluate and modify the aesthetic and technical elements in a production in process
Problem Solving	Sequence events for developing scripts; Plan a celebration day; Dramatize a current news story	Decide how to convince someone to buy a product; Analyze the qualities of creativity; Dramatize a theme or issue from current news	Dramatize a current topic that relates to the classifications of Chinese theatre in the Ming Dynasty; Plan rehearsal schedules; Produce a play for an audience
Characterization	Develop characters based on traits of animals; Use color as a motivation for character development	Analyze behavior to learn about characterization; Elaborate on given characters; Use emotional and sensory recall to develop characters	Practice making a character "real"; Use relaxation, breathing, and visualization to create characters; Use vocal tension and body tension for characterization; Recognize importance of make-up in developing a character; Act in a formal production

Subject	Grades K–1	Grade 2	Grade 3
	Students will		
Playmaking		Develop a beginning, middle, and end to a story and dramatize it; Create a simple sequence in a story; Investigate characteristics of theatre, TV, film, and radio and create and record a radio drama	Learn the structural differences between stories and plays, and create a play from a narrative; Create a "How and Why" story; Use the five W's and simple story analysis to create a dramatization; Present a dramatic performance for another class
Technical Elements		Create characters and stories using costumes and props; Visualize and draw pictures of settings; Work with a visiting theatre artist	Learn the difference between *drama* and *theatre*; Learn about puppetry used in other cultures; Build simple puppets

Subject	Grade 4	Grade 5	Grade 6
	Students will		
Playmaking	Analyze a story in terms of plot, conflict, climax, and resolution; Study criteria for changing a story into a play; Develop a play from a story; Develop a scene based on a story theme; Learn the vocabulary of stage directions; Develop a script; Make and use a shadow puppet	Create a detailed scene using developed settings and characters; Recognize the importance of creativity in playmaking; Analyze the suitability of elements in a story for play development; Write a two-character scene; Act out a scene using props; Act out a scene using a costume; Make and use a hand puppet	Analyze a script for stage movement; Understand the roles of protagonist and antagonist in a play; Study Stanislavsky's Method acting; Understand the purpose of, and practice auditioning; Develop a rehearsal schedule; Put on a formal performance for an audience
Technical Elements	Use sound effects to create a setting; Identify playing areas; Design a set and make a rendering; Use technical elements—lighting, sets, props, sound, make-up, and costumes—in developing a play; Use sound effects in dramatizing a story	Recognize the importance of creativity in developing technical elements; Create a drama vocabulary list and definitions for a notebook; Decide what props are needed for a scene; Develop a costume for a specific character in a play	Use make-up; Practice the role of director; Practice the skills needed by technical theatre personnel; Analyze a script for technical elements needed and develop a technical plan; Understand purpose of and conduct a technical rehearsal, a dress rehearsal, and a touch-up rehearsal; Use all the technical elements to produce a formal performance for an audience

Grade Four List by Component

AESTHETIC PERCEPTION

Lesson 1 Sensory Walk
Working in pairs, students experience a variety of visual, tactile, auditory, and olfactory sensations to increase their perception and sensory awareness.

Lesson 2 Sensory Associations
Students use sensory recall to convey weather conditions in improvising a scene.

Lesson 4 Creating Mood with Color
Students use color as motivation for movement and characterization activities.

Lesson 5 Emotions as Themes of Poems
Students listen to poetry to identify emotions used as themes in poetry, and create a scene that conveys an emotion.

Lesson 6 Movement Study
Students use animal comparisons to visualize behavioral traits for characterization.

Lesson 8 Communicating Emotion Through Movement
Students become aware of and respond to the communicative potential of drama/theatre by exploring nonverbal methods of communication.

Lesson 12 Practicing Concentration
Students practice their concentration skills with exercises stressing the ability to focus in the midst of distractions.

Lesson 13 Developing a Logical Sequence
Students arrange events in sequential order, and create a story from a given set of events or descriptions.

Lesson 20   Theatrical Stages
             Students identify and learn the terms for different types of
             performing areas, and experiment with performance in each
             one.

Lesson 27   Writing and Dramatizing a Scene
             Students become aware of the structural differences between
             stories and plays, and begin writing a playscript.

CREATIVE EXPRESSION

Lesson 3   Powers of Observation
             Students strengthen the observation skills needed in drama/
             theatre by focusing on sensory details of experiences.

Lesson 7   Controlled Movement
             Working in pairs, students concentrate on disciplined move-
             ments to give them aesthetic form.

Lesson 9   Character Study
             Students use perceptual skills to experience, create, under-
             stand, and evaluate drama/theatre as they transform what they
             have observed into aesthetic form.

Lesson 10   Nonsense Words
             Students communicate meaning through voice inflection as
             they give nonsensical directions for a set of actions.

Lesson 11   Improvisation from Literature
             Students use their imaginations to interpret and dramatize a
             famous nonsense poem.

Lesson 14   Sequential Development in Stories
             Students create a story using the five W's and a logical se-
             quence of events.

Lesson 15   Story Components in Drama
             Students learn appropriate drama/theatre terms and their
             meanings, and use the concepts to create and dramatize the
             beginning of a story.

Lesson 19   Sound Voyages

Students imagine and create auditory stimuli to tell and dramatize stories.

Lesson 24   Creating Characters with Costumes

Students use hats as costume pieces to create characters and improvise a story.

Lesson 30   A Special Celebration

Students use a story as motivation to plan a celebration, implementing ideas and techniques about drama/theatre that they have learned over the year.

HISTORICAL AND CULTURAL

Lesson 17   Themes and Stories

Students analyze and compare themes in children's literature, both folk tales and contemporary fiction.

Lesson 18   Common Themes in Literature

Students discover that throughout time people of diverse cultures have dealt with common themes, and then dramatize a story with the theme of good against evil.

Lesson 26   The Living Newspaper

Students create a dramatization from a current news event.

Lesson 28   Creating a Shadow Puppet

Students learn some of the techniques of shadow puppetry, make a shadow puppet, and experiment manipulating the puppet.

Lesson 29   Poetry in Chorus

Students learn some of the history of Greek chorus and perform poetry as a chorus.

APPENDIX

AESTHETIC VALUING

Lesson 16   Analyzing Stories for Dramatization
Students become aware of the techniques used to change a narrative story into a play, and make suggestions for dramatizing a particular story.

Lesson 21   Stage Areas and Directions
Students identify and use appropriate vocabulary to describe different areas of the stage and an actor's movement from one part of the stage to another.

Lesson 22   Designing a Set
Students learn the role of the set designer in drama/theatre, and practice designing a set by making a rendering for a drama.

Lesson 23   The Technical Element of Drama/Theatre
Students develop an understanding of and appreciation for the jobs necessary to aesthetic and technical theatre.

Lesson 25   Analyzing a Dramatic Work
Students use drama/theatre vocabulary and ethical standards when analyzing a dramatic performance.

Grade Five List by Component

AESTHETIC PERCEPTION

Lesson 1   Using the Senses
Students increase their perception and sensory awareness by imagining and pantomiming the lack of one of the senses.

Lesson 2   Giving and Following Directions
Students increase their perception and sensory awareness by completing an activity depending on another person for the sense of sight.

Lesson 3   Recalling Sensory Experiences
Students recall past sensory experiences to help them pantomime a particular weather condition.

Lesson 4   Personifying Objects
Students visualize and pantomime inanimate objects to increase body awareness and dramatization skills.

Lesson 5   Understanding the Emotions of Others
Students identify, respond to, and communicate different emotions.

Lesson 6   Recalling an Emotional Experience
Students recall emotional experiences and communicate their emotions through speech and movement.

Lesson 8   Vocalizing for Meaning
Students practice various vocal exercises to increase their ability to convey meaning, both with and without words.

Lesson 9   Stretching the Imagination
Students create mental pictures of past experiences and expand upon them to motivate dramatic movement and speech.

Lesson 10   Pantomiming in the Dark
Students use pantomime to portray a described scene, and then pantomime a passage from children's literature.

Lesson 16   Making Creative Choices
Students use a given work to stimulate mental images, then make choices concerning those images to create a story and dramatization.

Lesson 25   Using Theatrical Terms
Students learn appropriate drama/theatre vocabulary, create a drama vocabulary list for their notebooks, and plan a project.

CREATIVE EXPRESSION

Lesson 7   Developing a Character Role
Students analyze their own behavior to increase their awareness of the process of characterization.

Lesson 11   Improvising Original Stories
Students use given *who, what,* and *where* information to create original story improvisations.

Lesson 12   Variations on a Theme
Students work in pairs and in groups, using the idea of "Open Space," to improvise a story based on a suggested theme.

Lesson 13   Commercials as Mini-Dramas
Students dramatize a current commercial, and then create their own imaginary product or service and improvise a commercial for it.

Lesson 14   Creating Stories from Objects
Students work in groups to create and dramatize a story within a limited period of time, using given imaginary objects.

Lesson 17   Exploring Creativity
Students analyze the aspects of creativity and their relationship to drama/theatre.

Lesson 18   Creating Improvisations from Real-Life Situations
Working in groups, students create an improvisation from their own observations of a real incident.

Lesson 22   Setting Up Conflict in Drama
Students develop a dramatization from an original scenario.

Lesson 23   Developing Story Outlines for Drama
Students invent characters and conflicts to create and develop a story outline, and analyze its potential for dramatization.

Lesson 24   Analyzing and Writing Scripts
Students use a scripted drama to become familiar with the format, and then write and read their own two-character scene.

HISTORICAL AND CULTURAL

Lesson 19   Using Literature for Dramatization
Students learn about different kinds of stories from world cultures, and research and dramatize a story from a culture different from their own.

Lesson 20   Analyzing a Folk Tale
Students listen to a folk tale and improvise a scene that demonstrates one of the story components.

Lesson 21   Writing Haiku
Students learn about and write haiku, and improvise movement to this kind of poetry.

Lesson 30   Celebration! World Puppetry
Students learn about puppetry as part of drama/theatre in world cultures, participate in making a simple puppet, and dramatize part of a script to demonstrate a particular kind of puppetry.

AESTHETIC VALUING

Lesson 15   Creating Dialogue
             Students elaborate on given characters and create dialogue by
             making choices about how the characters would respond to
             each other.

Lesson 25   Using Theatrical Terms
             Students learn appropriate drama/theatre vocabulary, create a
             drama vocabulary list for their notebooks, and plan a project.

Lesson 26   Dramatizing with Props
             Students read and analyze a scene for the kinds of stage prop-
             erties that might be needed, and act out the scene using the
             props.

Lesson 27   Selecting Costumes for Characters
             Students learn about the role of the costumer in drama/theatre
             and improvise a scene to demonstrate an appropriate costume
             for a particular character.

Lesson 28   Evaluating a Performance
             Students use drama/theatre elements to evaluate a perfor-
             mance.

Lesson 29   Dramatizing Current Events
             Students research, form critical opinions on, and dramatize an
             issue from current events.

Grade Six List by Component

AESTHETIC PERCEPTION

Lesson 1   Exercising the Imagination
Students visualize objects, scenes, and activities in their minds' eyes to increase their perception and sensory awareness.

Lesson 2   Sharpening Observation Skills
Students practice observing detail in both objects and actions, and analyze their own point of view for its effect on their observation.

Lesson 3   Exploring Vocal Techniques
Students learn vocabulary terms related to the voice and practice vocal techniques to use their voices most effectively.

Lesson 4   Conveying Meaning Through Vocal Techniques
Students practice breath control and relaxation techniques as they use their voices to convey meaning through the spoken word.

Lesson 5   Planning Movement Onstage
Students interpret a script for the movements made by the actors onstage.

Lesson 6   Physical Movements Onstage
Students practice physical movements in relation to different situations and different characters.

Lesson 9   Switching Antagonist and Protagonist
Students identify and use appropriate drama/theatre vocabulary and dramatize a familiar story in which antagonist and protagonist are reversed.

Lesson 16   Real People, Imagined Characters
Students recognize the difference between the role played by an actor and the actor as a real person.

Lesson 11   Using Shakespearean Theatrical Devices
             Students learn about Shakespeare and the Elizabethan theatre,
             and experiment with some of Shakespeare's theatrical devices.

Lesson 12   Dramatizing a Mexican Folk Tale
             Students research information about Mexican folklore, select a
             story from a particular category, and present an improvisation
             of that particular type of tale from Mexico.

Lesson 13   World Theatre: China
             Students learn about theatre in China during the Ming Dy-
             nasty, and create a dramatization using current topics that fit
             the Chinese theatrical classifications.

Lesson 14   World Theatre: Japan
             Students study the stylized dance movements of Japanese Noh
             Theatre and create a pantomime with similar, carefully con-
             trolled dance movements.

Lesson 15   Russian Theatre and the Stanislavsky Method
             Students learn about Stanislavsky's place in drama history, and
             practice some of his Method acting exercises.

AESTHETIC VALUING

Lesson 20   Assuming Responsibility in the Theatre
             Students go through exercises that show the value of responsi-
             bility and trust.

Lesson 22   The Role of the Director
             Students learn more about the role of the director in drama/
             theatre, and apply the director's tasks to a particular script.

Lesson 23   Identifying Technical Elements in a Drama
             Students learn or review the tasks of technical theatre person-
             nel and plan the technical elements for a specific dramatic
             production.

Lesson 24   Technical Script Analysis
            Students analyze the script for their dramatic presentation,
            identifying the points in the production that will require the
            addition of a technical element.

Lesson 26   Scheduling and Holding Rehearsals
            Students learn how to schedule rehearsals, learn what kinds of
            rehearsals are necessary to put on a production, and practice
            for their performance.

Lesson 27   Holding a Technical Rehearsal
            Students practice the technical aspects of a dramatic produc-
            tion to be performed.

Lesson 28   Holding a Dress Rehearsal
            Students practice their dramatic production exactly as it is to
            be performed, with all the elements in place, to ensure a
            smooth performance.

Lesson 29   Polishing the Performance
            Students identify and adjust only those aspects of the produc-
            tion that need improvement before the performance.

Lesson 30   Celebration! The Performance
            Students present their performance to a live audience.